Objects of the Elements
The Art of
Elsa Thoresen

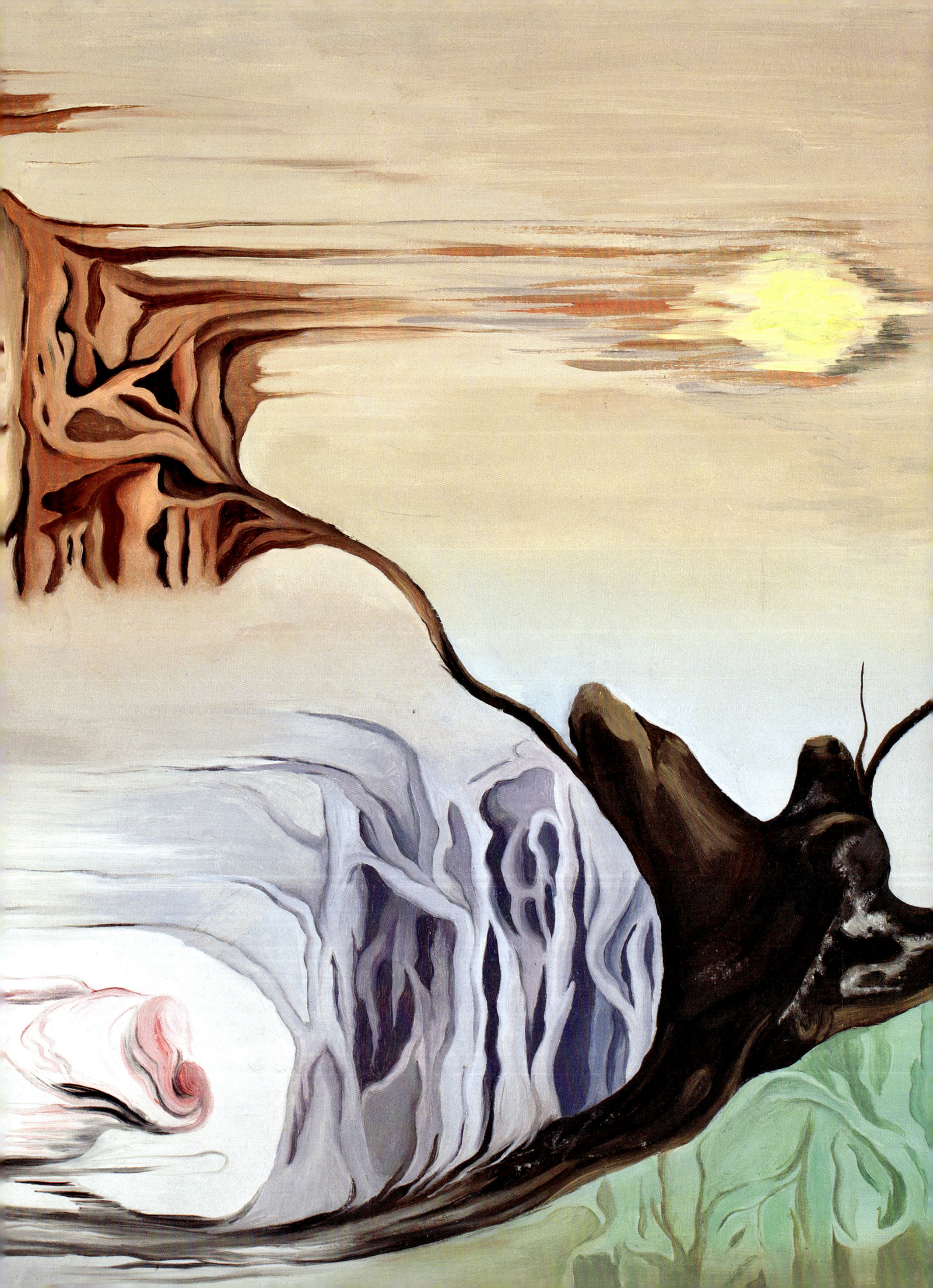

Objects of the Elements
The Art of
Elsa Thoresen

David F. Martin

CASCADIA ART MUSEUM

DISTRIBUTED BY UNIVERSITY OF WASHINGTON PRESS

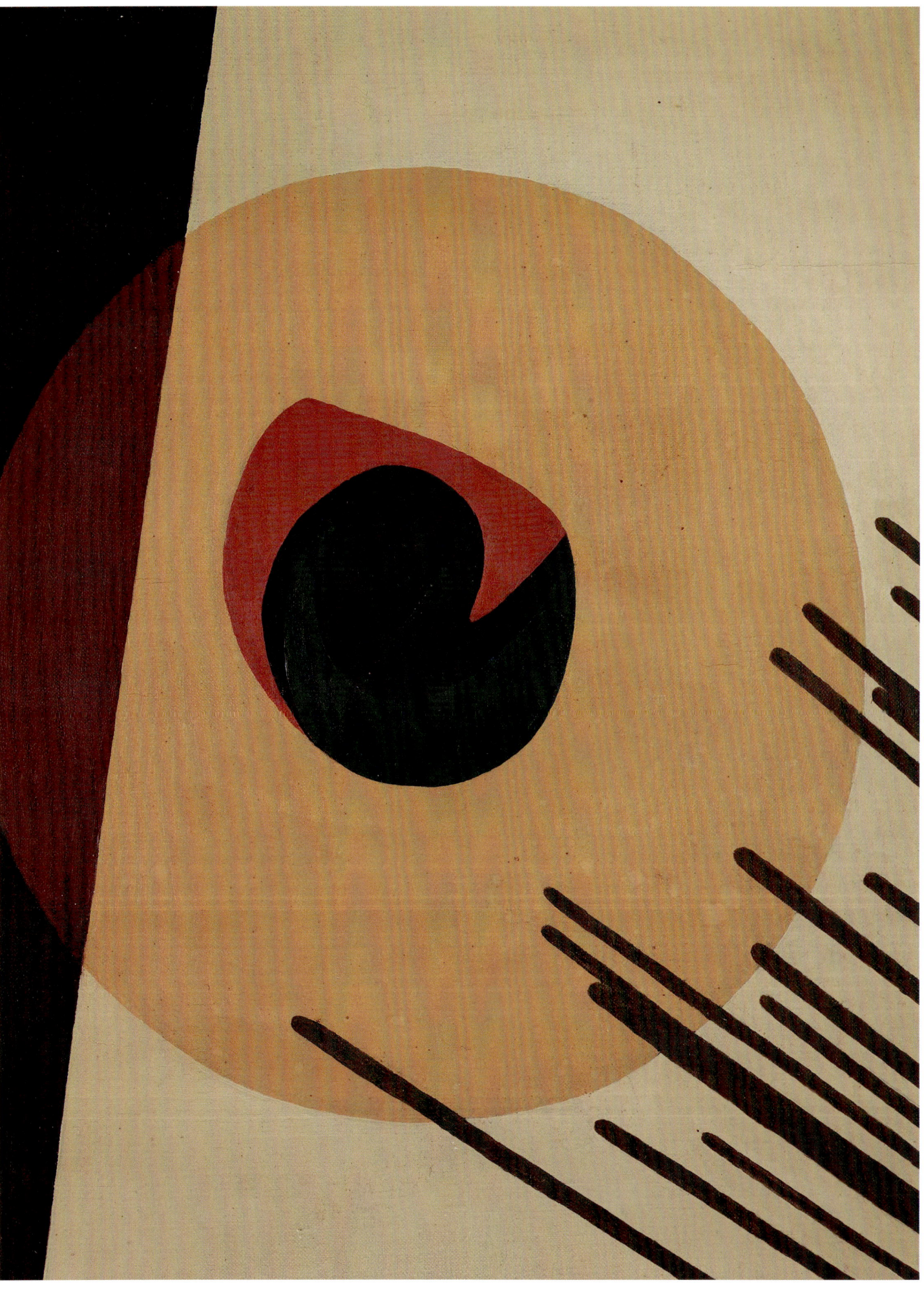

Contents

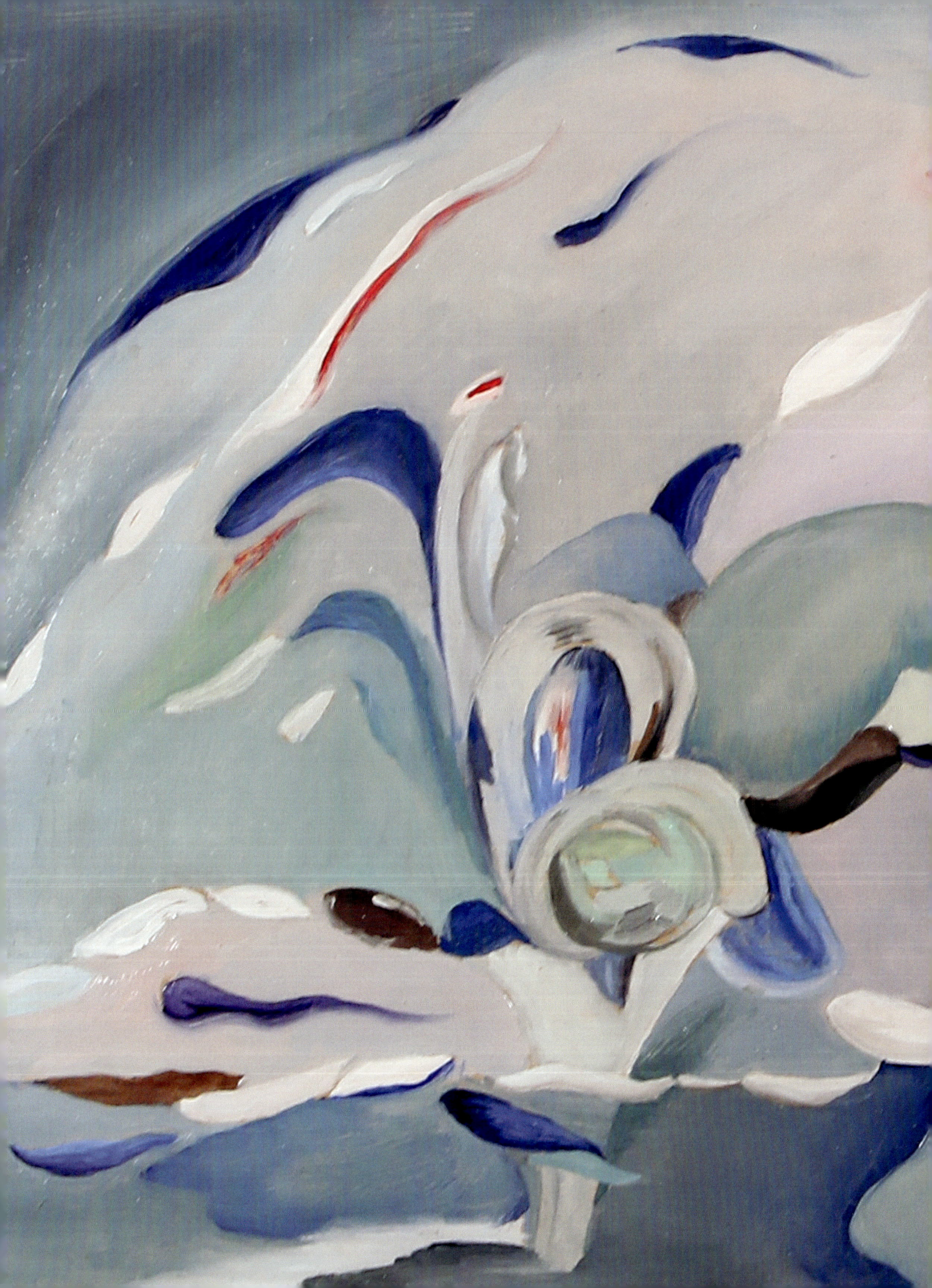

Foreword

SALLY RALSTON, EXECUTIVE DIRECTOR
CASCADIA ART MUSEUM

It is a joy to share this publication, *Objects of the Elements: The Art of Elsa Thoresen*, with you. This book and the exhibition reflect what Cascadia Art Museum does best, bringing to light the remarkable stories of artists who have shaped the cultural fabric of the Northwest.

Elsa Thoresen's journey—from her early acclaim in Europe to her creative life here in the Pacific Northwest—is inspiring. Her paintings show how art can transcend boundaries and connect us to something greater.

At Cascadia, we believe that telling these stories matters. They expand our understanding of history and ensure that artists like Thoresen are not lost to time. This publication, written with great care and insight by our curator, David F. Martin, is a testament to that mission. I am grateful for his scholarship and his passion for uncovering and celebrating artists whose legacies enrich us all.

Publishing has always been central to Cascadia's vision. In our ten years, we have proudly produced a growing library of art books that extend the reach of our exhibitions far beyond our walls. This publication joins that tradition, preserving Thoresen's legacy for generations to come. We are especially grateful to the University of Washington Press, whose partnership as distributor ensures that Elsa Thoresen's story will reach audiences worldwide.

As we celebrate the museum's tenth anniversary, I can think of no better way to honor this milestone than by presenting Elsa Thoresen's art to the public. I hope these pages inspire you, and that you come away with a deeper appreciation for the vibrant history of art in our region.

Finally, I want to thank the many friends and supporters whose generosity made this publication possible. Your belief in Cascadia's mission ensures that artists like Elsa Thoresen receive the recognition they so richly deserve.

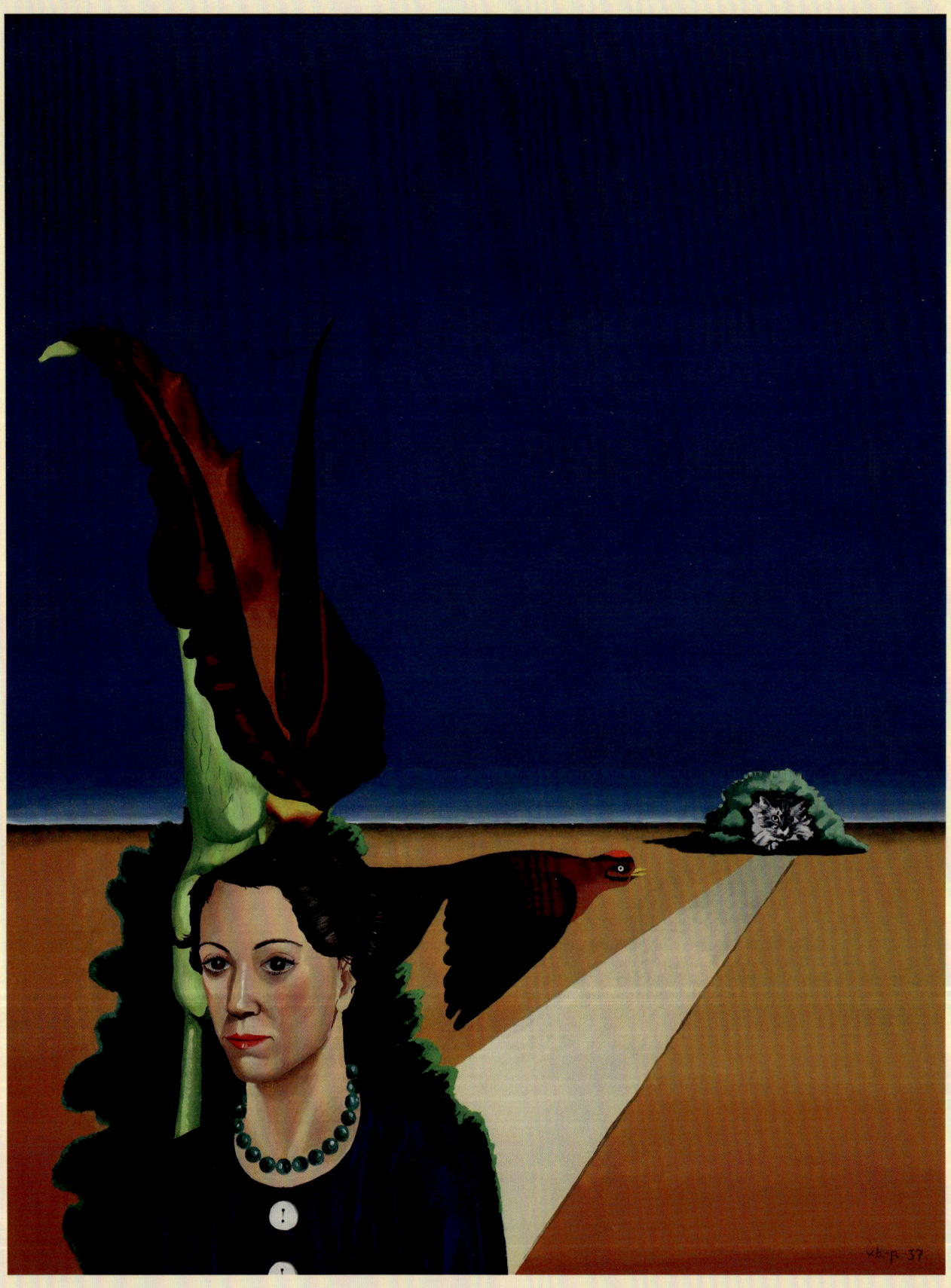

Vilhelm Bjerke-Petersen (1909–1957), *Portrait of the Painter Elsa Thoresen*, 1937. Oil on canvas, 45½ × 35⅜ in. (115.5 × 90 cm). Kunstmuseum Brandts, Odense, Denmark.

Objects of the Elements
The Art of
Elsa Thoresen

DAVID F. MARTIN

Elsa Cecilie Thoresen was born on May 1, 1906, in Benson, Minnesota, to Thore Nils Thoresen (1861–1933), a Norwegian immigrant, and Alice Josephine Johnson (1880–1978), an American. Thore was a physician when he emigrated to the United States in 1889, the year that Washington was granted statehood. He was practicing in Seattle by 1890, until he moved in 1898 to Minnesota, where he met and married Alice Johnson. Elsa was the middle of the couple's three children; the eldest was Marie (a.k.a. "Puss") (1903–1974) and the youngest, Nils (a.k.a. "Truls") (1910–1998).

Besides being a physician, Thore was an accomplished musician, specializing in the cello. The three Thoresen children were trained as classical musicians, with Marie on piano, Elsa on violin, and Nils on cello. While the family gravitated toward musical careers, Elsa had her heart set on becoming a painter. After living near Minneapolis, Minnesota, for several years, the Thoresens traveled to Oslo, Norway, for an extended visit with relatives. To undertake this crossing, Thore agreed to be the accompanying physician for the voyage on the passenger ship *Stavangerfjord*, part of the Norwegian American Line. The family arrived in Oslo in 1920, with no set plans of returning to the United States. Elsa maintained her artistic ambitions and, in 1924, enrolled at the Norwegian National Academy of Craft and Art Industry in Oslo, where she remained until 1927. One of her

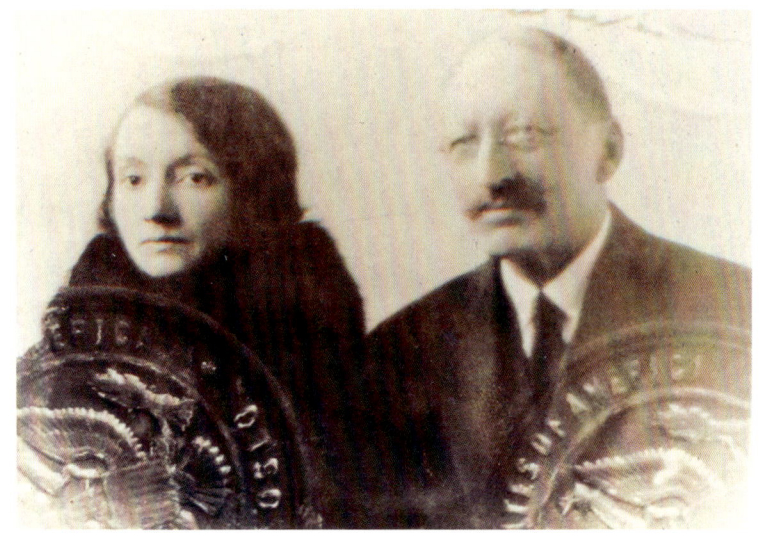

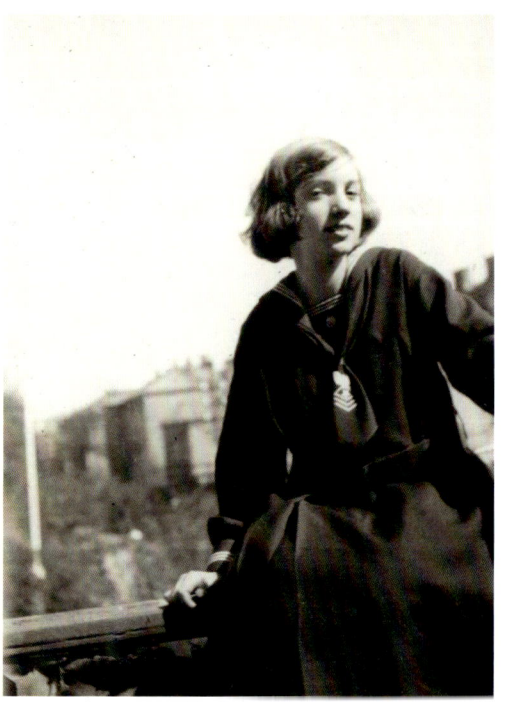

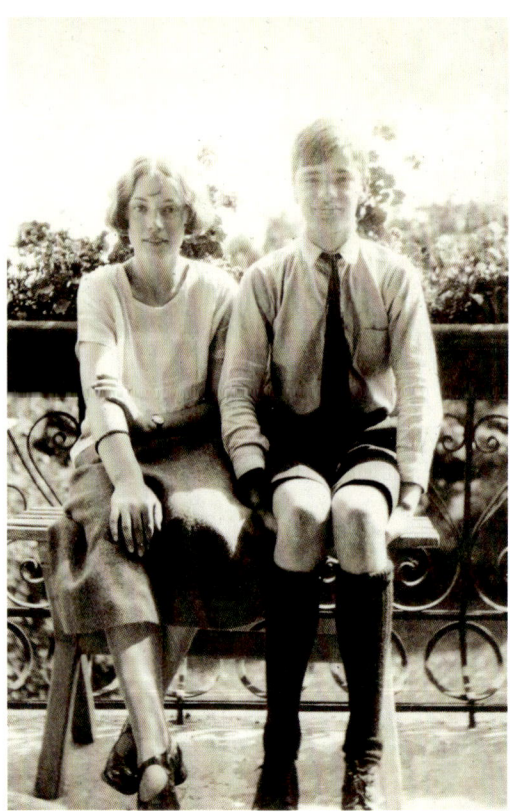

Elsa Thoresen's parents, Alice Josephine Johnson and
Thore Nils Thoresen.

Elsa Thoresen in Oslo, Norway, 1921.

Elsa Thoresen with her brother, Nils, known as "Truls," Oslo, 1921.

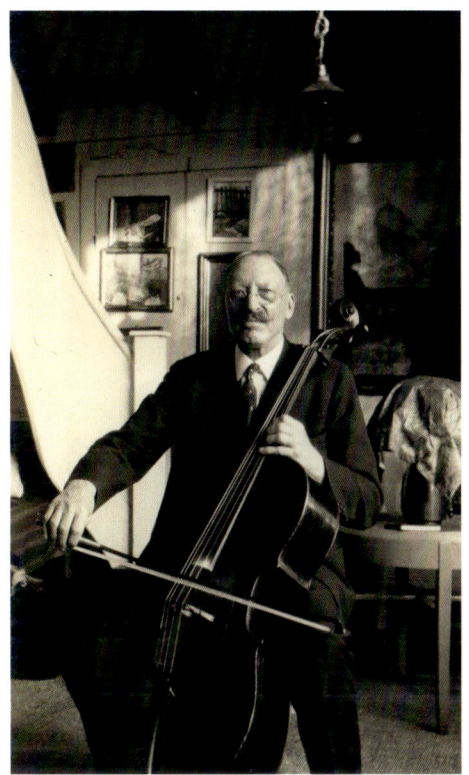
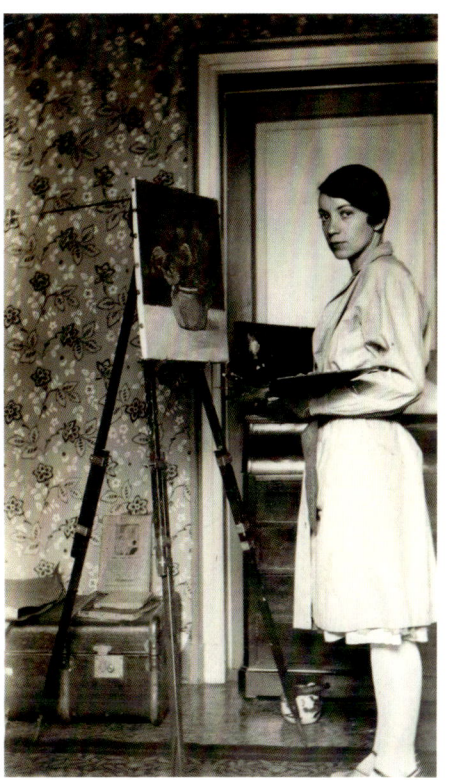

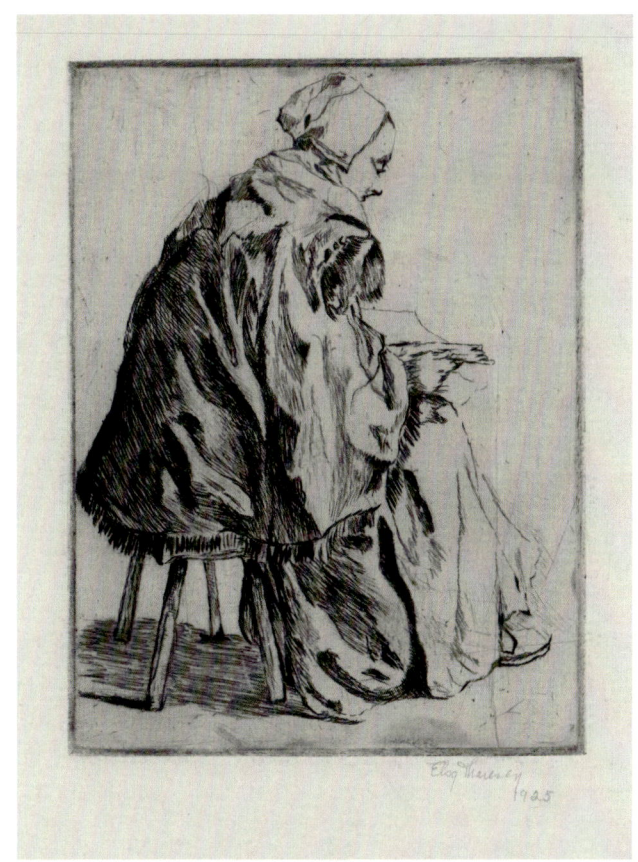

Thore Thoresen, date unknown.

Elsa Thoresen at her easel, circa 1925.

Elsa Thoresen (1906–1994), Untitled, 1925. Etching, 6¼ × 4¾ in. (15.9 × 12.1 cm).

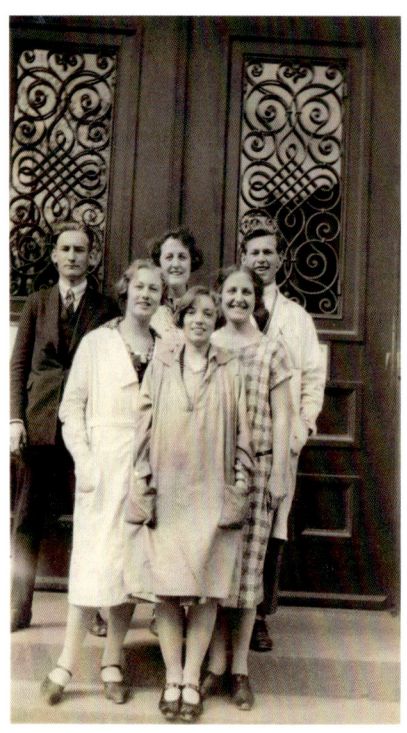

Elsa Thoresen (*front row center*) with students at the Norwegian
National Academy of Craft and Art Industry, Oslo, 1926.

classmates, Bjarne Rise (1904–1984), was also from Minnesota, but came to
Oslo at age five.

The few extant works by Elsa Thoresen that have survived from this period
indicate that she was trained in an academic, classical tradition of drawing and
composition. Several of her etchings and drawings attest to the success of her
education. Her 1926 self-portrait drawing, with its loose lines and spare use
of traditional modeling, indicates a growing interest in modern methods. Her
stark, analytical gaze displays a confidence in both her drawing abilities and her
serious determination. In contrast, her black-and-white study of Vermeer's 1665
painting *Girl with a Pearl Earring*, likely copied from a photograph, displays an
impressive tonal range and sensitivity to the subject, an unknown model whose
identity is lost to time.

After three years at the academy, Thoresen began classes at the Norwegian
National Academy of Fine Arts, Oslo, in 1927 and remained there on and off
until 1930. Her classmates included Johannes Rian (1891–1981) and the man
who would change the path of her artistic development and later become her
husband, Vilhelm Bjerke-Petersen (1909–1957). Her instructors at the academy
included Halfdan Strøm (1863–1949), a highly successful painter who worked

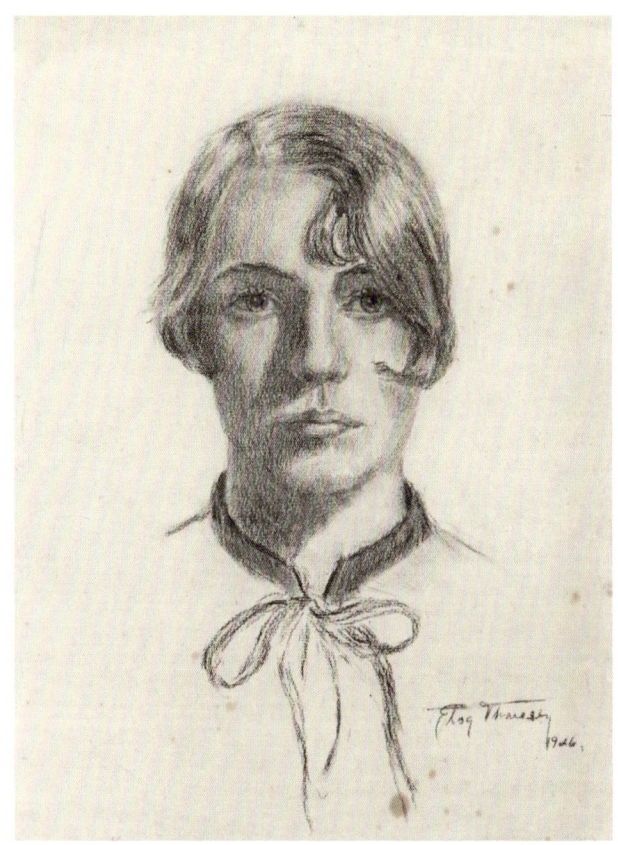

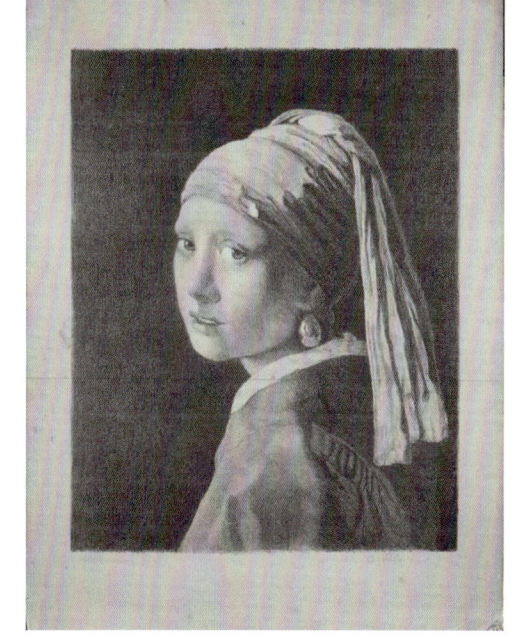

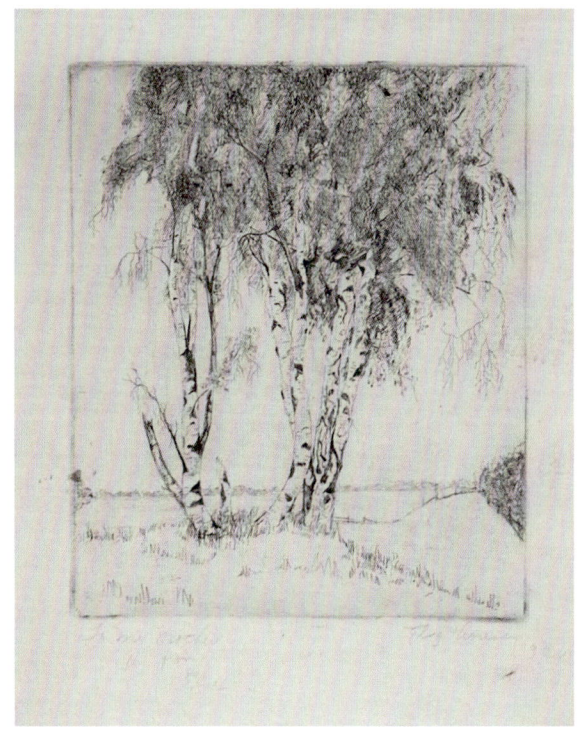

Elsa Thoresen (1906–1994), Self-portrait, 1926. Graphite drawing, 14½ × 10⅞ in. (36.8 × 27.6 cm).

Elsa Thoresen (1906–1994), copy of Vermeer's 1665 painting *Girl with a Pearl Earring*, 1925. Graphite drawing, 15 × 12 in. (38 × 30.5 cm).

Elsa Thoresen (1906–1994), Untitled, 1926. Etching, 8 × 6⅝ in. (20.3 × 16.8 cm). Inscribed "To my mother, from Elsa."

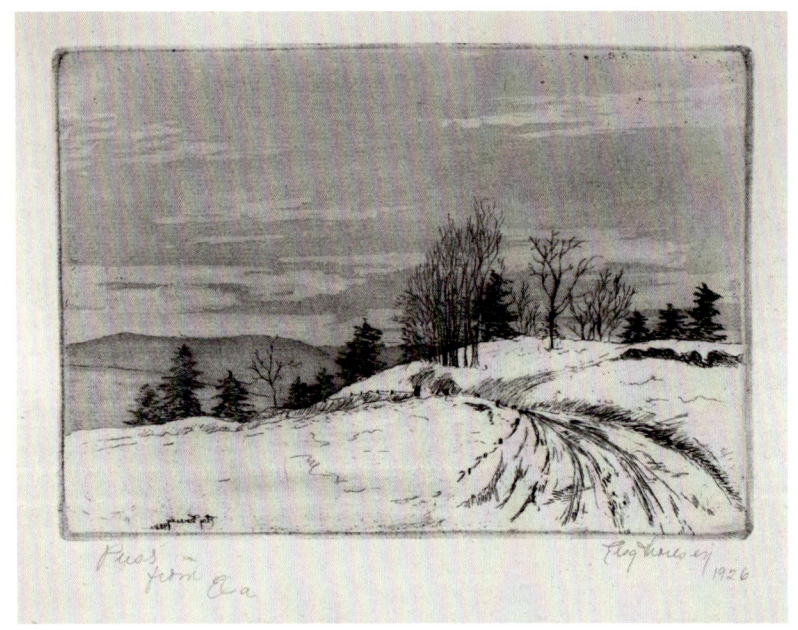

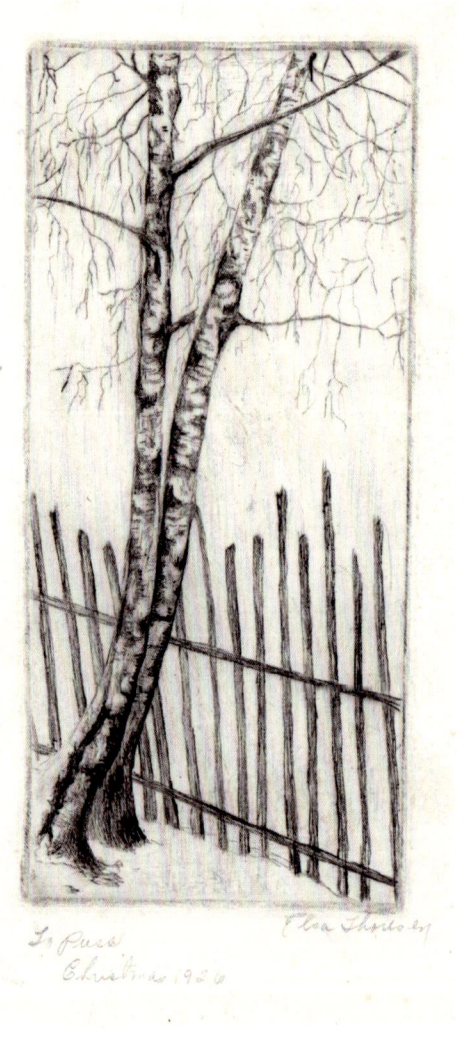

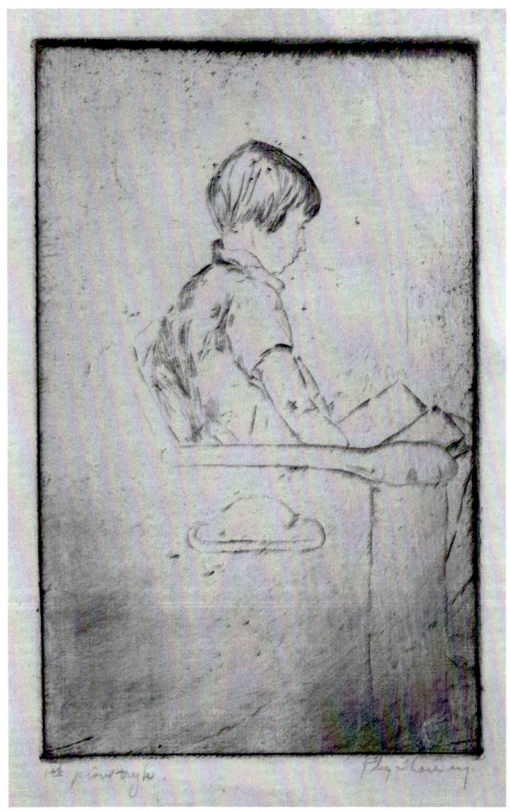

Elsa Thoresen (1906–1994), Untitled, 1926. Etching and aquatint, 4¾ × 6⅞ in. (12.1 × 17.5 cm). Inscribed "Puss from Elsa." "Puss" was the nickname for Thoresen's sister, Marie.

Elsa Thoresen (1906–1994), Untitled, 1926. Etching, 6⅝ × 3 in. (16.8 × 7.6 cm). Inscribed "To Puss, Christmas, 1926."

Elsa Thoresen (1906–1994), Untitled, 1926. Etching, 9⅝ × 6⅛ in. (24.5 × 15.6 cm). Inscribed "Prøvetrykk" (First proof).

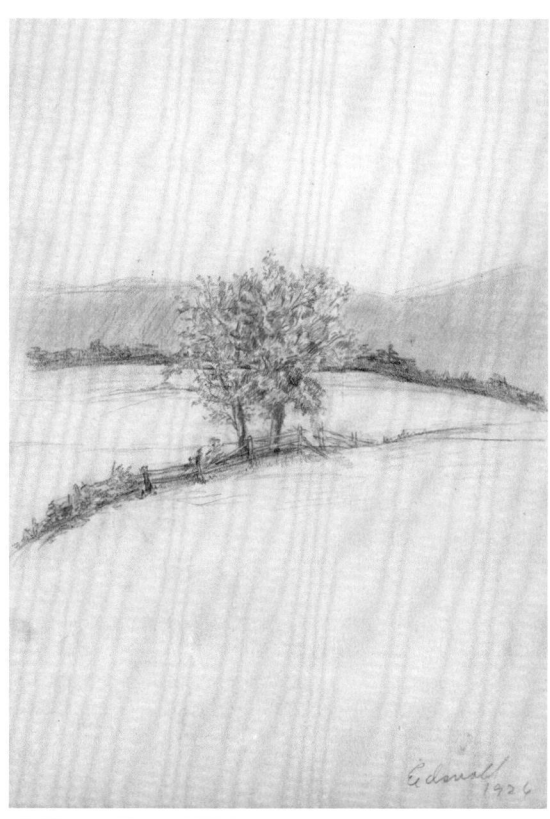

Elsa Thoresen (1906–1994), "Eidsvall" (Norway), 1926.
Graphite drawing, 10 × 7 in. (25.4 × 17.8 cm).

in a realist and somewhat impressionist style, and, on the other end of the spectrum, Axel Revold (1887–1962), who was open to more modern techniques, after studying with Henri Matisse for two years in Paris earlier in his career. From 1927 to 1929, Thoresen also took classes at the Académie Royale des Beaux-Arts in Brussels, Belgium, studying under Alfred Bastien (1873–1955), who was known for his large panoramic paintings and images of war. This period in Brussels corresponds to her younger brother Nils's enrollment at the Royal Conservatory in Brussels to study cello.

During the late 1920s, Thoresen's work began to evolve. A few of her earlier paintings have subjects that illustrate the Danish and Norwegian concept of *hygge*, a quality that engenders coziness, warmth, and contentment. These characteristics can be seen in her room interiors of 1927 and 1928. The 1928 drawing of Nils is sensitive and modern, with her quick, gestural diagonal lines and use of negative space to model his facial features. It was likely produced when both were in Brussels. For such a quick sketch, the portrait subtly conveys the sensitivity of the young musician.

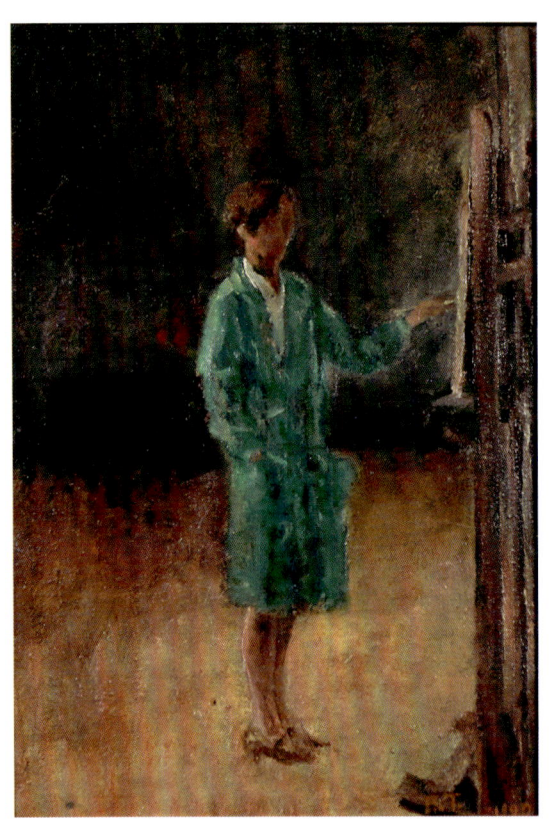
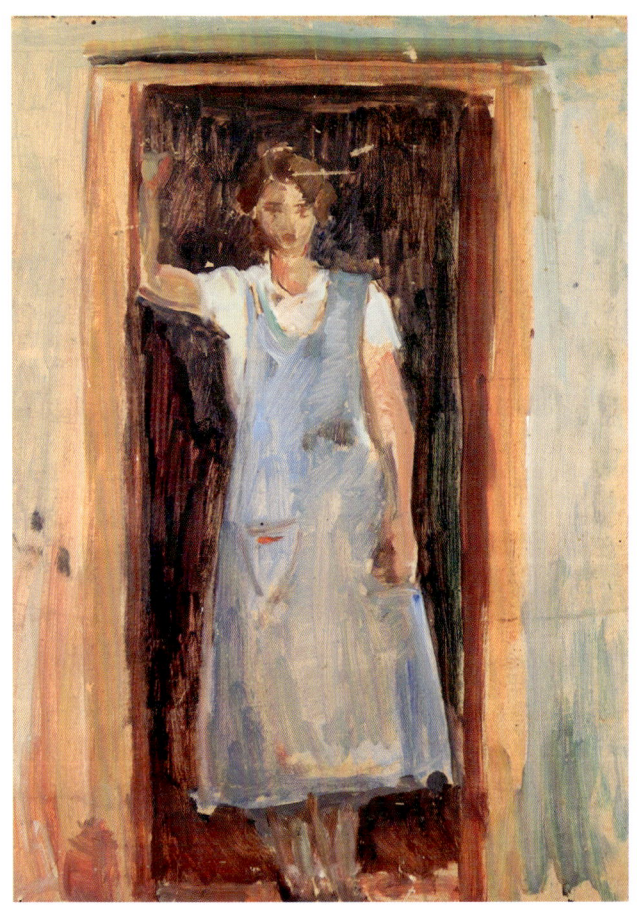
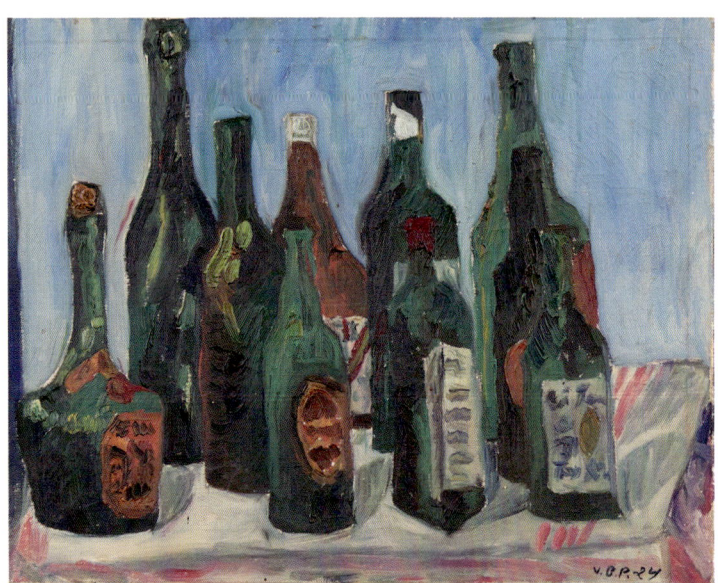

Elsa Thoresen (1906–1994), Self-portrait, 1927. Oil on board, 13½ × 9½ in. (34.3 × 24.1 cm).

Elsa Thoresen (1906–1994), Self-portrait, circa 1927. Oil on board, 16¾ × 12¼ in. (42.6 × 31.1 cm).

Vilhelm Bjerke-Petersen (1909–1957), Untitled, 1927. Oil on canvas, 14⅜ × 18½ in. (36.5 × 47 cm).

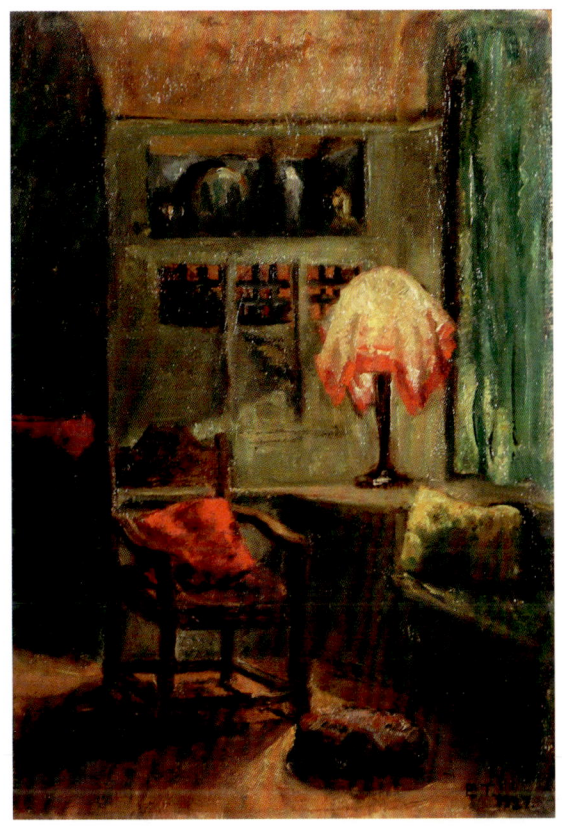
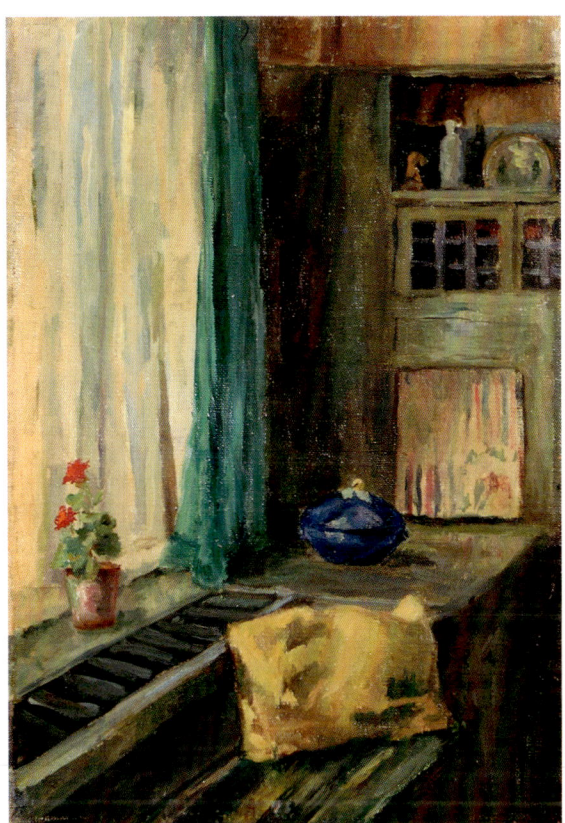
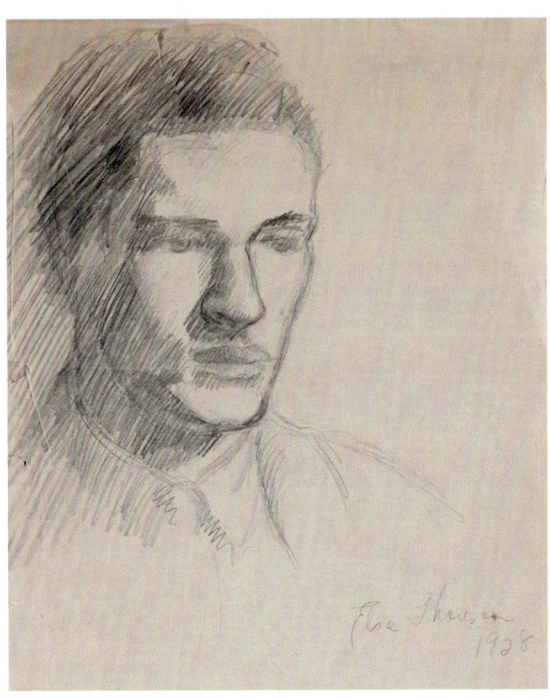

Elsa Thoresen (1906–1994), Untitled, 1927. Oil on board, 13½ × 9⅜ in. (34.3 × 23.8 cm).

Elsa Thoresen (1906–1994), Untitled, 1928. Oil on canvas, 13¾ × 10 in. (34.9 × 25.4 cm).

Elsa Thoresen (1906–1994), Portrait of Nils, the artist's brother, 1928. Graphite drawing,
15 × 10½ in. (38 × 26.7 cm).

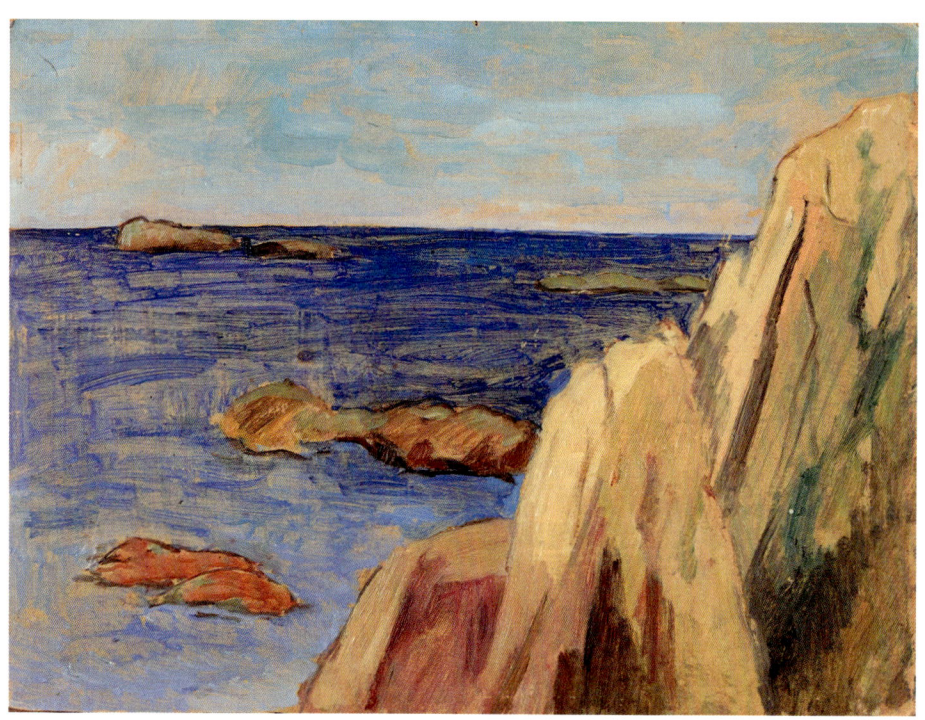

Elsa Thoresen (1906–1994), *Skjærgård billede #3*, circa 1928. Oil on board, 12⅜ × 16¾ in. (31.4 × 42.6 cm). ("Skjærgård painting," refers to the Norwegian coastal area south of Oslo.)

By 1928, Edvard Munch (1863–1944) was the most famous painter in Norway. He also attended the Norwegian National Academy of Fine Arts in Oslo, beginning in 1881. Although his work would likely have appealed to young artists in Oslo in the early twentieth century, only a few extant works by Thoresen show a hint of his influence. This can be seen in her *Skjærgård billede #3* (Skjærgård painting #3), one of a series of landscapes she made during a transitional phase, showing an awareness of Munch's work although using a much more subdued approach.

Two contrasting portraits of Thoresen created during this time illustrate the range of experimentation and practice at the school. In 1928, her classmate Rian depicted Thoresen in a somewhat cubistic style reminiscent of Picasso, with a palette of blue and rose, two periods of the artist's career that elevated his extraordinary reputation. In contrast, the more realistic unsigned portrait of around the same time uses naturalistic color in a loose, painterly application while conveying a sense of introspection and reserve.

In 1929, Bjerke-Petersen, now Thoresen's love interest, traveled to Paris, where he completed a beautiful modernist still life of lemons, which he annotated "Paris, 1929," and dedicated it to her. His father, the noted art historian Carl V.

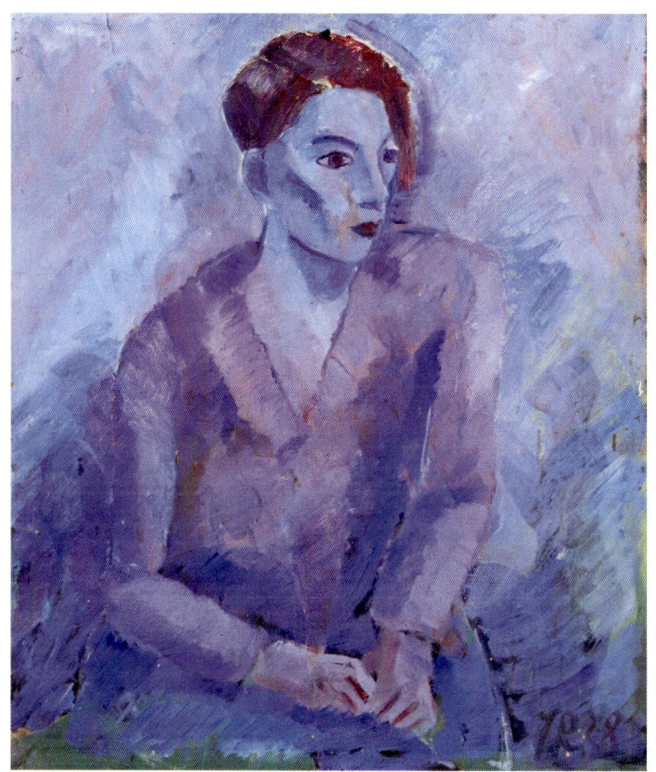
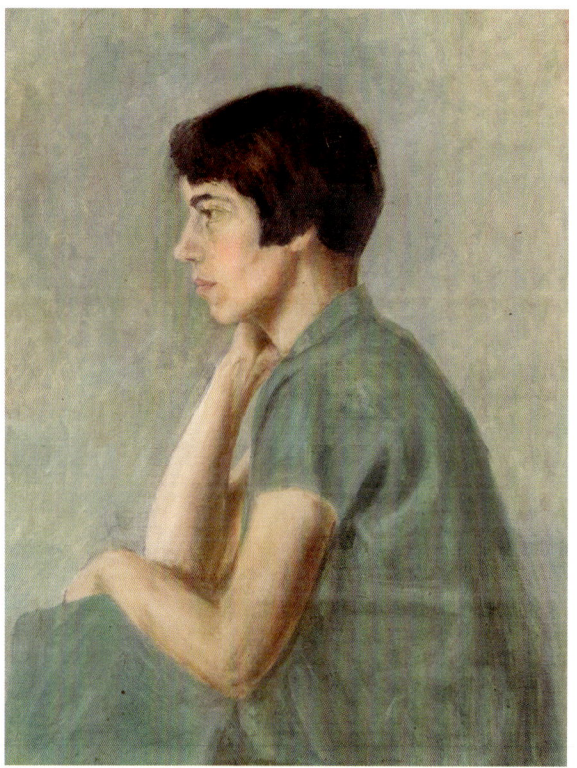
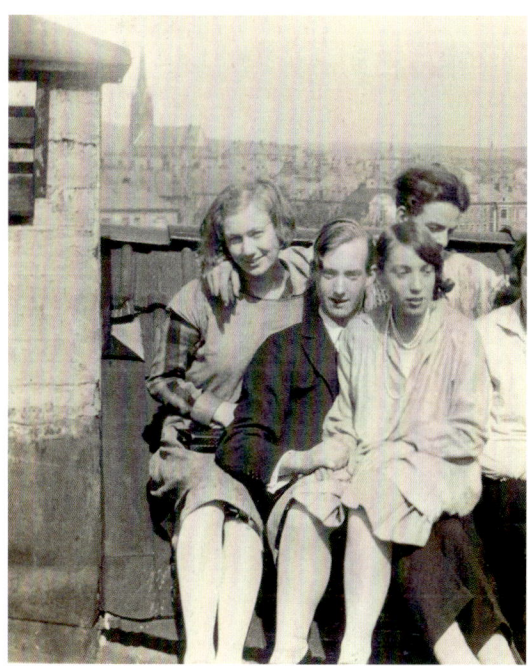

Johannes Rian (1891–1981), Portrait of Elsa Thoresen, 1928. Oil on board, 27 × 22⅞ in. (68.6 × 58.1 cm).

Artist unknown, Portrait of Elsa Thoresen, circa 1928. Oil on canvas, 25 × 19⅛ in. (63.5 × 48.6 cm).

Elsa Thoresen sitting on the lap of fellow student and boyfriend Vilhelm Bjerke-Petersen,
on the rooftop of the Norwegian National Academy of Fine Arts, Oslo, 1928.

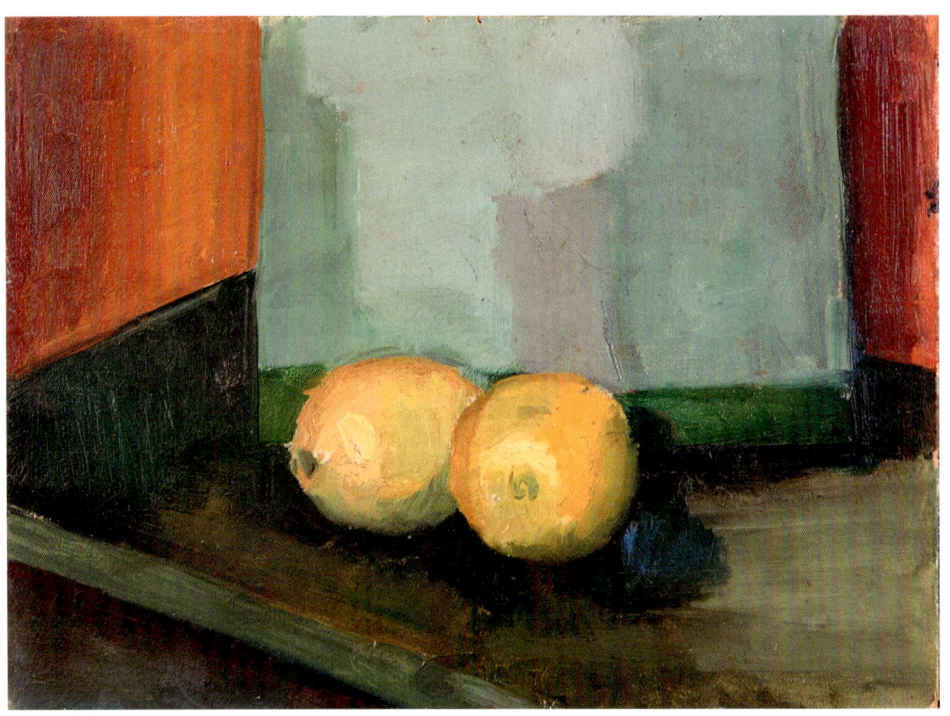

Vilhelm Bjerke-Petersen (1909–1957), Untitled, 1929. Oil on board, 9⅜ × 13 in. (23.8 × 33 cm). Inscribed verso "To Elsa" and annotated "Paris, 1929."

Petersen (1868–1938), encouraged him to advance his art studies by attending the Bauhaus school in Dessau, Germany, where from 1930 to 1931 he studied with Paul Klee (1879–1940) and Wassily Kandinsky (1866–1944). While Bjerke-Petersen was away, Thoresen continued her studies and was broadening her interest in modern art advancements throughout the world, especially in Paris. However, during this time, she did very little painting. Bjerke-Petersen, on the other hand, from his newfound inspiration at the Bauhaus, was actively creating and experimenting. A 1932 abstraction attests to his abandoning of figurative expressionist work in favor of a new concentration on color and form. The painting uses numerous contrasting shapes to infer a still-life composition, with the different forms lit from variant light sources. He flattened the planes, bisected the composition with an irregular, lightning-shaped geometric form, and limited the palette to a narrow range of colors. He also personalized the painting by placing a large V shape encapsulated in a form in the upper left quadrant of the painting. This was a clever way of representing the first initial of his name within the composition, which he signed with the conjoined initials of his full name. Within a short period of time, he would begin to introduce figurative Surrealist themes into his work.

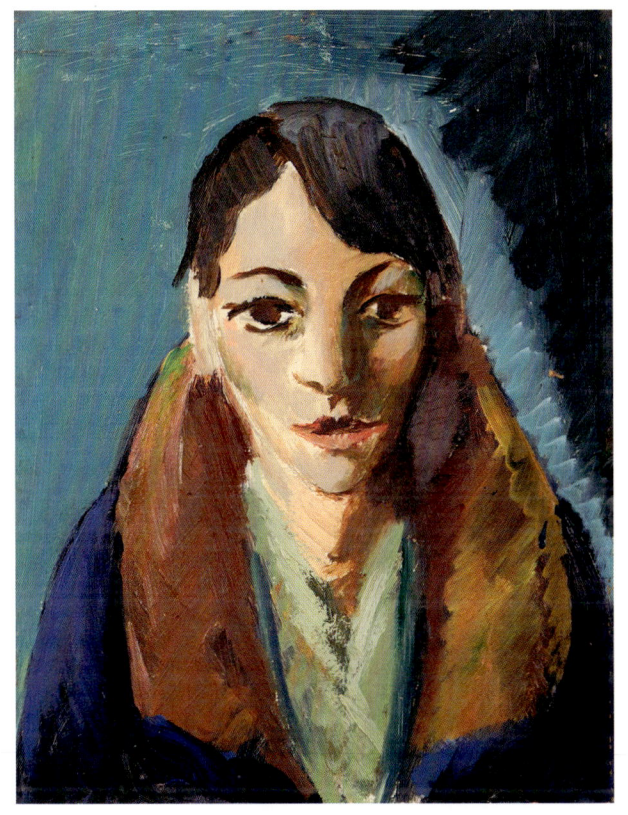

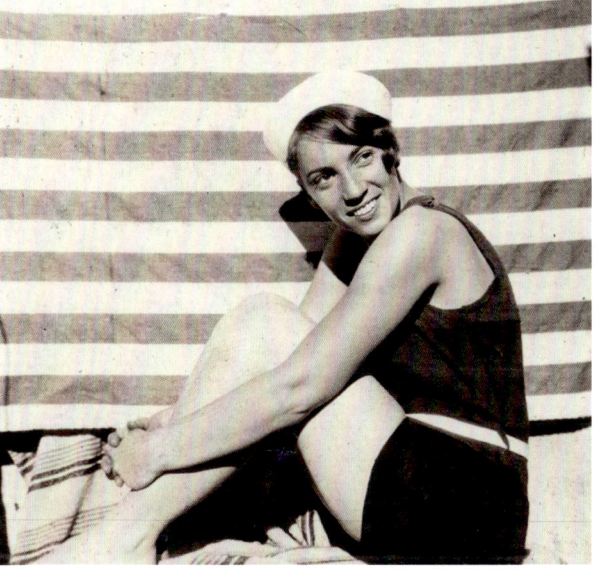

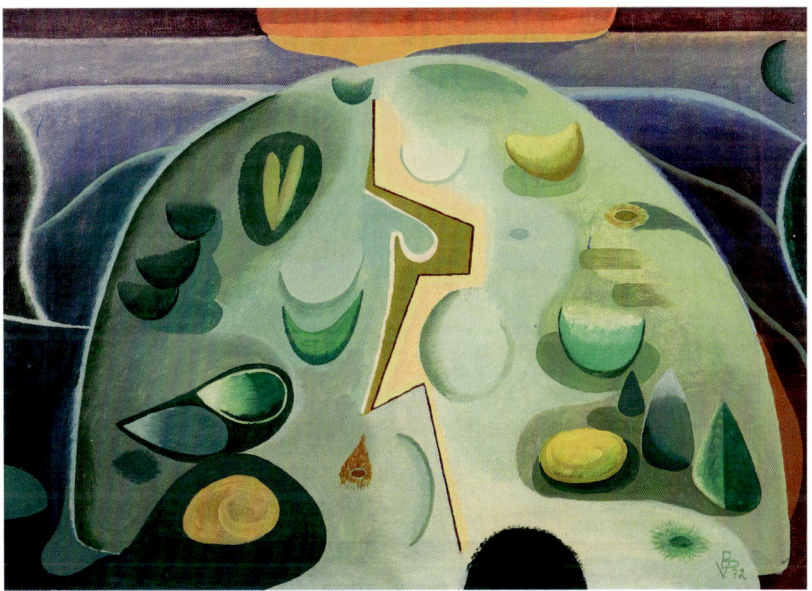

Artist unknown, possibly Bjarne Rise (1904–1984), Portrait of Elsa Thoresen, circa 1929. Oil on board,
16 × 12⅝ in. (40.6 × 32.1 cm).

Elsa Thoresen, 1929.

Vilhelm Bjerke-Petersen (1909–1957), Untitled, 1932. Oil on canvas, 26½ × 38 in. (67.3 × 96.5 cm).

Among Thoresen and Bjerke-Petersen's circle of friends was the Norwegian artist Karen Holtsmark (1907–1998), who attended the Norwegian National Academy of Craft and Art Industry from 1924 to 1927 and the Norwegian National Academy of Fine Arts from 1927 to 1930. Holtsmark credited their mutual instructor Axel Revold as an important mentor but also acknowledged Bjerke-Petersen as an inspiration, although her work does not fit into a strictly surrealist style. In 1932, she participated in a group exhibition at the Kunstnerforbundet in Oslo with Rise, Rian, and Bjerke-Petersen.[1]

In January 1934, Bjerke-Petersen became cofounder of the art association Linien (The Line), along with fellow Danish painters Ejler Bille (1910–2004) and Richard Mortensen (1910–1993). Their initial exhibition was held at Copenhagen's Kunsthal Charlottenborg and was accompanied by a collective journal. After a rift with Bille and Mortensen, Bjerke-Petersen withdrew his association with the group until after the war. By now, Bjerke-Petersen was an active writer on art and art theory, which culminated in his book *Surrealismen: Livsanskuelse, livsudfoldelse, kunst* (Surrealism: Outlook on life, expression of life, art) in 1934. After nearly eight years together, Thoresen and Bjerke-Petersen were married on February 20, 1935, in Copenhagen.

As one of the early advocates of Surrealism in Scandinavia, Bjerke-Petersen became highly influential as a writer, curator, and artist. His enthusiasm drew Thoresen into abandoning her figurative work for abstraction and, later, Surrealism. Initially, she began creating works such as Untitled, 1935 (page 63). This painting reflects an interest in Russian Constructivism, particularly the work of Aleksandr Rodchenko (1891–1956). Certainly, Bjerke-Petersen would have known of painters such as Rodchenko and also El Lissitzky (1890–1941) from his time at the Bauhaus, where their influence was significant. Less architectonic in concept, Thoresen's painting uses a large golden-yellow disk as the main component of the composition. Whether intentional or not, it suggests an impression of the sun, with an interior form that seems to be unfolding like a seed or a fetus. The left side of the painting shows a partial eclipsing of the light, while the forms on the right appear to be elongated shadows thrown across the canvas by a glaring light source. These

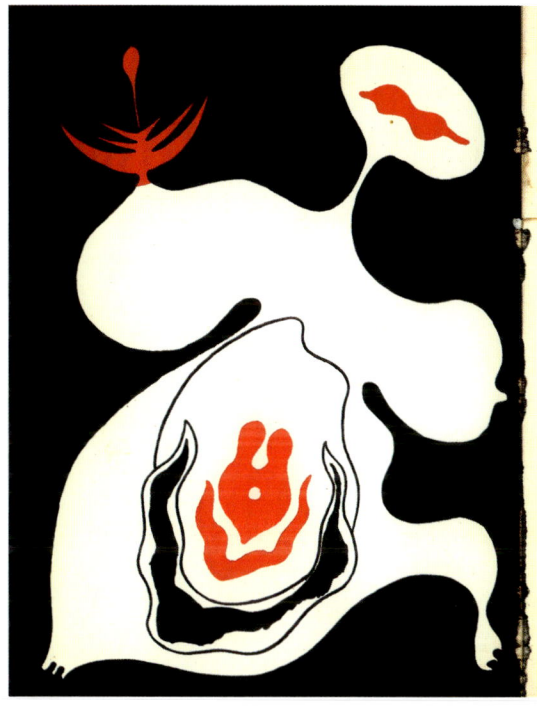

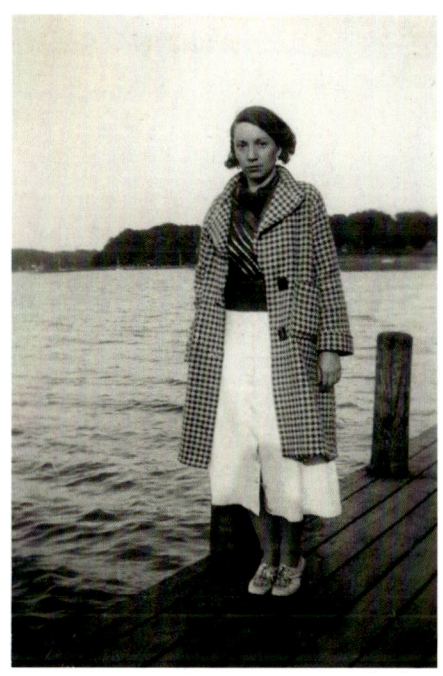

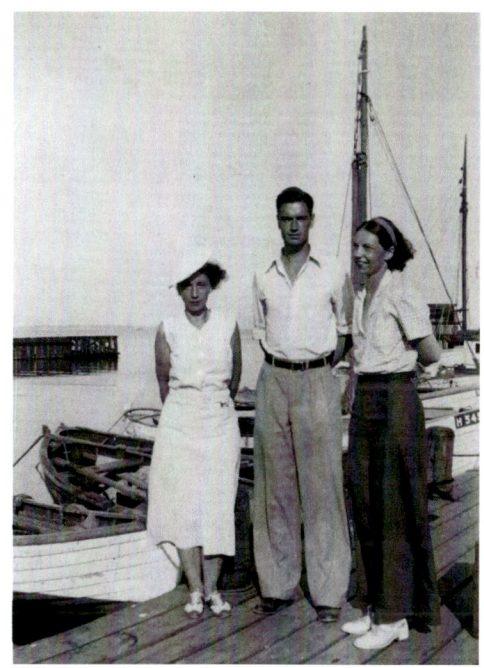

Vilhelm Bjerke-Petersen, *Surrealismen: Livsanskuelse, livsudfoldelse, kunst* (Copenhagen, 1934), frontispiece. The University of Iowa Art Library, scan courtesy of James C. Hall.

Elsa Thoresen at Furesøen, the deepest lake in Denmark, 1935.

From left: Elsa Thoresen; her brother, Nils; and her sister, Marie, known as "Puss," 1936.

shapes and forms will reappear in Thoresen's compositions throughout her life, especially in the later part of her career.

In 1935, Bjerke-Petersen curated the *International Art Exhibition: Cubism = Surrealism* at Den Frie Udstillingsbygning (The Free Exhibition Building) in Copenhagen. It was credited as the first international Surrealist exhibition in Scandinavia and featured works by some of the leading figures of the period. They included, among others, René Magritte (1898–1967), Salvador Dalí (1904–1989), Max Ernst (1891–1976), Man Ray (1890–1976), Yves Tanguy (1900–1955), and Paul Klee, Bjerke-Petersen's former instructor at the Bauhaus. The exhibition's accompanying catalogue included a short essay by André Breton (1896–1966), the leading voice of the movement through his *Surrealist Manifesto* of 1924. Not only was this milestone exhibition an important introduction to Surrealism in Denmark, but it also had a decisive impact on the work of Bjerke-Petersen and Thoresen's own creative output and standing within the community of already established artists.

> *Surrealism is not an art form or art movement, but an outlook on life of a highly revolutionary nature, as we absolutely distance ourselves from sexual restraints of any kind, from all snobbery and admiration pertaining to individual persons, whether Hitler or Lenin, from any class division, from all coercion in general and finally, in a narrower sense within the visual arts, from all imitation and portrayal of persons, instead proclaiming our goal to be man's freest expression, recognising only the direct personal experience of everything.*[2]
> Vilhelm Bjerke-Petersen

Also in 1935, Bjerke-Petersen edited the first of six issues of *Konkretion: Interskandinavisk tidsskrift for kunsten af i dag* (Concretion: An inter-Scandinavian journal for the arts of the day). The journal included influential essays and poetry by Breton, Paul Éluard (1895–1952), and Benjamin Péret (1899–1959). It contained illustrations by Jean Arp (1886–1966), Dalí, Kandinsky, Picasso, and many other

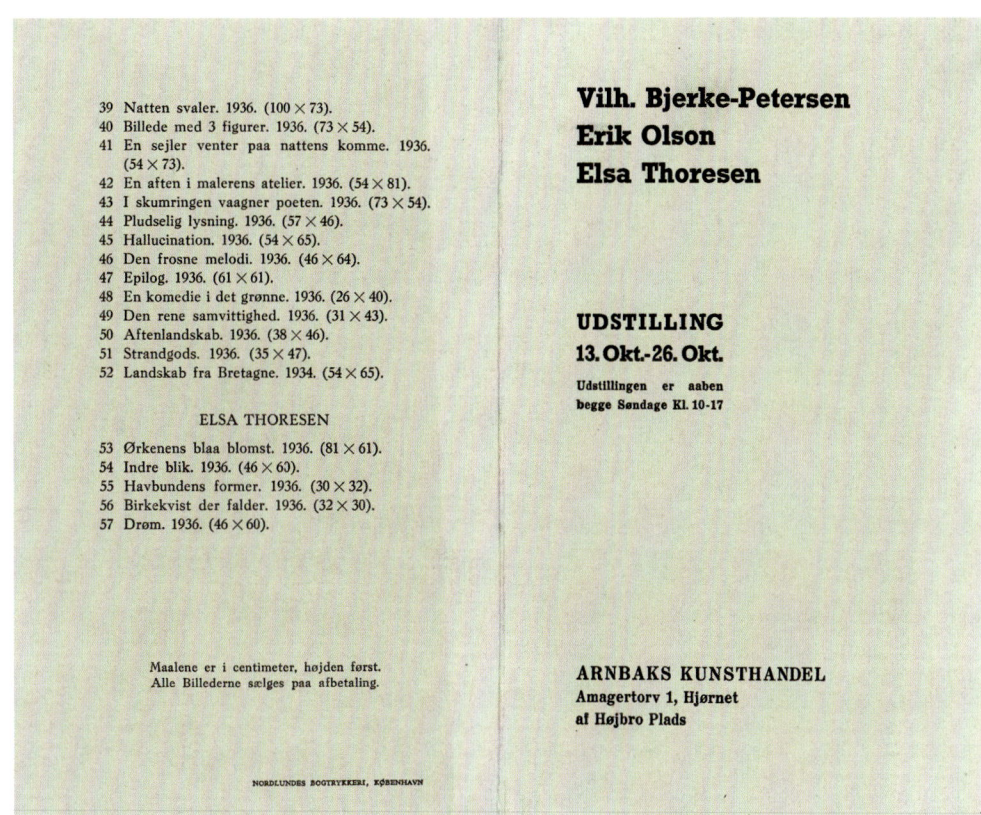

Catalogue for three-person exhibition with husband Vilhelm Bjerke-Petersen and Erik Olson, Arnbak Art Gallery, Copenhagen, 1936.

leading figures of the time. *Konkretion* also included Bjerke-Petersen's own work and that of his contemporaries in Scandinavia, such as Esaias Thorén (1901–1981) and Axel Olson (1899–1986) of Sweden's Halmstad Group. Concurrent with these activities, Bjerke-Petersen began creating anti-fascist and anti-Nazi collages and drawings, prefiguring the Nazi invasion of Denmark in 1940.

By 1936, Thoresen had assembled an impressive group of new paintings reflecting her shift into Surrealism. Contrary to the work of her husband and many of the male Surrealists, Thoresen's work is devoid of any overt sexual or sociopolitical references. Her subject matter was much more personal and guided by dreams and analytical associations. That year, she debuted her work in a three-person exhibition with Bjerke-Petersen and the Swedish modernist Erik Olson (1901–1986) at Arnbak Art Gallery in Copenhagen.

In a rare extant newspaper interview with Thoresen at this time, she spoke freely to a reporter about her career.

At Arnbak, three artists will open a small Surrealist exhibition: the well-known Swedish Surrealist Erik Olson, the Dane Vilhelm Bjerke-Petersen and his young wife, who is of Norwegian American descent. This is the first time we will see pictures of Mrs. Elsa Bjerke-Petersen, b. Thoresen, and we therefore find it appropriate to have a little compassion with the hypermodern painter.

[Being] an abrupt transplant, do you now feel American, Norwegian or Danish? We ask the chic little artist, whose brown tresses roll away from her forehead in fashionable, elegant curls.

"I haven't thought about that," says the painter. "I was born and raised in the States, in Minneapolis to be exact. My father, Dr. Thoresen, was a Norwegian, but my mother is American. I came to Norway at age fifteen. I could not speak the language, but although the change was enormous, I soon found myself at home in the new surroundings. I joined the Academy and started painting, and it captured all of my interest."

Have you been to the States since you moved to Norway?
"Yes, on a visit, but it's not the same. I don't know any American painters. There are undoubtedly several Americans among the Surrealists who exhibit in Paris, but a name doesn't tell you whether the artist is English or American. In America, there is also great interest in Surrealism, museums buy Surrealist paintings for their collections and pay well for them."

Have you always been a Surrealist?
"No, the movement hasn't been advanced up here in the North so dangerously long. However, I am now completely absorbed in Surrealism and therefore cannot think of any other form of artistic expression, but that's how it always is when a certain movement has swallowed you up."

Had you exhibited in Oslo?

"Yes, several times, but I'm only starting here now after being a sudden transplant, a year and a half here."

And your Danish husband, where did you meet him?

"In Oslo, at the Academy up there, and Surrealism is our great common interest. I saw the Surrealist exhibition here at Den Frie, and it was brilliant. However, I am only exhibiting eight canvases now at Arnbak, while my co-exhibitors are showing many more pictures. My husband has twenty-eight paintings. . . ."

And are you comfortable in Copenhagen?

"Yes, it's absolutely lovely here. The Danes are so gentle and compliant; you meet kindness everywhere. I am quite satisfied with once again having changed my place of residence, but besides, it is not far from here to Oslo, where my American mother still has her home, and where I have a sister and a brother who live there."[3]

Although Thoresen mentioned having eight paintings in the Arnbak exhibition, the catalogue lists only five, all from 1936: *Ørkenens blå blomst* (The blue flower of the desert); *Drøm* (Dream); *Indre blik* (Inner gaze); *Havbundens former* (The shapes of the seabed) (page 64); and *Birkekvist der falder* (Falling birch twig). It is interesting to note that the extant images of works from this exhibition show Thoresen using only her lowercase initials to sign her works.

The following year, in 1937, Bjerke-Petersen's father, Carl V. Petersen, the director of the Hirschsprung Collection, wrote an introductory essay for the eleventh volume in the series Danske kunstnere (Danish artists), a themed publication on the leading Surrealists in Denmark. The book is credited as an important introduction to the art careers of Rita Kernn-Larsen (1904–1998), Harry Carlsson (1891–1968), and Wilhelm Freddie (1909–1995), as well as Thoresen and

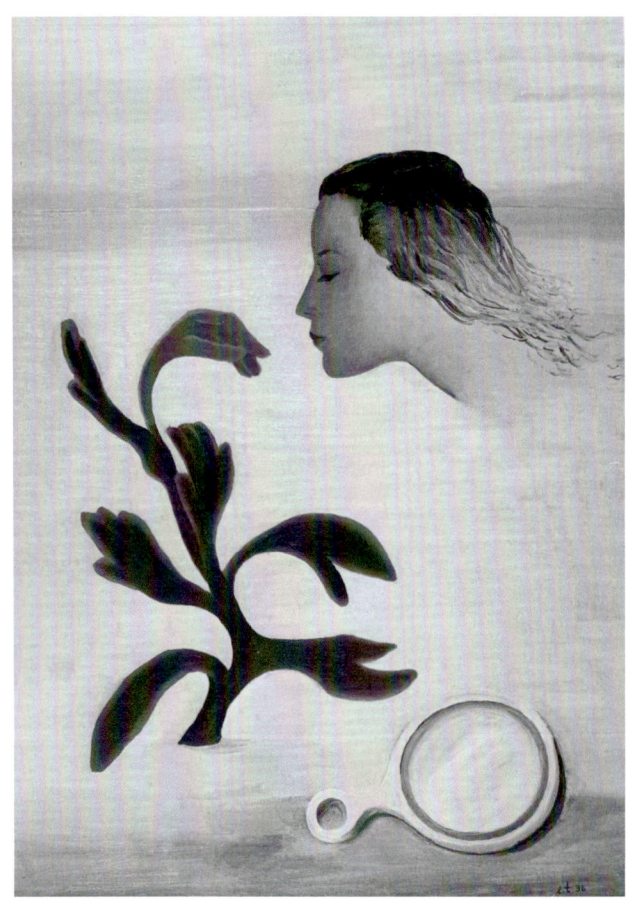

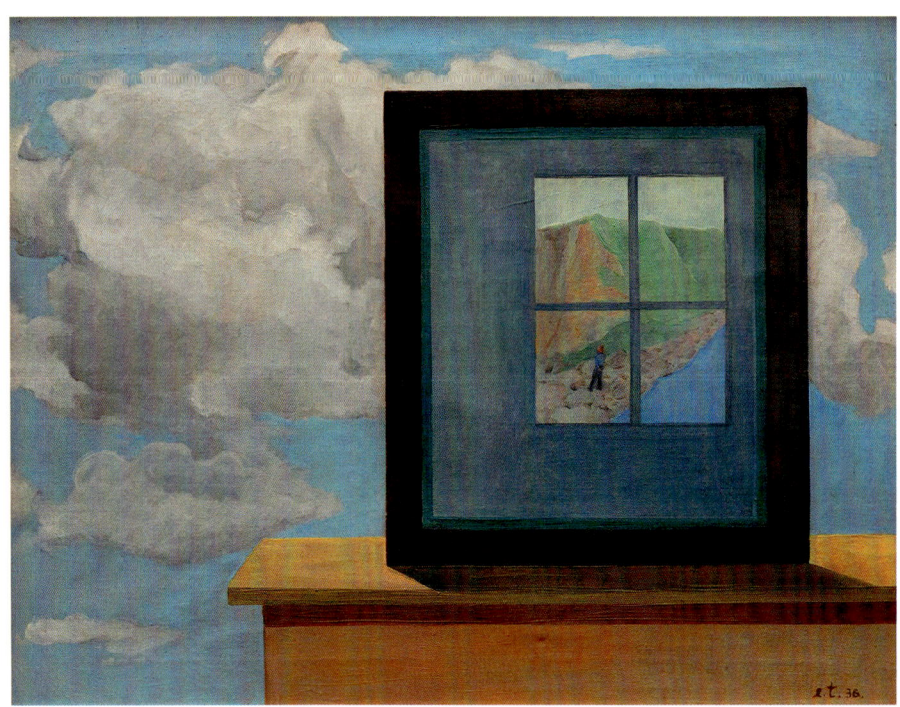

Elsa Thoresen (1906–1994), *Ørkenens blå blomst* (The blue flower of the desert), 1936. Oil on canvas, 31⅞ × 24 in. (81 × 61 cm). Current whereabouts unknown.

Elsa Thoresen (1906–1994), *Indre blik* (Inner gaze), 1936. Oil on canvas, 18 × 23½ in. (45.7 × 59.7 cm). Private collection.

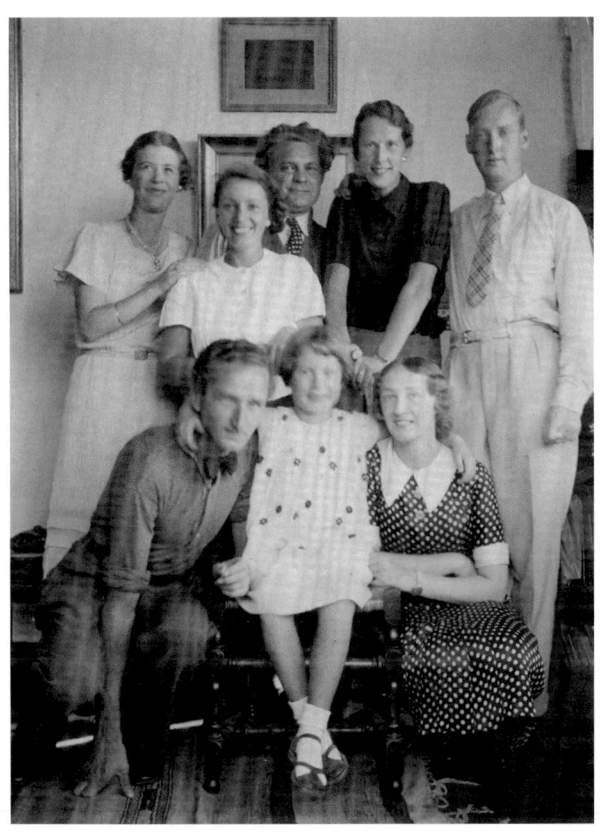

At the home of the Swedish Surrealist painter Erik Olson, Taarbæk, Denmark, 1936. *Standing left to right:* Solvig Sven-Nilsson Olson (wife of Erik Olson), Elsa Thoresen, Egon Östlund, Anna-Lisa Falk (married Axel Olson in 1944), and Vilhelm Bjerke-Petersen. *Bottom, left to right:* the painter Axel Olson, brother of Erik; Erik's daughter Viveka Olson Bosson; and Karin Östlund (Egon Östlund's second wife).

Bjerke-Petersen.[4] Thoresen had a great love for her father-in-law and honored him in a later interview.

> *Carl V. Petersen was one of the most remarkable and interesting men anyone could have known. His intelligence, his great love of art, and his respect for the artist were unequaled. He was also highly respected throughout the Scandinavian countries. His linguistic abilities helped V. Bjerke-Petersen with the translation of texts and in his correspondence and dealings with French artists. Carl V. Petersen certainly had a great influence on his son's career. He introduced him to art from an early age, and their family life was very invigorating for a young artist. All sorts of interesting people were around them, not only artists, poets, and writers, but also men like Niels Bohr, Peter Freuchen, etc.*[5]

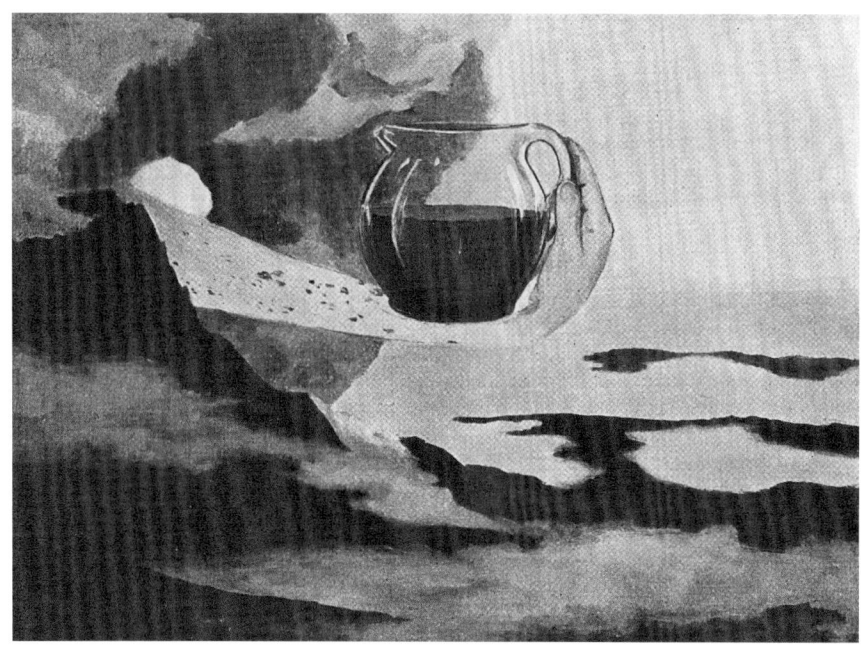

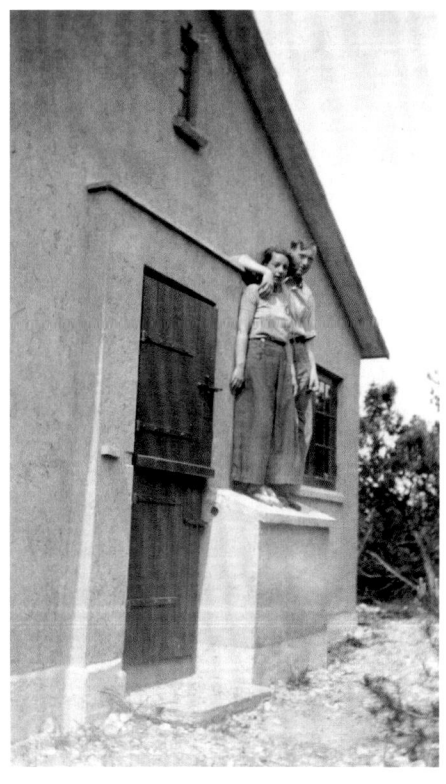

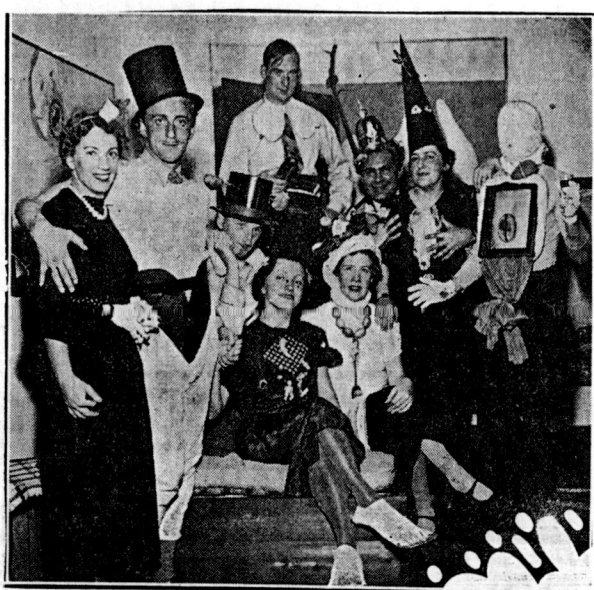

Elsa Thoresen (1906–1994), *Paysage atmosphérique* (Atmospheric landscape), 1936. Oil on canvas,
18⅛ × 24¾ in. (46 × 63 cm). Current location unknown. Scanned from a copy in the artist's papers.

Elsa Thoresen and Vilhelm Bjerke-Petersen at their home in Denmark, 1936.

"Party with the Surrealists," *Ekstra Bladet*, October 15, 1936. Newspaper clipping from Thoresen's papers.
The Surrealists partied in Elsa Thoresen and Vilhelm Bjerke-Petersen's attic studio at Højbro Plads
15, Copenhagen, Denmark. The occasion was the couple's joint exhibition with Erik Olson at the
prominent Arnbaks Kunsthandel, located at Bredgade 24. *From left:* Thoresen, Wilhelm Freddie, Axel
Olson, Bjerke-Petersen, Egon Östlund, Franciska Clausen, Erik Olson, and, seated, Rita Kernn-Larsen
and Solvig Olson.

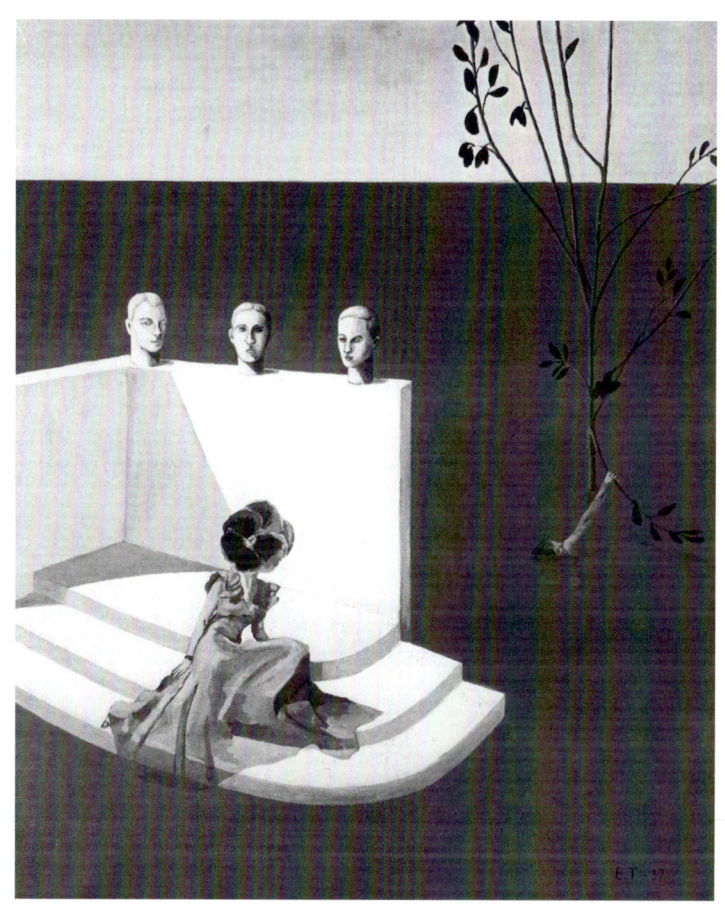

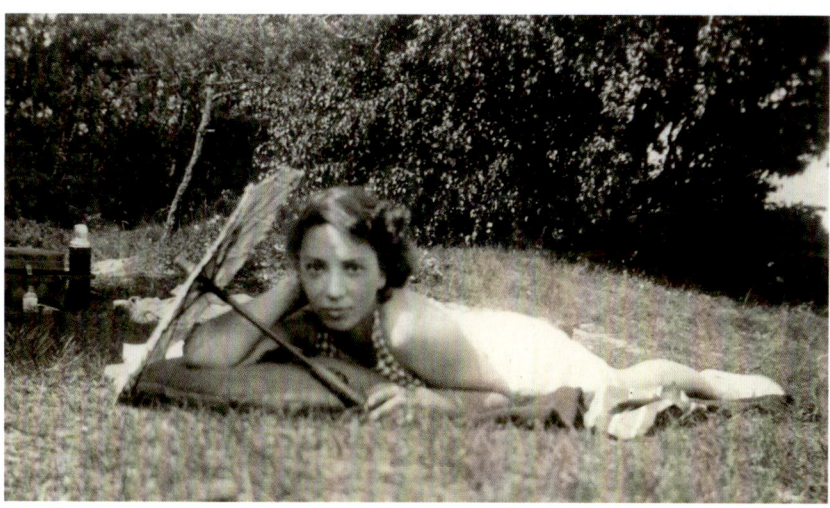

Elsa Thoresen (1906–1994), *Oliventræet* (Olive tree), 1937. Oil on canvas, 27½ × 23⅝ in. (70 × 60 cm).
Present location unknown.

Elsa Thoresen, 1937.

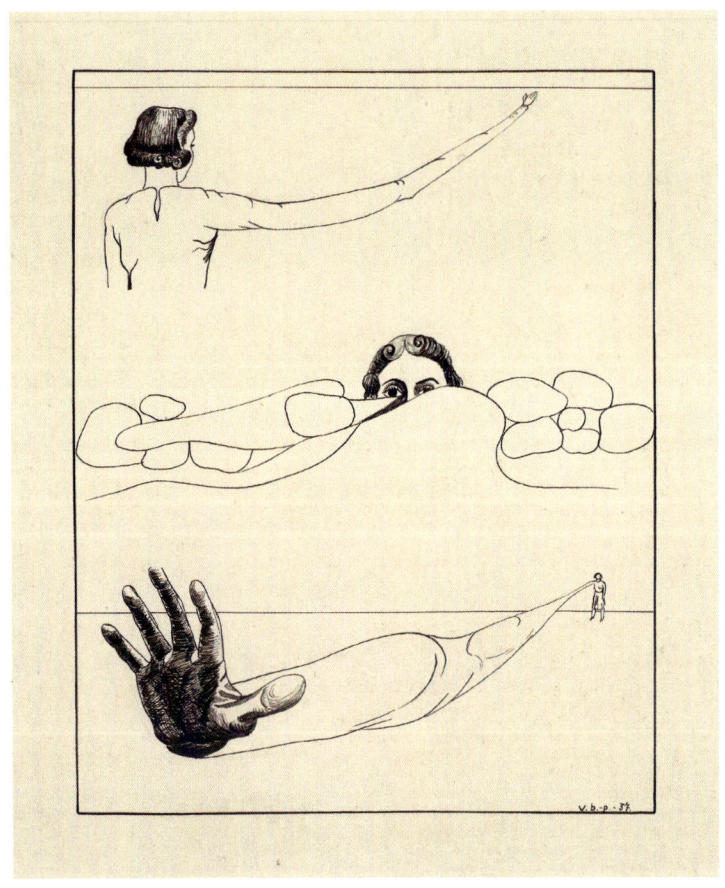

Vilhelm Bjerke-Petersen (1909–1957), Untitled, 1937. India ink on paper, 15 × 12½ in. (38 × 31.6 cm). Musée National d'Art Moderne / Centre Georges, Pompidou/Paris/France. Digital Image © CNAC/MNAM, Dist. RMN–Grand Palais / Art Resource, NY. Asset image: AR6204199. Asset source: 21-535918. Photo: Cecilia Laulanne.

Bjerke-Petersen used Elsa Thoresen, his wife, as the model for this drawing.

Integrating their personal and professional lives, the couple now began using each other as models for their individual Surrealist compositions. Bjerke-Petersen's unusual Daliesque drawing of Thoresen with her arms and hands magically elongated stands in sharp contrast to his portrait of her, painted in a realistic manner, surrounded by an improbably placed cat and bird, with a giant dragon lily looming above her. Thoresen's clever use of Bjerke-Petersen painting their collaborative mural is incorporated into her composition, but he is painting on the still water as canvas and casting a large misshapen shadow that looks similar to the contour of the dragon lily he painted in her portrait. The allusion to Bjerke-Petersen's love of sea glass is represented by his hand dipping into a fishbowl to collect his naturally weathered gems. The couple also collaborated on a mural for the Højdevangens School in Copenhagen and produced a series of thirteen panels for the residential building Ved Volden in Christianshavn in 1938–39.[6]

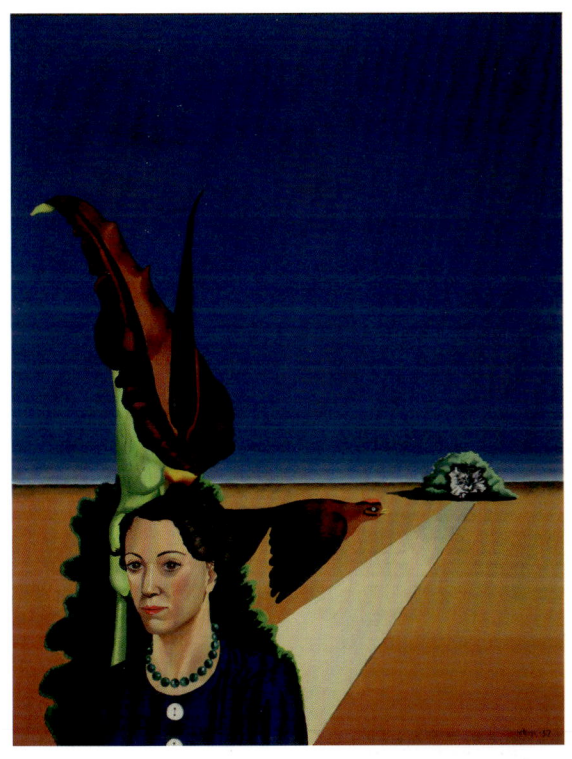

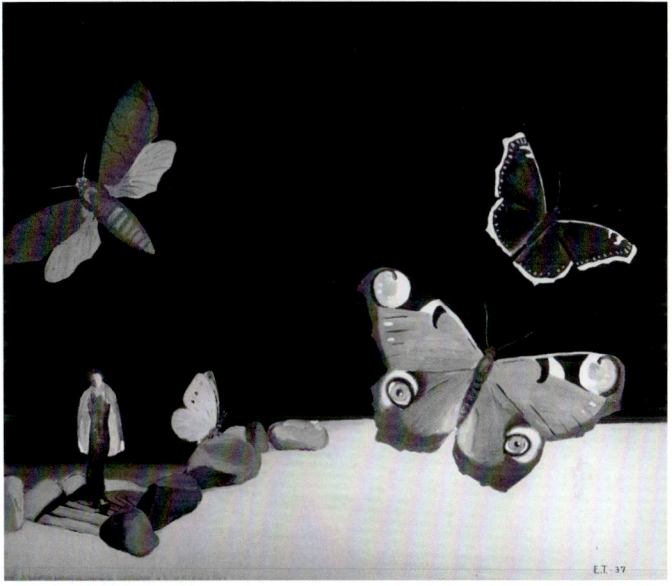

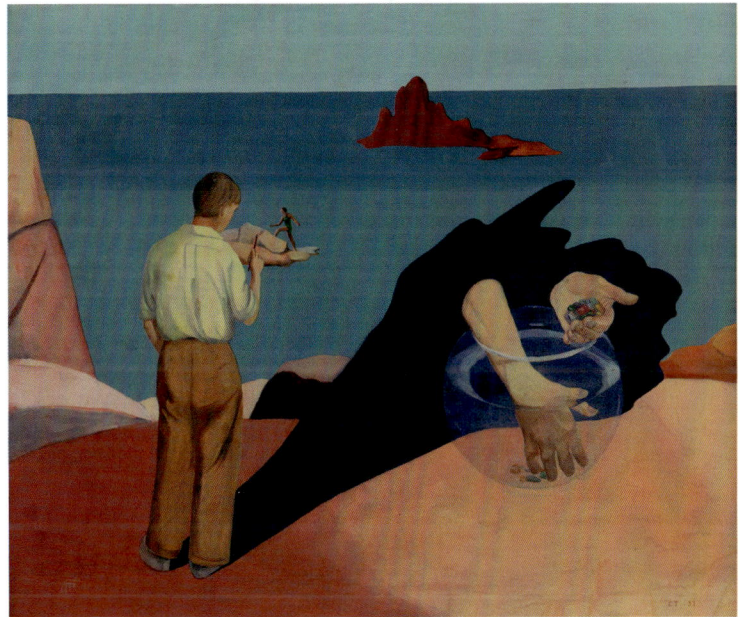

Vilhelm Bjerke-Petersen (1909–1957), *Portrait of the Painter Elsa Thoresen*, 1937. Oil on canvas, 45½ × 35⅜ in. (115.5 × 90 cm). Kunstmuseum Brandts, Odense, Denmark.

Elsa Thoresen (1906–1994), *Naubemere* (Neighbors), 1937. Oil on canvas, 23½ × 27½ in. (59.7 × 70 cm). Present location unknown.

Elsa Thoresen (1906–1994), *Bjerke-Petersen maler* (Bjerke-Petersen painting), 1937. Oil on canvas, 31⅛ × 38⅝ in. (79 × 98 cm). Private collection, Scandinavia. Photo by Torben Eskerod.

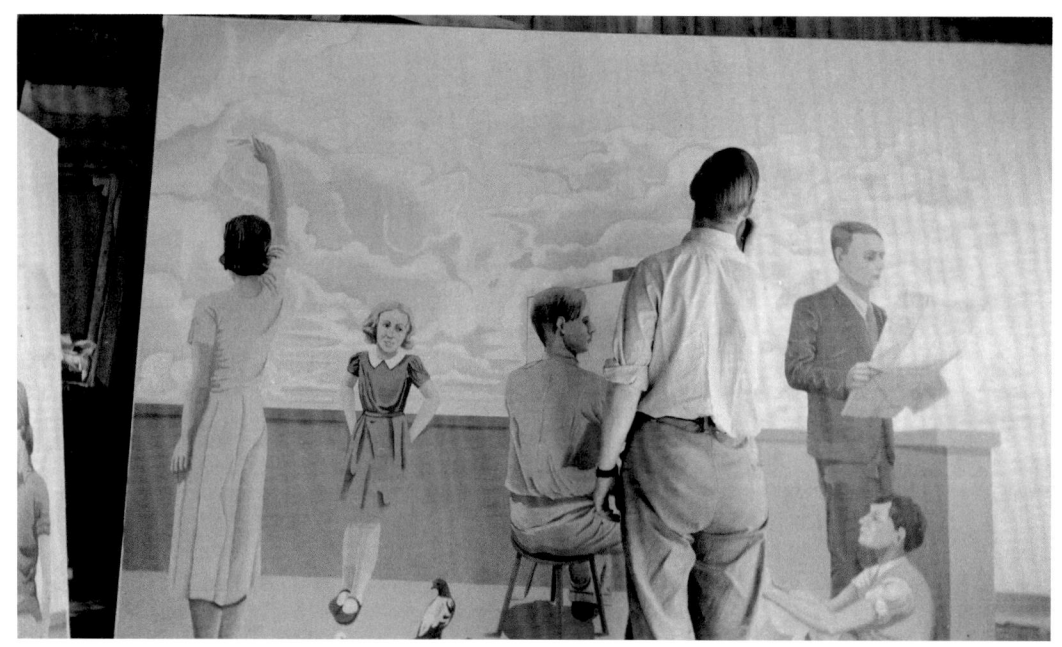

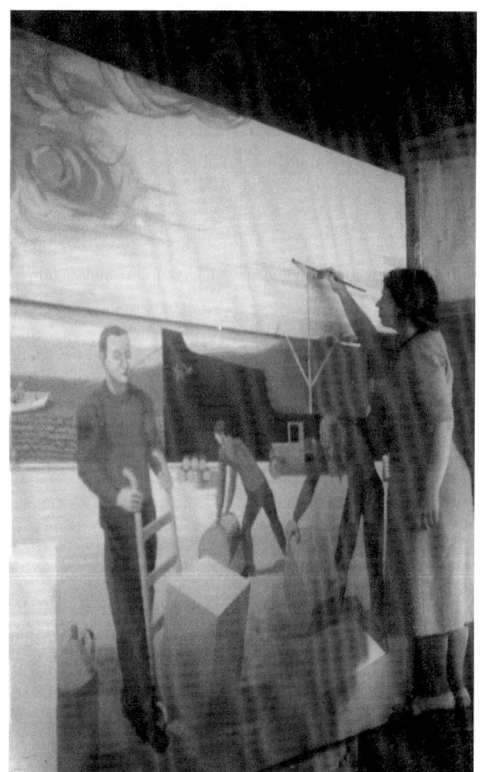

Vilhelm Bjerke-Petersen painting one of the mural panels for the Højdevangens School in his and Elsa Thoresen's studio in Birkerød, Copenhagen, 1937.

Elsa Thoresen painting one of the mural panels for the Højdevangens School in her and Vilhelm Bjerke-Petersen's studio in Birkerød, Copenhagen, 1937.

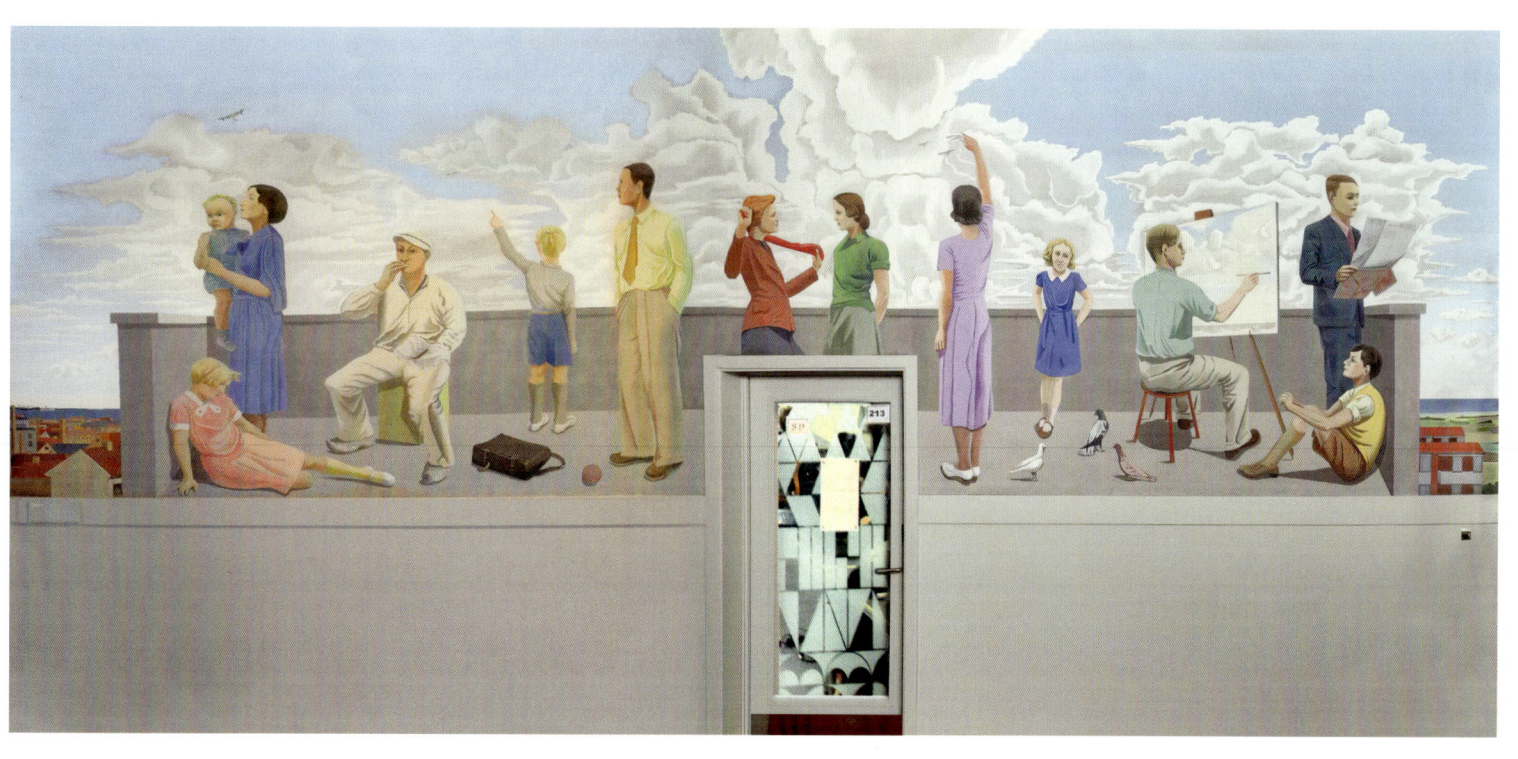

Elsa Thoresen (1906–1994) and Vilhelm Bjerke-Petersen (1909–1957), Completed murals for the
Højdevangens School in Copenhagen, 1939. Photo provided by Thomas Millroth.

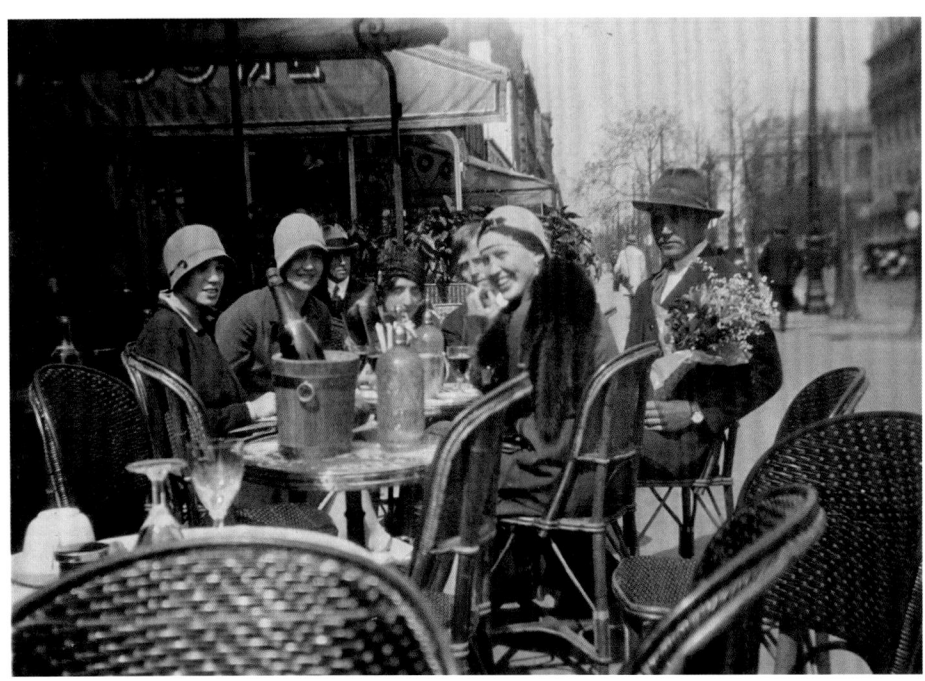

Elsa Thoresen (far left) and friends at the Café du Dôme, Paris, circa 1937/38.

In 1937, Thoresen and Bjerke-Petersen left for Paris. In a 1976 interview, Thoresen stated: "I accompanied my husband to Paris in 1937–38, and we met Max Ernst, (Yves) Tanguy, (Kurt) Seligmann, Jean Arp, Sophie Taeuber-Arp, (Benjamin) Péret, Marcel Duchamp, André Breton, (Wassily) Kandinsky, and others, perhaps not as important, whose names I cannot remember. V. Bjerke-Petersen and Erik Olson visited Dalí. Language was still a barrier; neither of us spoke much French. We both spoke English, and Vilhelm spoke German fluently."[7]

Thoresen and Bjerke-Petersen were selected to be included in *L'exposition internationale du surréalisme* organized by Breton and the poet Paul Éluard. The landmark exhibition took place in the Galérie Beaux-Arts, January 17–February 24, 1938, and featured the leading Surrealist painters of the period. Thoresen's two paintings in the exhibition were *Verdenslyset—mørkets lys* (The light of the world—the light of darkness), painted in Paris in 1937, and *Jeb ved det ikke* (I do not know), 1937. Although Thoresen was Norwegian American, Breton selected her as part of the Danish group of Surrealists, whose work he admired. One of Thoresen's closest friends was the painter Rita Kernn-Larsen, whose work was also included in the show. Kernn-Larsen later recalled the struggles that she and her fellow Scandinavian Surrealists encountered early in their careers: "We had everyone against us as young surrealists. They were furious and the critics were very hostile. It was incomprehensible to me because it seemed so

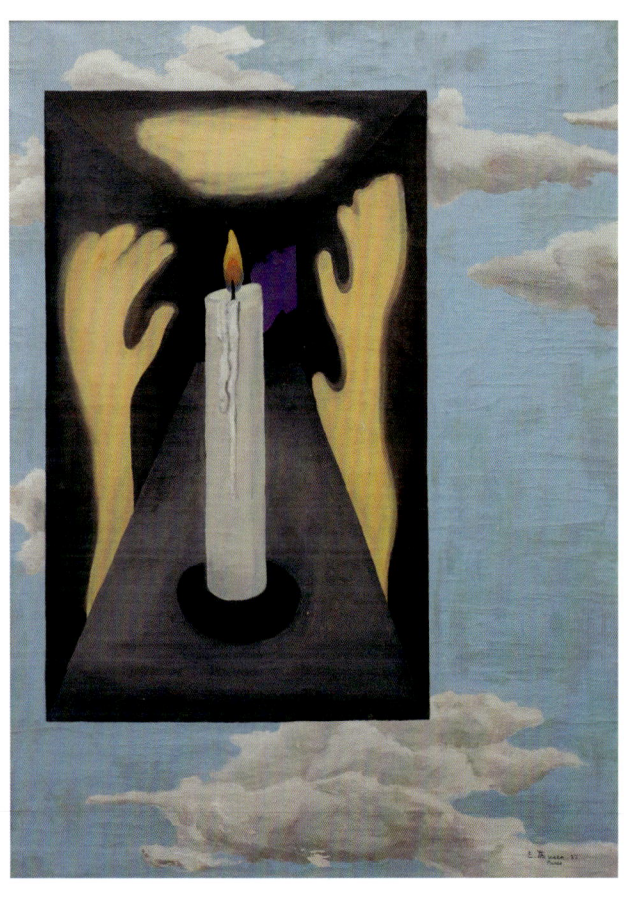

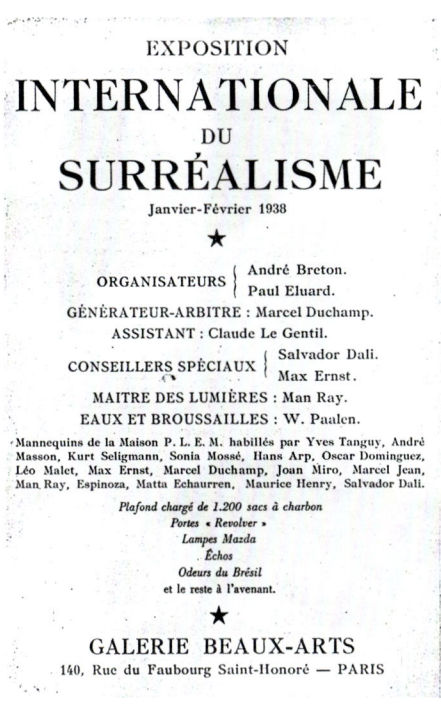

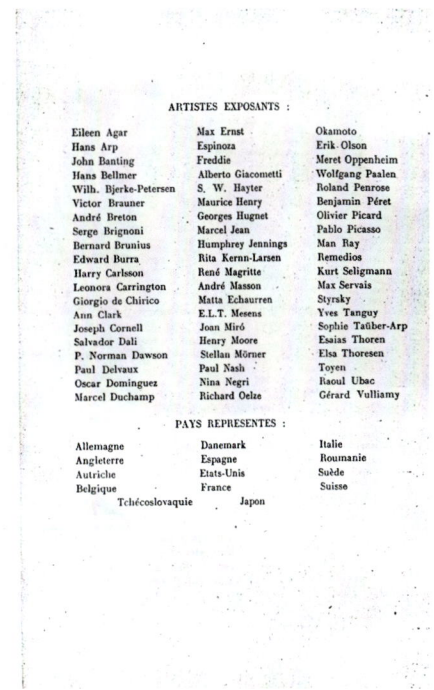

Elsa Thoresen (1906–1994), *Verdenslyset—mørkets lys* (The light of the world—the light of darkness),
1937. Oil on canvas, 30⅞ × 22⅞ in. (78.5 × 58 cm). Private collection, Denmark.
Photo by Torben Eskerod.

Scanned photocopy of *L'exposition internationale du surréalisme* catalogue from Elsa Thoresen's papers.

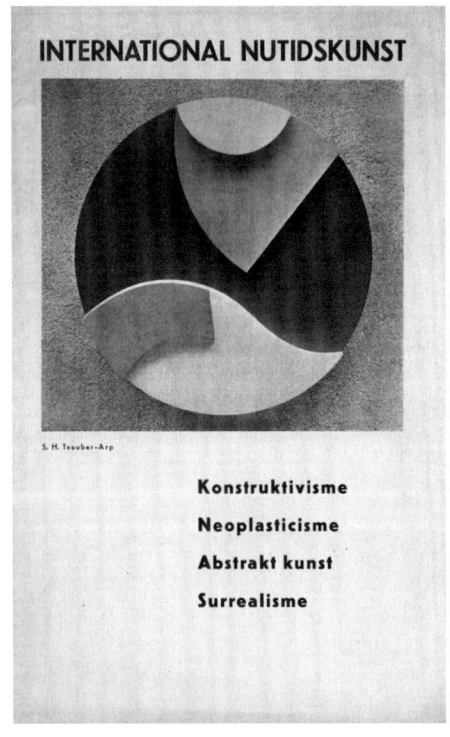

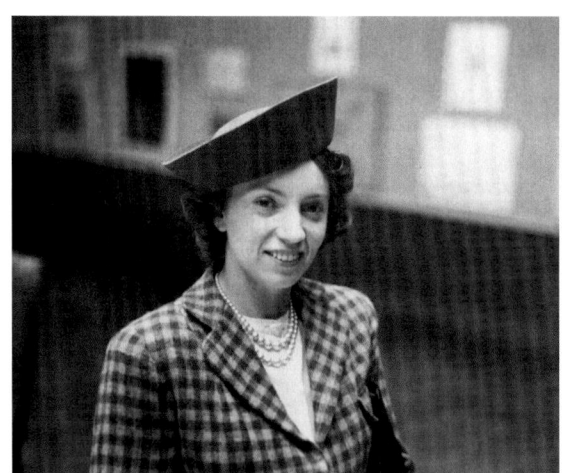

Cover of the *International nutidskunst: Konstruktivisme, neoplasticisme, abstrakt kunst, surrealisme*
(International contemporary art: Constructivism, neoplasticism, abstract art, surrealism)
catalogue, Oslo, 1938. Catalogue design by Vilhelm Bjerke-Petersen. Scan provided by Dr. Jana
Teuscher, curator, Stiftung Arp e.V., Berlin, Germany.

Elsa Thoresen at the *International nutidskunst: Konstruktivisme, neoplasticisme, abstrakt kunst,
surrealisme* exhibition, Kunstnerforbundet, Oslo, 1938.

natural! It was in the air, it was inevitable, it was the times, and we had to
participate in it."[8] As a result of Thoresen's inclusion in the exhibition, Breton
reproduced her painting *Atmosfaerisk landskab* (Atmospheric landscape, 1936) in
his *Dictionnaire abrégé du surréalisme* (Abridged dictionary of Surrealism) in 1938.
That year also found her painting *Abstrakt komposition* (Abstract composition)
of 1935 illustrated in Sophie Taeuber-Arp's magazine *Plastique*, issue 3 (1938).[9]

After their Paris success and with newfound important connections,
Thoresen and Bjerke-Petersen became involved in the exhibition *International
Contemporary Art: Constructivism, Neoplasticism, Abstract Art, Surrealism*, which
ran September 16–October 2, 1938, at the Kunstnerforbundet in Oslo. The show
was organized by Arp, Taeuber-Arp, and Bjerke-Petersen, who also designed
the catalogue, and with Thoresen assisting in the installation. The exhibition
featured major artists of the period, including Dalí, Ernst, Magritte, Man Ray,
Kurt Schwitters (1887–1948), and Bjerke-Petersen's teachers Kandinsky and
Klee, among others. Schwitters had just recently been included in the exhibition

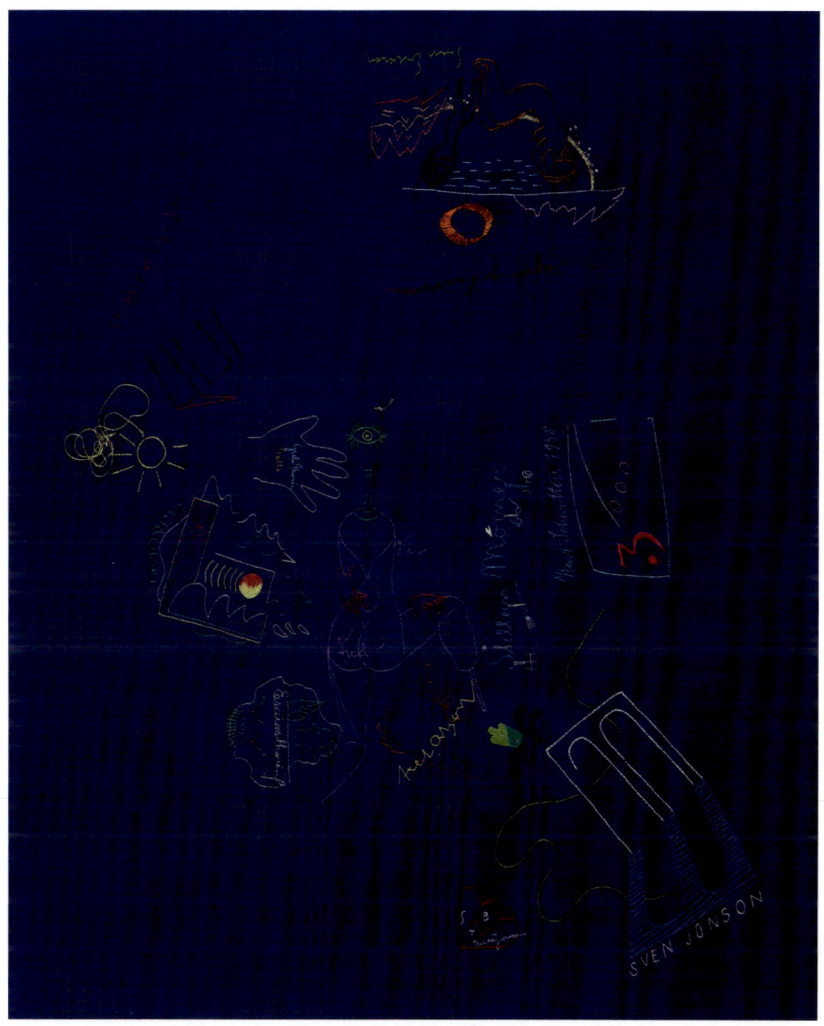

Elsa Thoresen (1906–1994), Fabric with embroidered sketches and signatures of artists, 1938.
Cloth, 57 × 54 in. (144.8 × 137.2 cm).

Twentieth Century German Art at the New Burlington Galleries in London, which was organized in protest against the Nazi *Degenerate Art* exhibition of 1937. After the 1938 Oslo exhibition, Schwitters traveled to Stockholm, Copenhagen, and Göteborg, Sweden, where he met with some of the Swedish Surrealists from the Halmstad Group and their spouses, and with Bjerke-Petersen and Thoresen in attendance. An interesting artifact from that time is an embroidered cloth with drawings and autographs by Schwitters, Stellan Mörner (1896–1979), Sven (X:et) Erixson (1899–1970), Sven Jonson (1902–1981), Brita Jonson, Ingeborg Ericson, Wilhelm Freddie, Esaias Thorén, Greta Cembraeus Thorén, Axel Olson, and Erik Olson. Thoresen had the artists draw on the cloth with chalk, which she later embroidered to preserve the occasion. Some of the original chalk drawings remain where Thoresen had intended to complete the embroidering.[10] Considering the 1938 travel date of Schwitters, Bjerke-Petersen and Thoresen

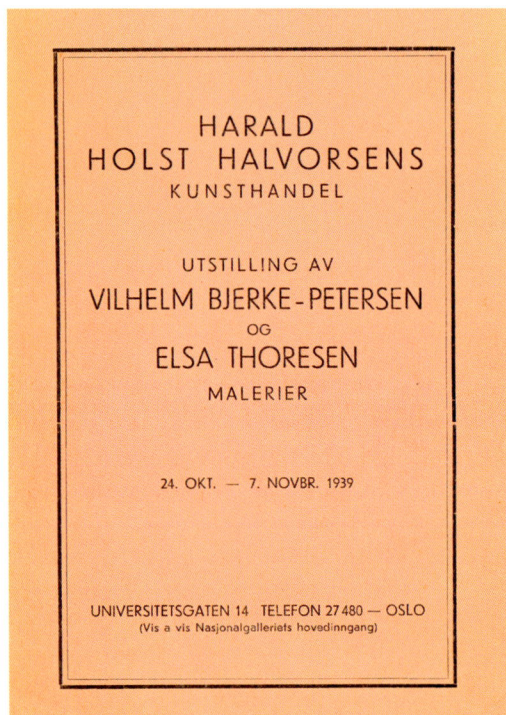
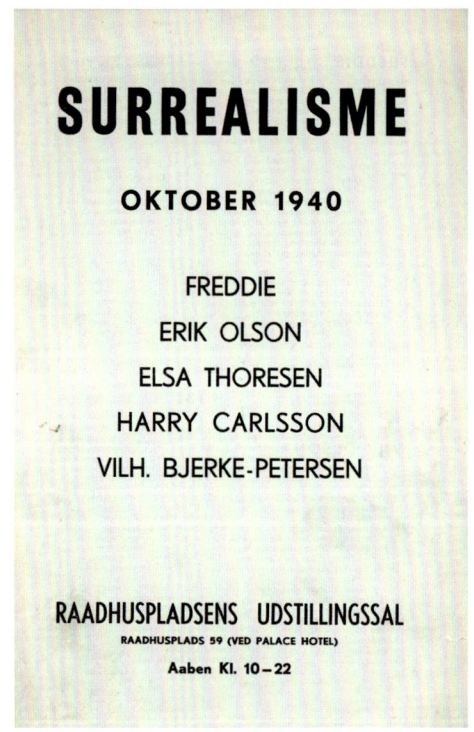

Harald Holst Halvorsen Gallery exhibition brochure for Thoresen and Bjerke-Petersen paintings exhibition, 1939.

Exhibition catalogue of Surrealist works at Raadhuspladsens Exhibition Hall, Copenhagen, 1940.

must have been visiting Sweden during that time, having known members of the Halmstad Group previously. The pioneering modernist group had formed in 1929 and held their first exhibition in 1930 at Göteborg Konsthall. Although the group were certainly advanced in their art production, the women artists in their circle remained mainly ancillary figures and were never invited to formally exhibit with the male-only organization.[11]

In 1939, Thoresen and Bjerke-Petersen were given a two-person exhibition at Harald Holst Halvorsen's art gallery in Oslo. Halvorsen was an important dealer, collector, and preservationist of the works of Edvard Munch and other leading Norwegian artists of the period. For this exhibition Bjerke-Petersen, as usual, had more of his work included, with twenty-one paintings, and Thoresen with fifteen.[12]

On April 9, 1940, Denmark became occupied by Nazi Germany. Three months later, on July 6, Bjerke-Petersen and Thoresen's son, Kai, was born in Copenhagen. That same year, Thoresen's brother, Nils, became a messenger

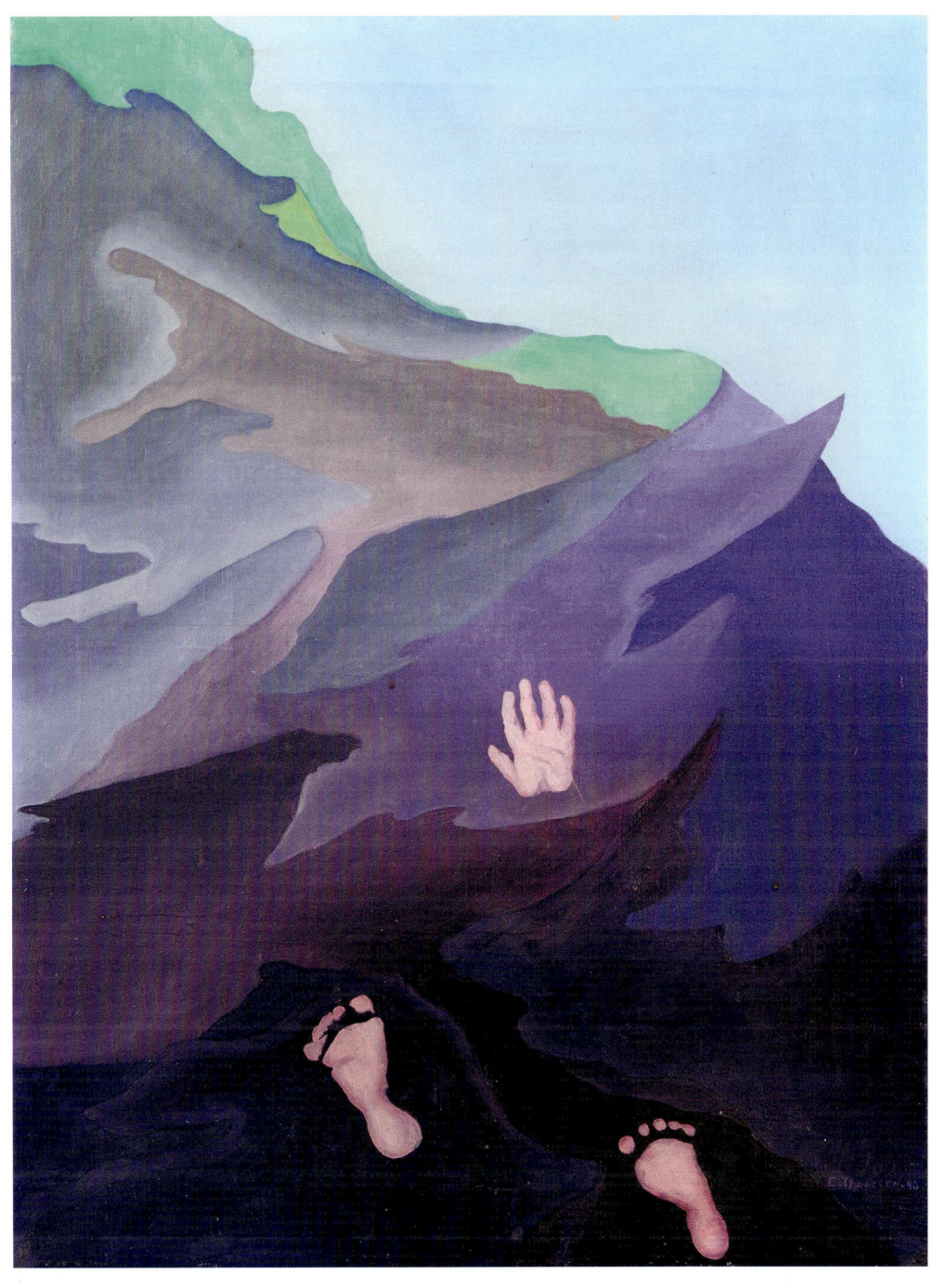

Elsa Thoresen (1906–1994), Untitled, 1940. Oil on canvas, 23¾ × 18¼ in. (60.3 × 46.4 cm).

For this painting, Thoresen painted the hand and feet of her newborn son, Kai, and imprinted them onto the canvas.

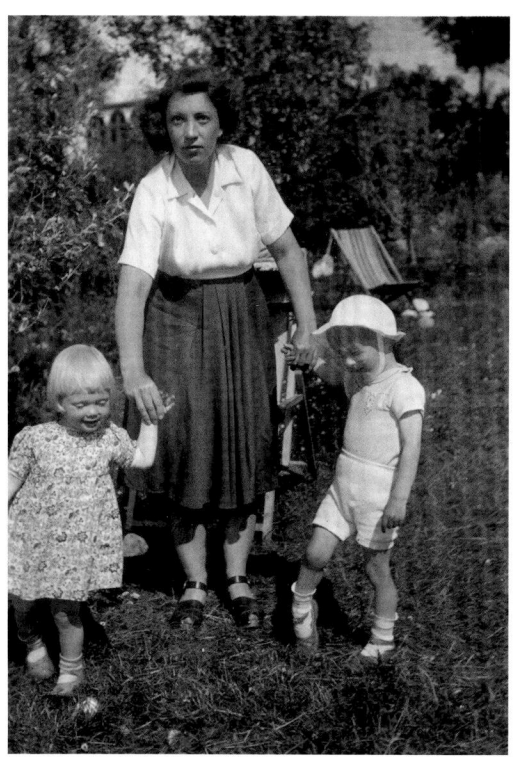

Elsa Thoresen with her children, Alice and Kai.

for the American Consulate General in Oslo, and her sister, Marie, served as a clerk in the office. In October, Thoresen and Bjerke-Petersen were included in a group exhibition along with Wilhelm Freddie, Erik Olson, and Harry Carlsson at Raadhuspladsens Exhibition Hall, Copenhagen. Once again, Thoresen had the fewest number of works shown, with thirteen paintings and no biographical sketch, compared to the men.[13]

By 1941, Thoresen and Bjerke-Petersen had a second child, a daughter named Alice (after Thoresen's mother) Louise (in case they stayed in France) Tove (in case they stayed in Scandinavia). Greta Cembraeus Thorén, the wife of Esaias Thorén, was Alice's godmother.[14] For the next few years, Thoresen was busy raising the children, which left her very little time to paint. Denmark was still under Nazi occupation, and Bjerke-Petersen's political and artistic statements against fascism and Nazi Germany began to catch up with him. As his daughter recalled: "My father was doing propaganda against the Nazis, political cartoons in the newspapers. The Danish national security (intelligence agency) found his name on the blacklist. They put us on a ship and got us over to Sweden."[15]

According to a recently located family history, "In late 1943 or early 1944, when Kai was 3½ and Alice a bit over two, the family, with the assistance of the Danish police, boarded a boat loaded with Danish beer and outbound from Copenhagen across Øresund and transferred to a boat flying the Swedish flag but clearly manned by Danes and went into the harbor at Helsingborg, Sweden. . . . An interesting side note is that the Danes, aware of the effects of cocaine, routinely dusted the decks of their ships going to Sweden. Thus, when the Germans inspected individual vessels with their guide dogs, several sniffs and the dog was, from an olfactory standpoint, totally paralyzed and within seconds, was unable to smell anything."[16]

Several accounts have the family arriving in southern Sweden by spring 1944. Assisted by artist friends, the family lived in the town of Söndrum and then various locations in and around Halmstad and Stockholm. Being on the western coast, so near to the sea, the family would find solace from the uncertainty of their future by visiting the peaceful beaches and shoreline. During this time, Thoresen began collecting small pieces of driftwood that had been eroded and sculpted by the sea. These objects would soon be incorporated into her paintings and provided her with a unique and personal iconography. Thoresen and Bjerke-Petersen were welcomed to the community of Swedish artists from the Halmstad Group, and they were part of an exhibition with the Norwegian artists Alf-Jørgen Aas (1915–1981) and Henrik Finne (1898–1992) and the Danish artist Egon Möller-Nielsen (1915–1959) in 1944.[17]

A year later, the couple were part of a group exhibition called *From Five Nations* at the God Konst (Good Art) Gallery at the Göteborg Concert Hall, May 25–June 10, 1945. The accompanying catalogue, written by the artist Jørgen Nash, stated: "The refugees and the Swedes, who together exhibit their different works here in God Konst, have both as people and as artists been part of Nazism's hideous joy of conquest. Now, however, this destructive 'swöbe' is unharmed and the persecuted can return to their respective countries and continue the fight against the reaction. 'From Five Nations' would rather not be the last time Göteborg saw their faces."[18] The term "swöbe" likely referenced Swabia,

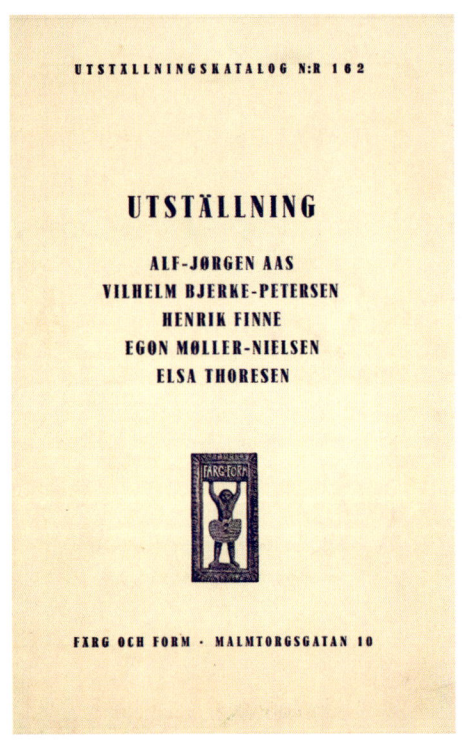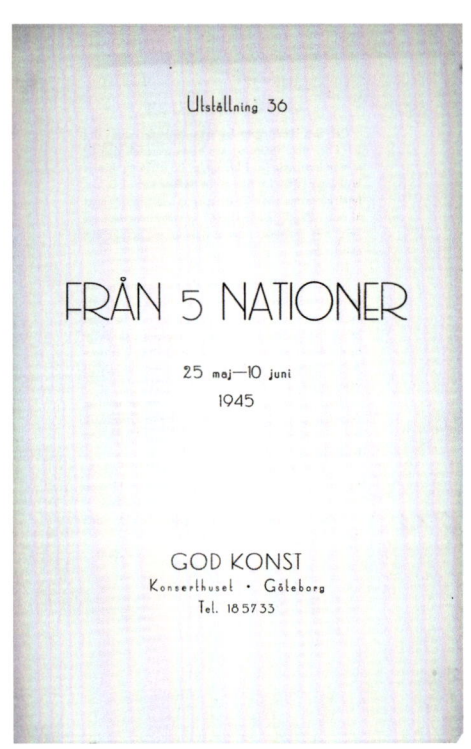

Exhibition catalogue #162, group show featuring Bjerke-Petersen and Thoresen, Color and Form Gallery, Stockholm, 1944.

Catalogue for Exhibit 36, *From Five Nations*, Good Art, Göteborg Concert Hall, Sweden, 1945.

which was a Nazi administrative district in Germany during this time. Besides Thoresen and Bjerke-Petersen, the other artists in the exhibition included Erik Asmussen and Erik Ortvad from Denmark; Endre Nemes from Hungary; Ernst Martin, Lennart Rodhe, and Uno Vallman from Sweden; Peter Weiss from Czechoslovakia; and Werner Worbs from Germany.[19] That same year, 1945, the couple's work was also featured in a two-person exhibition at the Lidköping Art Association in Lidköping, Sweden. Thoresen's three paintings were titled *Stenens mirakel* (The miracle of the stone), *Skogens poesi I* (The poetry of the forest I), and *Skogens poesi II* (The poetry of the forest II).

With the war now over and constraints lifted, Bjerke-Petersen won a Guggenheim Fellowship to travel to New York City and brought along the family, sailing on the ship *Stavangerfjord* and arriving on June 11, 1946. Bjerke-Petersen's teacher and inspiration, Kandinsky, had died in 1944, and in spring of 1945 the *Kandinsky Memorial Exhibition* was held at the Museum of Non-Objective Painting, the forerunner of the Guggenheim Museum. During the couple's 1946/47 time in New York City, two important books were translated by Kandinsky student Hilla Rebay; Kandinsky's *On the Spiritual in Art* (1911) was translated into English for

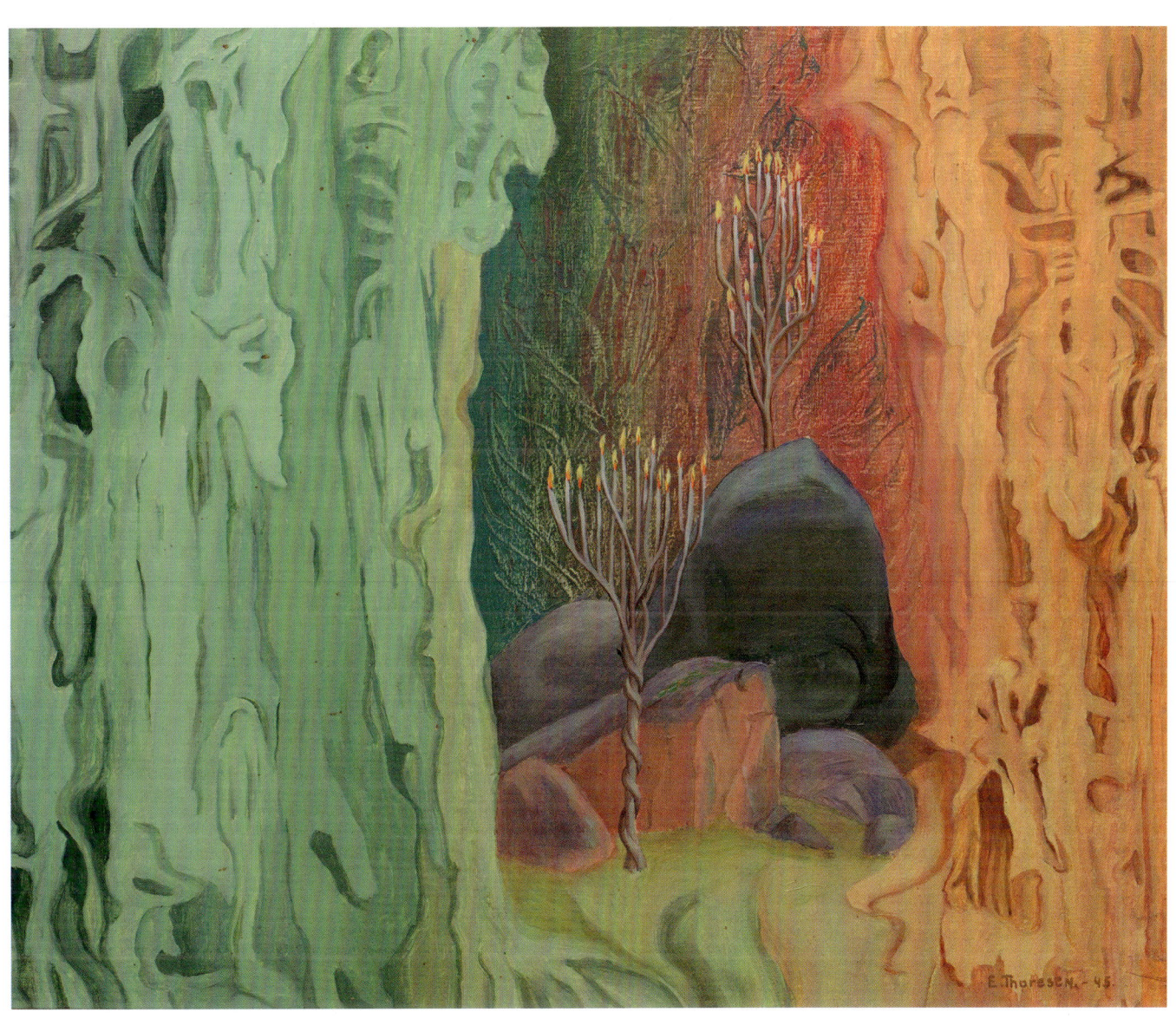

Elsa Thoresen (1906–1994), *Surprising Appearance of Candelabras in a Landscape*, 1945. Oil on canvas, 19⅝ × 24 in. (50 × 61 cm). Private collection, Denmark. Photo by Torben Eskerod.

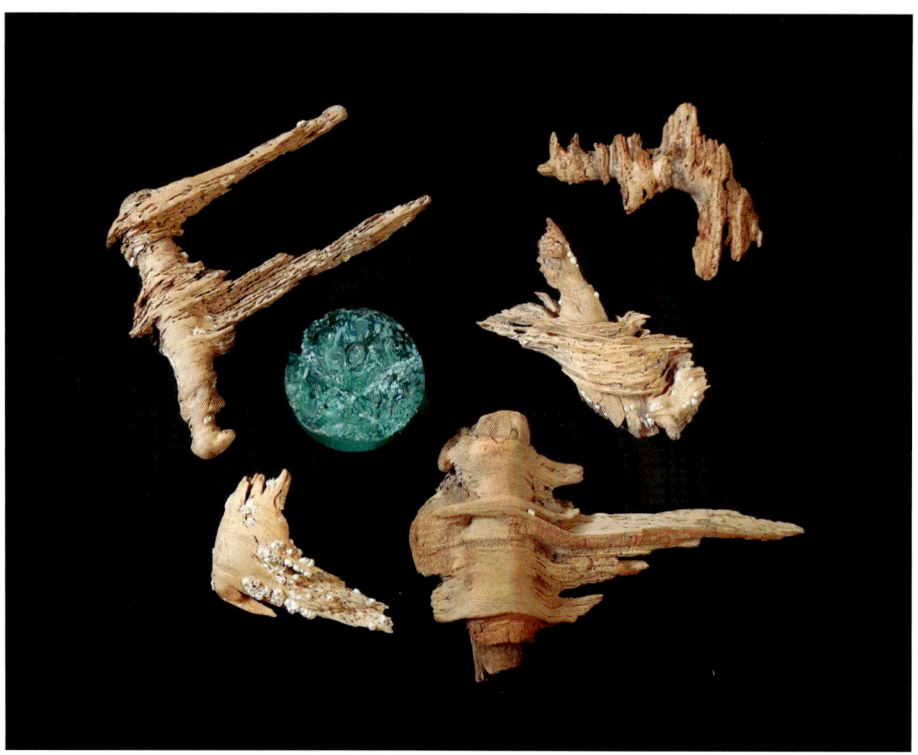

Glass paperweight and various pieces of driftwood collected by Elsa Thoresen for reference use in her paintings.

the first time in 1946, and the following year, his *Point and Line to Plane* (1926) was translated and released by the museum. Bjerke-Petersen was included in the Guggenheim's *Loan Exhibition #56*, which opened on February 12, 1947, and where he exhibited under the name V. B. Petersen. During their time in New York City, the couple met a man named Johnny Gouveia (1913–2007), who had just returned from serving in the military during the war and had enrolled in art classes under the G.I. Bill of Rights. The couple befriended him and bonded over their mutual love of art. Gouveia studied with Bjerke-Petersen and grew close to Thoresen and their children.

When the family returned to Sweden on June 30, 1947, Thoresen learned that her work was being included in a major show in Paris, the 1947 *International Surrealist Exhibition* organized by André Breton and Marcel Duchamp and held at Gallery Maeght. Although there is ample evidence of her participation in this exhibition, any titles of her works from this show have not been verified.

Around this time, Bjerke-Petersen returned to a non-objective style, reminiscent of the period after his studies at the Bauhaus, with Kandinsky being an important influence. Thoresen continued to produce paintings in her Surrealist style, such

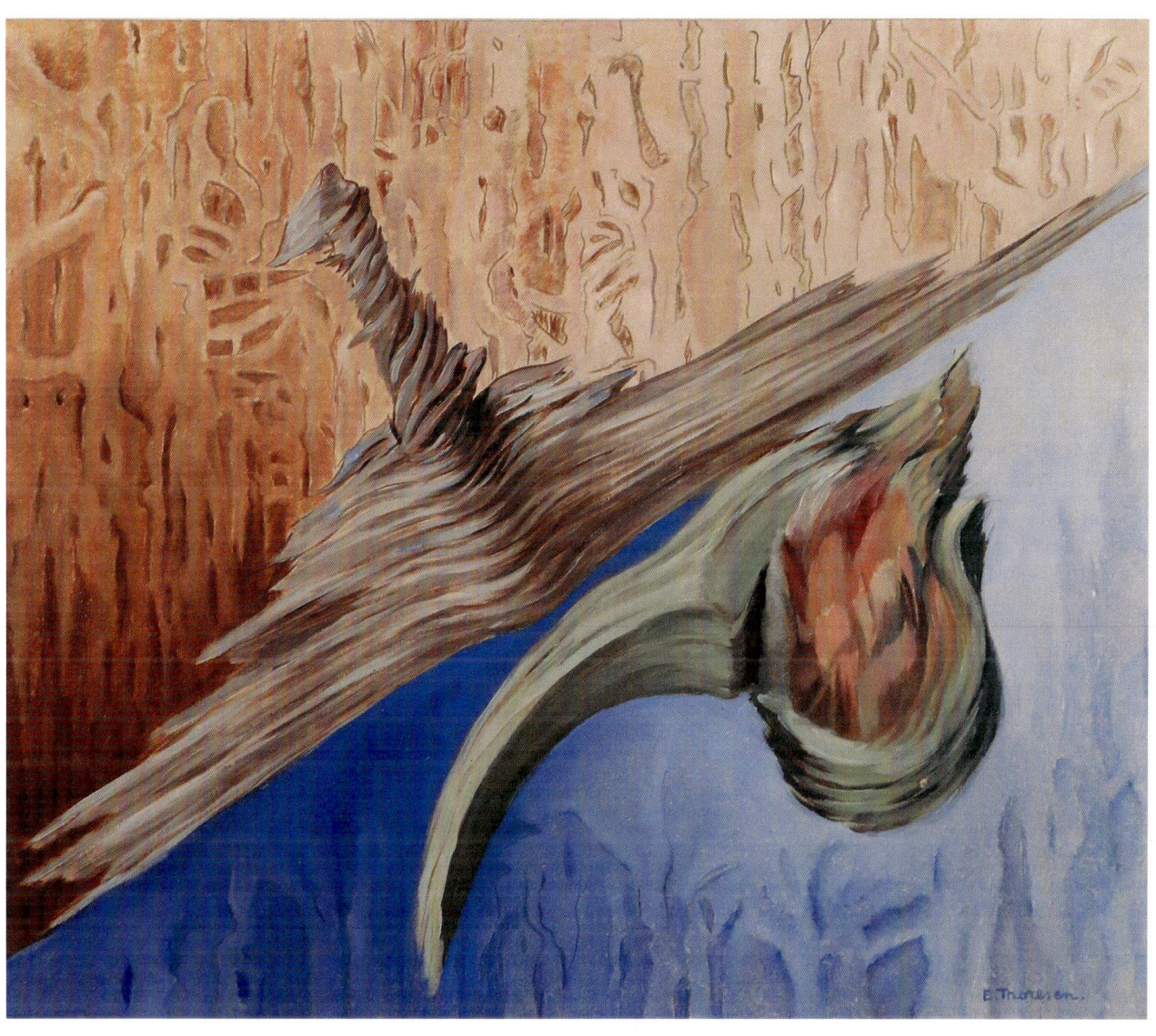

Elsa Thoresen (1906–1994), Untitled, circa 1945. Oil on canvas, 18¼ × 21¾ in. (46.4 × 55.3 cm).

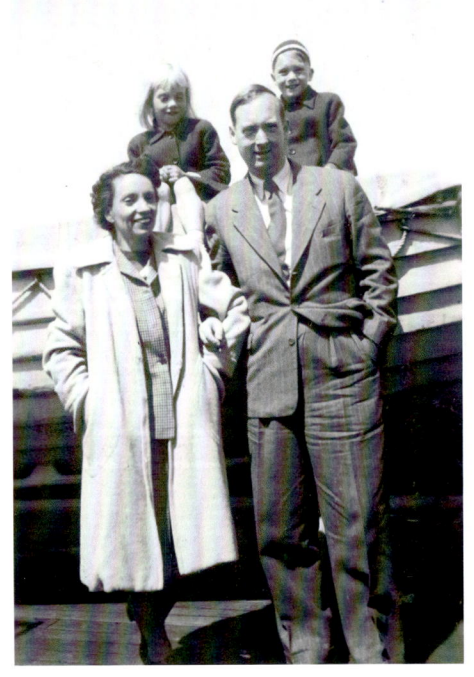
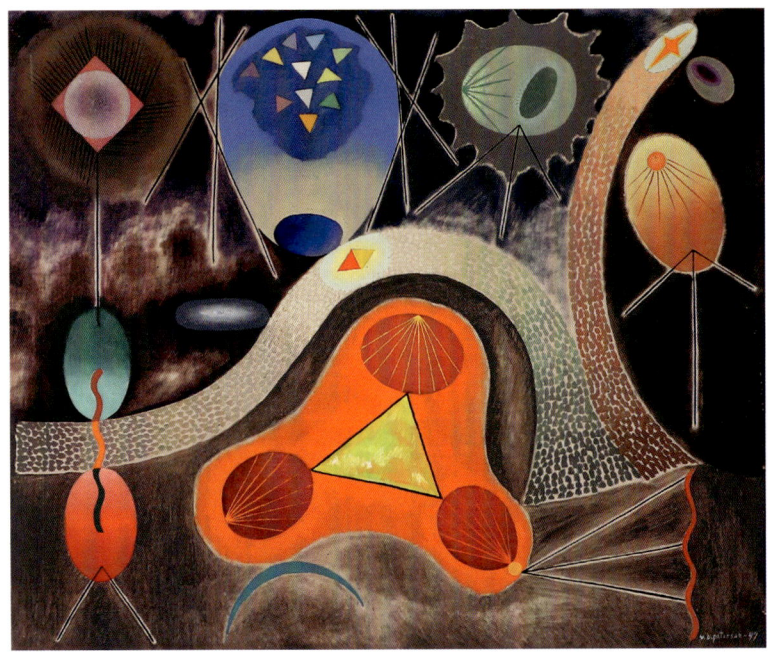

Elsa Thoresen and Vilhelm Bjerke-Petersen with their children, Alice and Kai, aboard the ship *Stavangerfjord* on the way to America, 1946.

Vilhelm Bjerke-Petersen (1909–1957), *Dramatiske hændelser* (Dramatic events), 1947. Oil on canvas, 23¾ × 29 in. (60.3 × 73.7 cm).

as the untitled 1947 work depicting a floating driftwood object impressed with her own lip prints. Bjerke-Petersen's painting *Dramatiske hændelser* (Dramatic events) was also created in 1947 and uses geometric forms to indicate the couple's recent disrupted lives due to the war. The large treelike form filled with broken brushstrokes starts out united but soon diverges into two separate directions. Perhaps with Surrealism starting to fade and a renewed interest in non-objective art from a high-profile New York museum dedicated exclusively to it, Bjerke-Petersen may have been inspired to return to his non-objective roots.

By this time, Gouveia had joined the family in Sweden to extend his studies with Bjerke-Petersen and continued his friendship with the couple's children. In April–May 1948, Thoresen and Bjerke-Petersen were given a two-person exhibition at the Halmstad Music Hall in Halmstad, Sweden. In the 1948 July–August exhibition catalogue of The Line, Bjerke-Petersen's *Dramatiske hændelser* was illustrated along with one of Thoresen's versions of *Brinnande jord* (Burning Earth) (page 83), revealing the new discrepancy in the couple's styles.

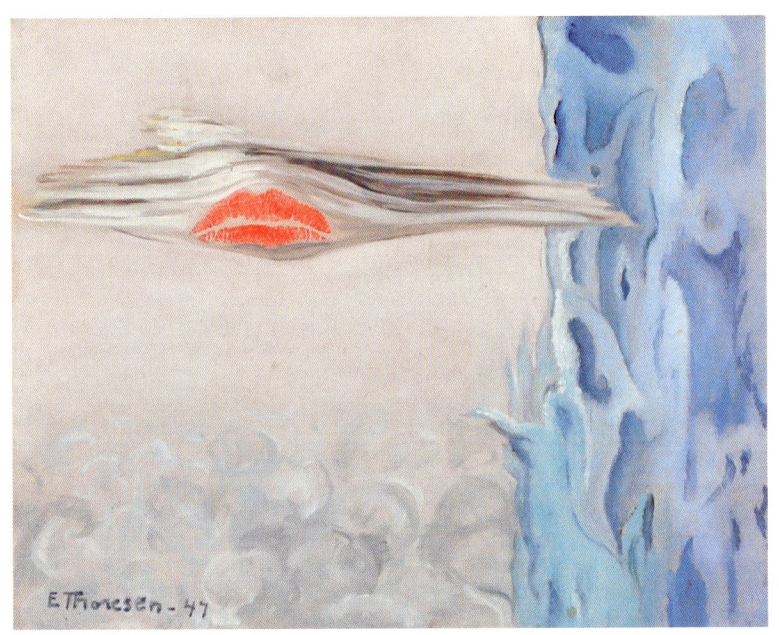

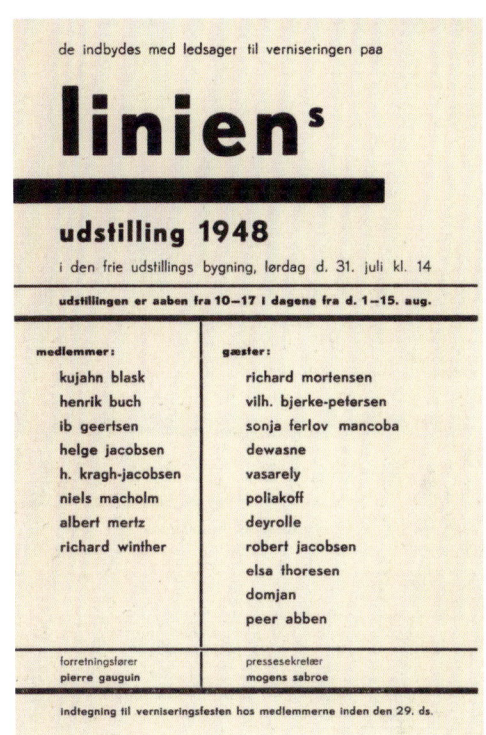

Elsa Thoresen (1906–1994), Untitled, 1947. Oil on board with artist's painted lip print,
7½ × 9½ in. (19.1 × 24.1 cm).

Opening invitation for the 1948 group exhibition by members and guest exhibitors of
The Line (2), Denmark.

In May 1950, Thoresen had a solo exhibition at the prestigious Louis Hahne Gallery in Stockholm. She was finally able to have an entire exhibition, with thirty-three works, rather than being relegated to a smaller number as in her group exhibitions with Bjerke-Petersen or other male artists.[20] That same month, Bjerke-Petersen and Thoresen exhibited along with Yves Tanguy at the London Gallery, at 23 Brook Street, London, W.1. This prominent commercial gallery had been operating since the 1930s, specializing primarily in Surrealism. However, this exhibition would be the gallery's last, as it was forced to close due to financial reasons.

The following spring, in 1951, Bjerke-Petersen and Thoresen were included in the exhibition *Foreign Artists in Sweden*, at the Artist's House Gallery in Stockholm. The couple were also given a two-person exhibition at the Örebro Castle grounds, in Örebro, Sweden, in 1952. In September 1952, one of their final two-person exhibitions was held at the Värmlands Museum in Karlstad, Sweden. Bjerke-Petersen showed thirty-eight paintings and a selection of ceramics he had designed for Rörstrand Pottery. In keeping with their usual discrepancy, Thoresen displayed seventeen works.[21]

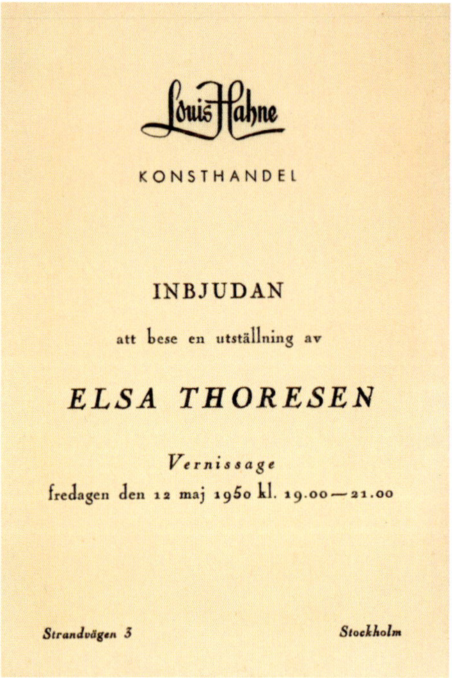
Louis Hahne

KONSTHANDEL

INBJUDAN

att bese en utställning av

ELSA THORESEN

Vernissage

fredagen den 12 maj 1950 kl. 19.00—21.00

Strandvägen 3 *Stockholm*

Opening invitation for the Elsa Thoresen solo exhibition at the Louis Hahne Gallery, Stockholm, Sweden, May 12, 1950.

Their collaborative exhibitions ended along with their relationship when Bjerke-Petersen fell in love with the entertainer Eva-Lisa Lennartsson (1910–1999), thus ending his marriage to Thoresen in 1953. Distraught by the betrayal, Thoresen took the children to visit her mother and sister, who were living in the United States, in Washington, DC, at the time. After Thoresen reunited with Gouveia in New York, the two developed a relationship after her divorce from Bjerke-Petersen. Gouveia had a stable job as a civil servant in the Department of the Navy, and he and Thoresen married on November 14, 1953. Thoresen and the children followed Gouveia to his new job assignment in Scotia, New York, where they lived for a brief period. During their short time in New York, Thoresen did not produce any work. Also in 1953, Thoresen's brother, Nils, moved to Seattle, Washington, to work for the Boeing Company. He soon sent for his mother and his sister Marie to join him. The region had a substantial population of Norwegian and Scandinavian immigrants, so there was an element of cultural familiarity that was reassuring. Because Gouveia was able to transfer easily within his profession to another location, the Puget Sound area presented a logical opportunity for relocation due to the substantial naval activity in the region. He, Thoresen, and the children moved to Seattle around 1954 to rejoin the rest of her family. As the family acclimated to their new environment, Thoresen slowly began to paint again.

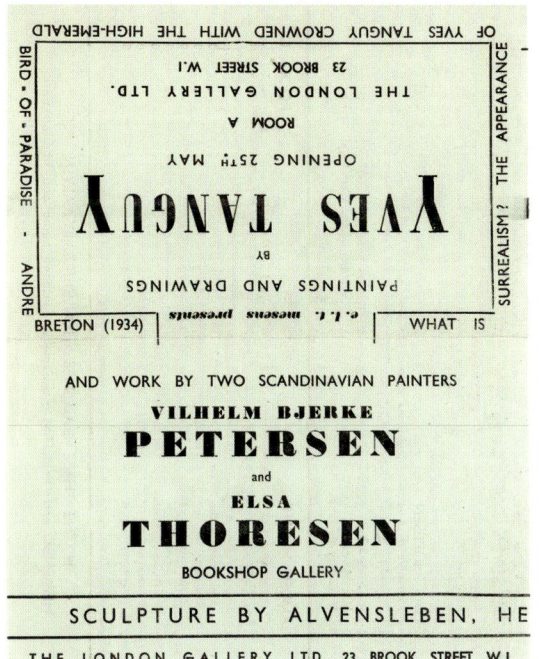

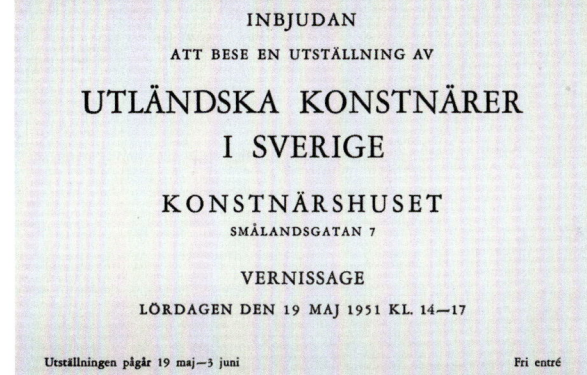

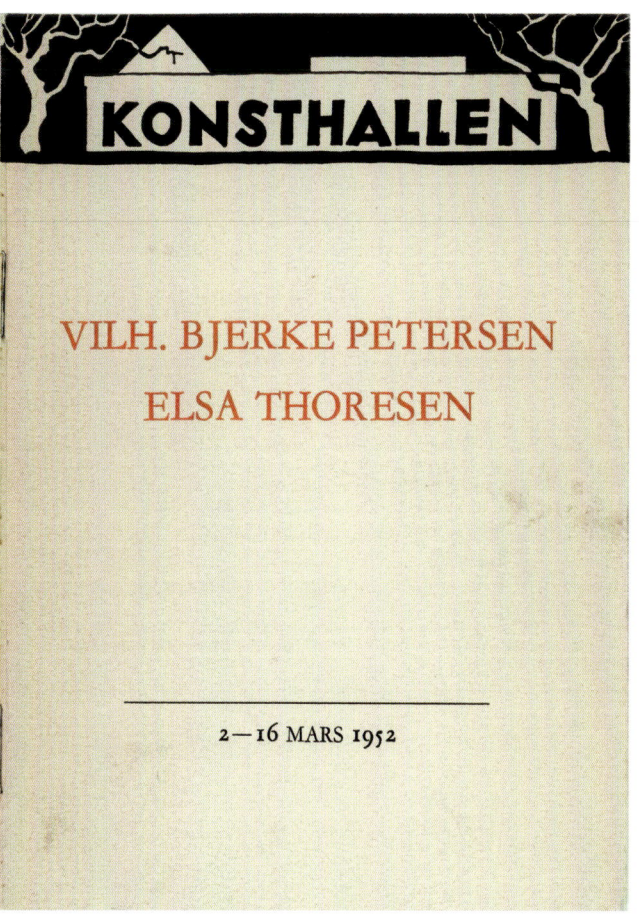

Postcard for Thoresen and Petersen exhibition with Yves Tanguy. The London Gallery,
May–June, 1950.

Opening invitation for the exhibition *Foreign Artists in Sweden*, Artist's House Gallery,
Stockholm, Sweden, 1951.

Catalogue cover for a two-person exhibition of Bjerke-Petersen and Thoresen, Örebro Castle
grounds, Örebro, Sweden, 1952.

Surrealism in Seattle

I have never taken drugs—since I am the drug! I don't talk about hallucinations . . . I evoke them. I am hallucinogenic! I am the drug![22]
Salvador Dalí

When Thoresen arrived in Seattle, there were an impressive number of regional artists who had local, national, and even international success. Surrealism in Seattle began with the artist Malcolm Roberts (1913–1990) in the mid-1930s as part of the region's Works Progress Administration (WPA) art programs. His life partner at that time, Morris Graves (1910–2001), also utilized surrealistic conventions in his work but not in the figurative manner that Roberts did.[23]

In the United States, Surrealism was cautiously accepted in the Federal Art Projects of President Franklin Roosevelt's New Deal programs, especially in Seattle. The government mostly encouraged artists to paint realistic depictions of historical events that reflected the corresponding region's culture and industries. The director of Washington state's WPA was the artist Robert Bruce Inverarity (1909–1999), who had been a leading modernist in Seattle since the 1920s. In 1938, Inverarity began a series of Surrealist paintings that were truly unique within the genre. Drawing on his study and collecting of Northwest Coast Native American objects, he personalized his subject matter and influenced other local artists, such as Helmi Juvonen (1903–1985) and Julius "Land Elk" Twohy (Two-vy-nah-auche) (1902–1986), a Ute Indian whose work sometimes incorporated non-objective designs as filtered through Kandinsky.[24] Other noted Surrealists in Seattle included the Los Angeles–born Margaret Tomkins (1916–2002), who was also part of Washington state's WPA programs, and Blanche Morgan Losey (1912–1981). Losey and Malcolm Roberts both turned to stage, costume, and set designs, with Losey active with Seattle's Federal Theatre Project and the Negro Repertory Company and Roberts with the Cornish Ballet in Seattle. Both artists went on to impressive careers in interior and commercial design, which often maintained elements of surrealism.

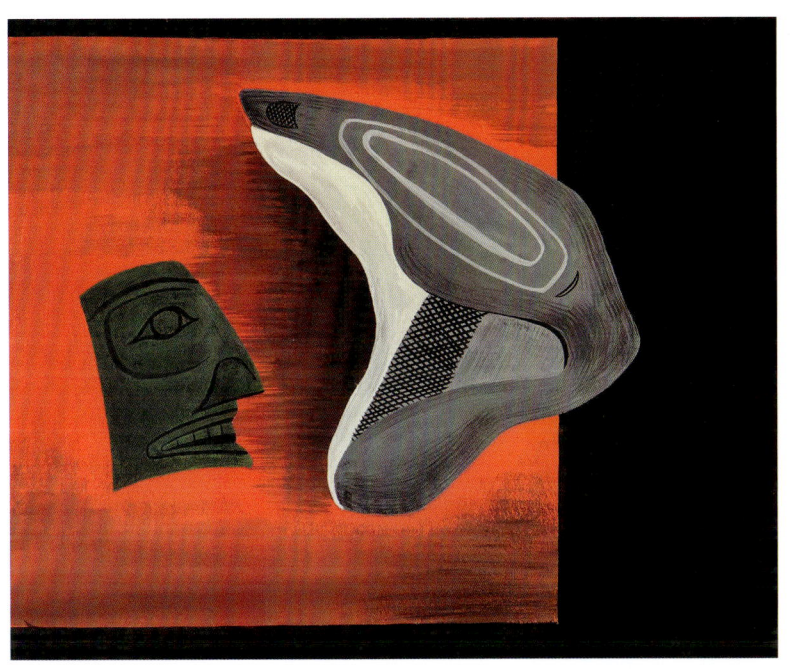

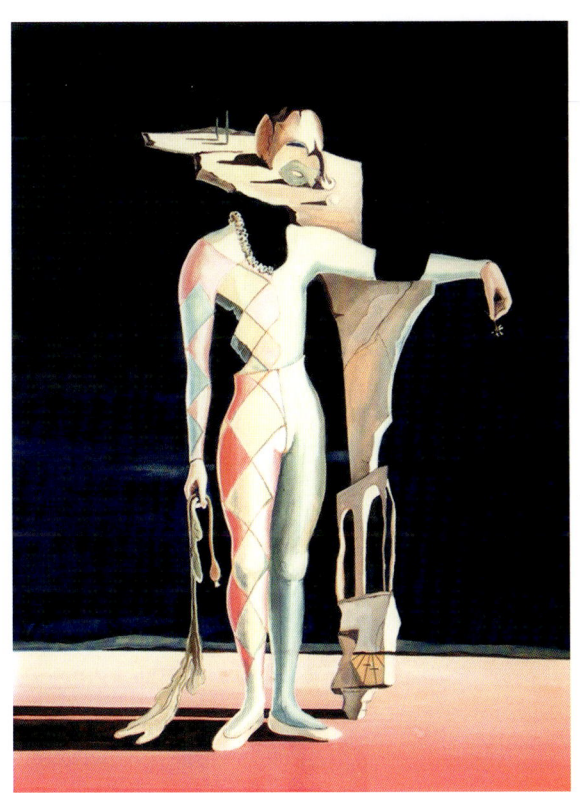

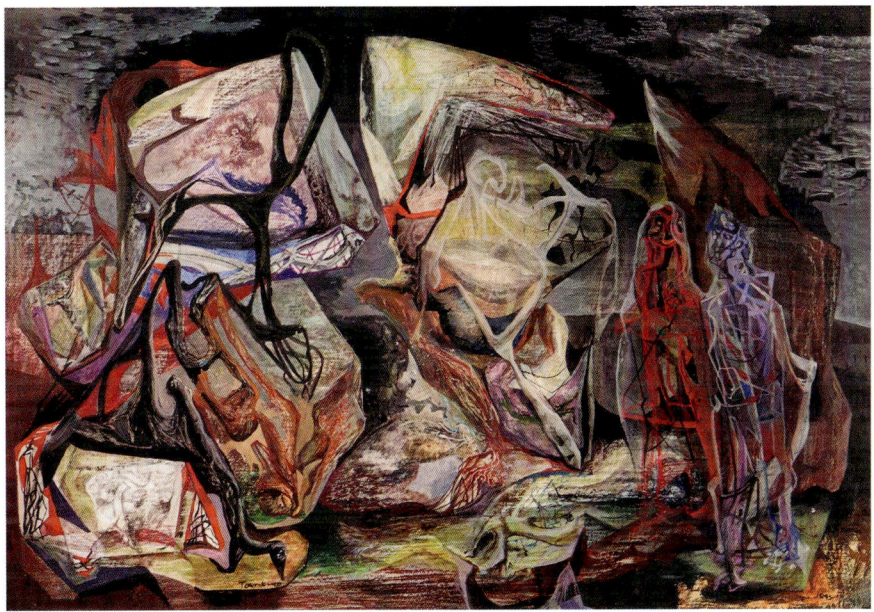

Robert Bruce Inverarity (1909–1999), *Northwest Coast Indian Forms*, circa 1938. Tempera on board, 16 × 20 in. (40.6 × 50.8 cm). Private collection. Courtesy of C. W. American Modernism Gallery, Los Angeles, CA.

Margaret Tomkins (1916–2002), *Penetration of Emergent Life*, 1945. Tempera on board, 18 × 27 in. (45.7 × 68.6 cm). Collection of Lindsey and Carolyn Echelbarger, Woodway, WA.

Blanche Morgan Losey (1912–1981), *Tired Harlequin*, circa 1945. Tempera on illustration board, 20 × 16¼ in. (50.8 × 41.3 cm). Private collection, Seattle, WA.

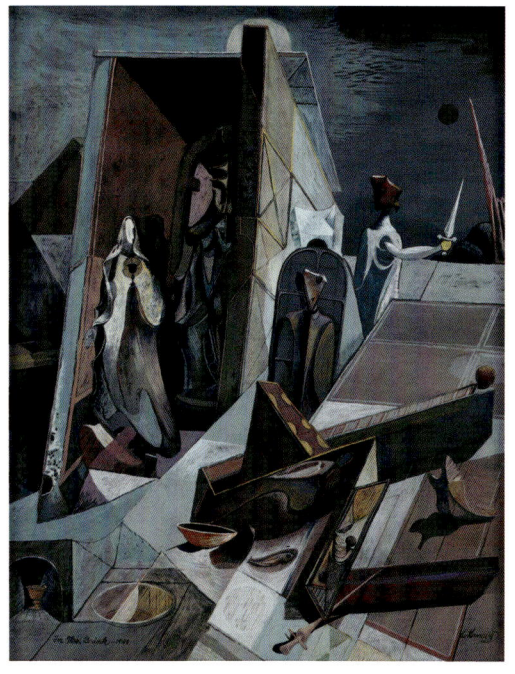

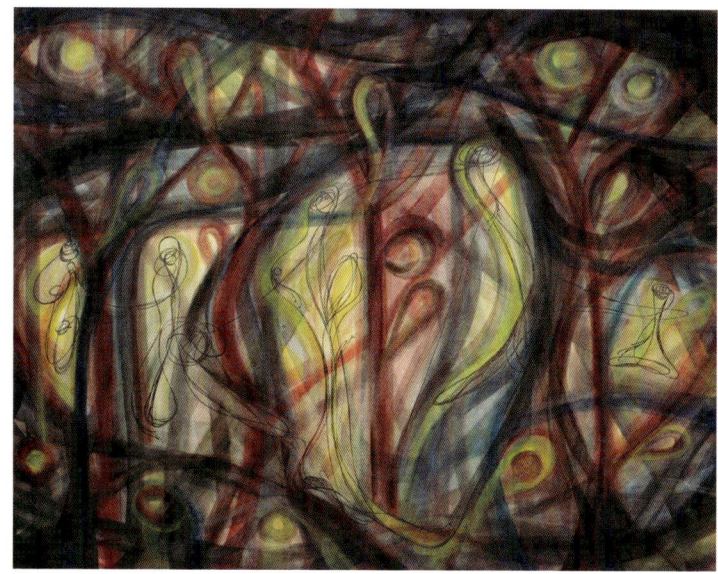

Leo Kenney (1925–2001), *Protected Grail*, 1949. Gouache on paper, 15½ × 12 in. (39.4 × 30.5 cm).
Collection of Merch and Alice Pease, Seattle, WA.

Maria Frank Abrams (1924–2013), *Ghosts Among Cinnamon Trees*, 1953. Casein and ink on paper,
21⅞ × 28 in. (55.6 × 71.1 cm). Cascadia Art Museum, 2022.10.26. Gift of the Estate of
Maria Frank Abrams.

In the months before Elsa Thoresen arrived in Seattle, *Life* magazine featured an article titled "Mystic Painters of the Northwest" in its September 28, 1953, issue. The article focused on four male artists: Mark Tobey (1890–1976), Morris Graves, Kenneth Callahan (1905–1986), and Guy Anderson (1906–1998). This brought a national focus to the region and implied a dominant "Northwest School" that used a limited color palette and showed influences of Asian and Native American art, assigning a false air of mysticism to the artists and their style. All four of these artists dabbled in Surrealism at some point in their careers, but their subdued palette and abstracted, almost monotonous iconography dominated the region's aesthetic for decades.[25] In truth, Washington state, and Seattle in particular, boasted a wide range of artists who worked outside of the dominant style, which was heavily promoted for a perceived cohesiveness to distinguish the region artistically. Although true, there was also an underlying commercial motivation. Two artists of great talent in the postwar era in Seattle were Leo Kenney (1925–2001), whose early work was indebted to Surrealism, and Maria Frank Abrams (1924–2013), a painter of extraordinary optimism, in

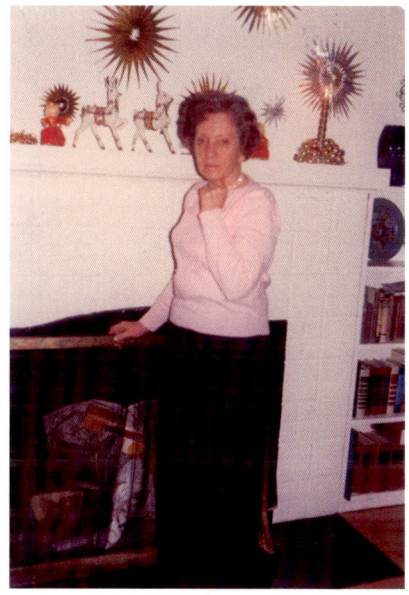

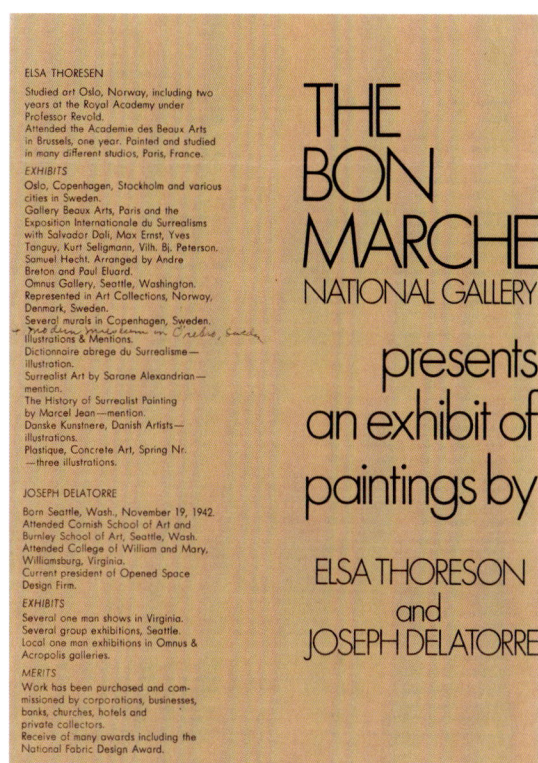

Elsa Thoresen, Seattle, WA, 1973.

Exhibition brochure for a two-person exhibition of the work of Elsa Thoresen and Joseph Delatorre, Bon Marche Department Store, National Gallery, Seattle, WA, 1975.

List of Elsa Thoresen's paintings for sale, the Bon Marche Department Store's National Gallery, Seattle, WA, 1975.

light of the fact that she survived three Nazi death camps before arriving in Seattle in 1948.

Under the leadership of the Seattle Art Museum's founder and director, Richard E. Fuller (1897–1976), regional artists received a great deal of support. The museum's Northwest Annuals featured the best regional artists, beginning in 1914 and through the early 1970s. Many of these artists also received solo exhibitions at the museum. Alice Tompkins, Thoresen's daughter, recalled that her mother attended many of the local art exhibitions but never participated in any, nor did she seek commercial gallery representation.

When Thoresen resumed painting after moving to Seattle, she rarely included any of her surrealist imagery. She had left that behind in favor of a personal and lyrical style of abstraction. "The realistic, literary, and macabre aspects of Surrealism finally tired me, and also the plastic limitations of literary Surrealism made me gradually evolve towards abstract art. Although I now paint in a

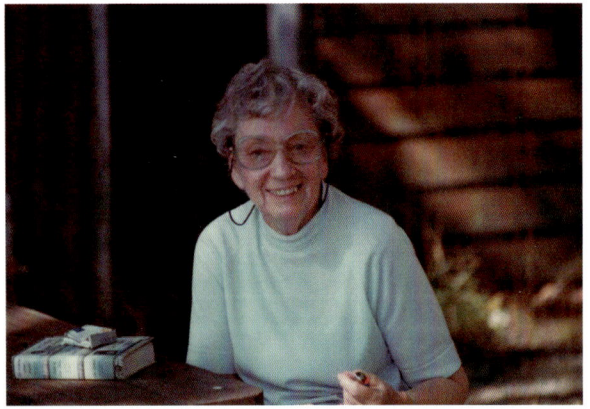
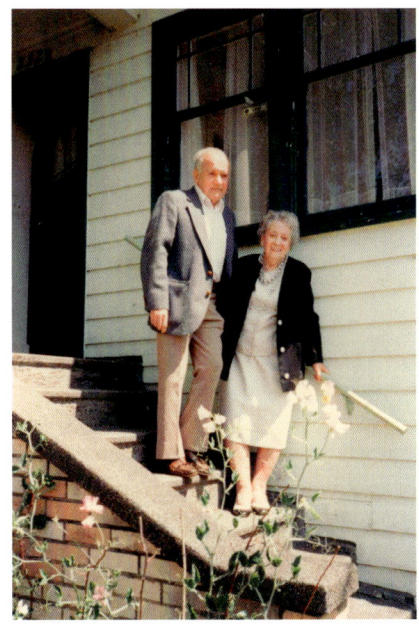

Elsa Thoresen, Orcas Island, WA, 1982.
Elsa Thoresen with husband Johnny Gouveia at their home in Seattle, WA, 1989.

non-objective way, I consider the time I spent in the Surrealist movement to be very interesting as a research experience, and I believe that Surrealism had a great influence on modern abstract art."[26]

Thoresen went on to produce a highly accomplished body of work during her time in Seattle, which exceeded her time in Scandinavia. Why she chose to work in isolation remains a mystery. Never one for self-promotion, and perhaps with Bjerke-Petersen not around to encourage her, she held only a few exhibitions in small venues during her forty years in Seattle, even though her talent and reputation surpassed many of her Northwest contemporaries. To augment her husband's income, Thoresen worked for the Bon Marche, a large Seattle department store, in the lighting and gallery departments. She was part of a two-person exhibition there in 1975, but she received no reviews or publicity. By that time, she and Gouveia had purchased a small cabin on Orcas Island, in Washington, where she and her family spent a great deal of time in the extraordinary natural beauty that the island provided. Her last recorded Northwest exhibition came in July 1981 at Washington Federal Savings and Loan in Eastsound, Orcas Island.[27]

Thoresen continued to paint until her death on August 20, 1994. Gouveia remained in their home until his death on November 18, 2007.

NOTES

1   Wikipedia, "Karen Holtsmark," last modified November 10, 2024, https://en.wikipedia.org/wiki/Karen_Holtsmark.

2   Jens Tang Kristensen, "Shock—Vilhelm Bjerke Petersen and His Surrealist Exhibition at Den Frie in 1935," *Perspective* (National Gallery of Denmark), March 2021, https://www.perspectivejournal.dk/en/shock-vilhelm-bjerke-petersen-and-his-surrealist-exhibition-at-den-frie-in-1935.

3   "Surrealistens Københavns debut Elsa Bjerke-Petersen fortæller *Ekstra Bladet*" [The Surrealist's Copenhagen debut Elsa Bjerke-Petersen tells *Ekstra Bladet*], *Ekstra Bladet*, October 12, 1936, p. 2 (Women's Page).

4   Thoresen's paintings illustrated in the volume were titled *Oliventræet* (Olive tree), 1937; *Naubemere* (Neighbors), 1937; *Paysage atmosphérique* (Atmospheric landscape), 1936; *Indre blik* (Inner gaze), 1936; *Ørkenens blå blomst* (The blue flower of the desert), 1936; and *Klassisk landskab* (Classic landscape), 1937.

5   "La femme surréaliste," special issue, *Obliques* (Éditions Borderie, Paris), no. 14–15 (1 janvier 1977): 57.

6   Thomas Millroth, *Good Luck Elsa Thoresen* (Stockholm: Carlsson Bokförlag, 2024), 48–61.

7   "La femme surréaliste," *Obliques*, 56.

8   "La femme surréaliste," *Obliques*, 50.

9   Nathalie Ernoult, "Three Scandinavian Surrealist Women Artists in Paris," AWARE: Archives of Women Artists, Research and Exhibitions, January 12, 2019, https://awarewomenartists.com/en/magazine/trois-artistes-femmes-surrealistes-scandinaves-a-paris.

10   Alice Tompkins, Thoresen's daughter, claims a memory of her mother embroidering the cloth, so it is possible that Thoresen worked on the piece intermittently over several years, since it remains unfinished. Alice and Chuck Tompkins, interview by David F. Martin, at the Tompkins's home, Camano Island, WA, June 28, 2025.

11   Johan Zimsen Kristiansen, "The Halmstad Group and Scandinavia," in *The Halmstad Group: Pioneers of Swedish Surrealism* (Halmstad, Sweden: Mjellby Art Museum, 2024), 89–94.

12   Thoresen's paintings in the exhibition had these titles:

> *Ørkenens blå blomst* (The blue flower of the desert; 1936), 81 × 61 cm
> *Luftens og vannets forening* (The union of air and water; date unknown), 46 × 61 cm
> *Verdenslyset—mørkets lys* (The light of the world—the light of darkness; 1937), 78.5 × 58 cm
> *Verdenslyset—lysets lys* (The light of the world—the light of light; 1938), 81 × 60 cm
> *Nattsvermere* (Night warmth; 1937), 60 × 70 cm
> *Et glimt* (It glows; 1938), 65 ×70 cm
> *Fantasilandskap I* (Fantasy landscape I; 1939), 45 × 60 cm
> *Fantasilandskap I* (Fantasy landscape I; 1939), 46 × 55 cm
> *Sfærisk dans* (Spherical dance; 1939), 70 × 60 cm
> *Strandens ansikt* (The face of the beach; 1939), 81 × 60 cm
> *Skogen* (The forest; 1939), 33 × 46 cm
> *Det bryter løs* (It breaks loose; 1939), 64 × 81 cm
> *Improvisasjon I* (Improvisation I; 1939), 61 × 50 cm
> *Improvisasjon II* (Improvisation II; 1939), 54 × 73 cm
> *Eventyrskogen* (The fairy forest; 1939), 65 × 100 cm

13   The exhibited paintings by Thoresen had these titles:

> *Eventyrskoven* (The fairy forest)
> *Skovens billede* (The picture of the forest)
> *Det genfundne landskab* (The rediscovered landscape)
> *Sfærisk dans* (Spherical dance)
> *Det bryder løs* (It breaks loose)
> *Bjerke-Petersen maler* (Bjerke-Petersen painting)
> *Verdenslyset* (The light of the world)
> *Natsvarmere* (Night warmth)
> *Nattens ansigter* (Faces of the night)
> *Horisontalt* (Horizontal)
> *Det ubevidstes landskab* (Landscape of the unconscious)
> *I sfærisk fangenskab* (In spherical captivity)
> *Mod lyset* (Toward the light)

14   Alice and Chuck Tompkins, interview.

15   Alice and Chuck Tompkins, interview.

16   "The Bjorn Andersson Haller and Marta Andersdotter Haller Lineage: A Genealogic Study of the Family and History of Its Members" (unpublished manuscript, n.d.).

17   Thoresen's paintings for the 1944 exhibition had these titles:

> *Utbrott* (Outbreak)
> *Lagor i havet* (Flames in the sea)
> *Drömskogen* (The dream forest)
> *Trädet höjer sig I* (The tree rises I)
> *Trädet höjer sig II* (The tree rises II)
> *Duvornas moln I* (Clouds of doves I)
> *Duvornas moln II* (Clouds of doves II)
> *Vinden frän berget* (Wind from the mountain)
> *Stenens mirakel* (The miracle of the stone)
> *Undergäng i skönhet* (Destruction of beauty)
> *Skenet i skogen* (Light in the forest)

18   Jørgen Nash, introduction to *From Five Nations*, exhibition catalogue (Good Art, Göteborg Concert Hall, 1945).

19   The paintings by Thoresen for the exhibition had these titles:

> *Utbrott* (Outbreak)
> *Duvornas moln* (Clouds of doves)
> *Trädet höjer sig* (The tree rises)
> *Skogens poesi* (The poetry of the forest)

20   The paintings Thoresen exhibited had these titles:

> 1. *Blå värld* (Blue world)
> 2. *Vegetativa former, blå* (Vegetative forms, blue)
> 3. *Vegetativa former, röd* (Vegetative forms, red)
> 4. *Vegetativa former, grön* (Vegetative forms, green)
> 5. *Brinnande jord* (Burning Earth)

6.–22. *Skogens, havets och luftens poetiska object* (The poetic objects of the forest, the sea and the air)

23. *Blommande rymd I* (Blooming space I)

24. *Blommande rymd II* (Blooming space II)

25. *Vegetativa former, svart* (Vegetative forms, black)

26. *Vegetativa former, orange* (Vegetative forms, orange dominant)

27. *Mörkrets vegetation* (Vegetation of darkness)

28. *Blå rytmer* (Blue rhythms)

29. *Mánljusets fjäril I* (Moonlight butterfly I)

30. *Mánljusets fjäril II* (Moonlight butterfly II)

31. *Två fjärilar* (Two butterflies)

32. *Skogens fjäril* (Butterfly of the forest)

33. *Fjäril mot sol* (Butterfly against the sun)

21 The titles of Thoresen's paintings for the exhibition, by catalogue number:

39. *Havets fjäril* (Butterfly of the sea)

40. *Två fjärilar* (Two butterflies)

41. *Vegetativa former, orange* (Vegetative forms, orange dominant)

42. *Vegetativa former, svart* (Vegetative forms, black)

43. *Mánljusets fjäril* (Moonlight butterfly)

44. *Blå rytmer* (Blue rhythms)

45. *Berget i natten* (The mountain at night)

46. *Eruption*

47. *Skogens kandelabrar* (Candelabra in the forest)

48.–54. *Skogens, havets och luftens poetiska object* (The poetic objects of the forest, the sea and the air)

55. *Färgkomposition* (Color composition)

22 Salvador Dalí, "Hello, Dali!," interview by Michael Delon, 1980, excerpted in *New Surrealism: The Liberation of Images in Consciousness*, by Akhter Ahsen (New York: Brandon House, 1992), 61.

23 David F. Martin, *The Lavender Palette: Gay Culture and the Art of Washington State* (Edmonds, WA: Cascadia Art Museum; Seattle: distributed by University of Washington Press, 2020), 218–27.

24 David F. Martin, *Territorial Hues: The Color Print and Washington State, 1920–1960* (Edmonds, WA: Cascadia Art Museum; Seattle: distributed by University of Washington Press, 2017), 37, 39, 50, 132–36.

25 Martin, *Lavender Palette*, 87–93.

26 "La femme surréaliste," *Obliques*, 56.

27 *The Islands' Sounder*, July 1, 1981, p. 14.

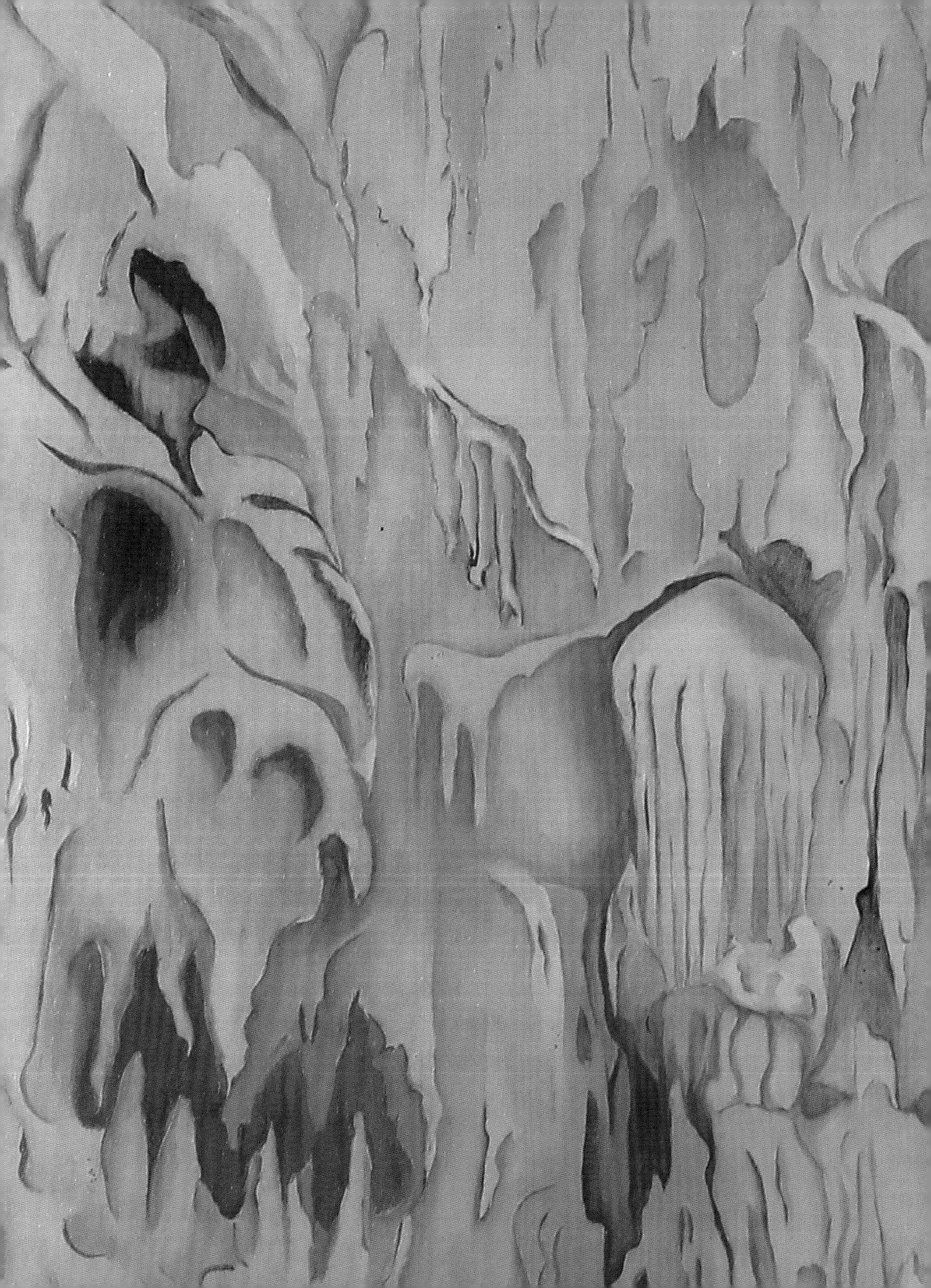

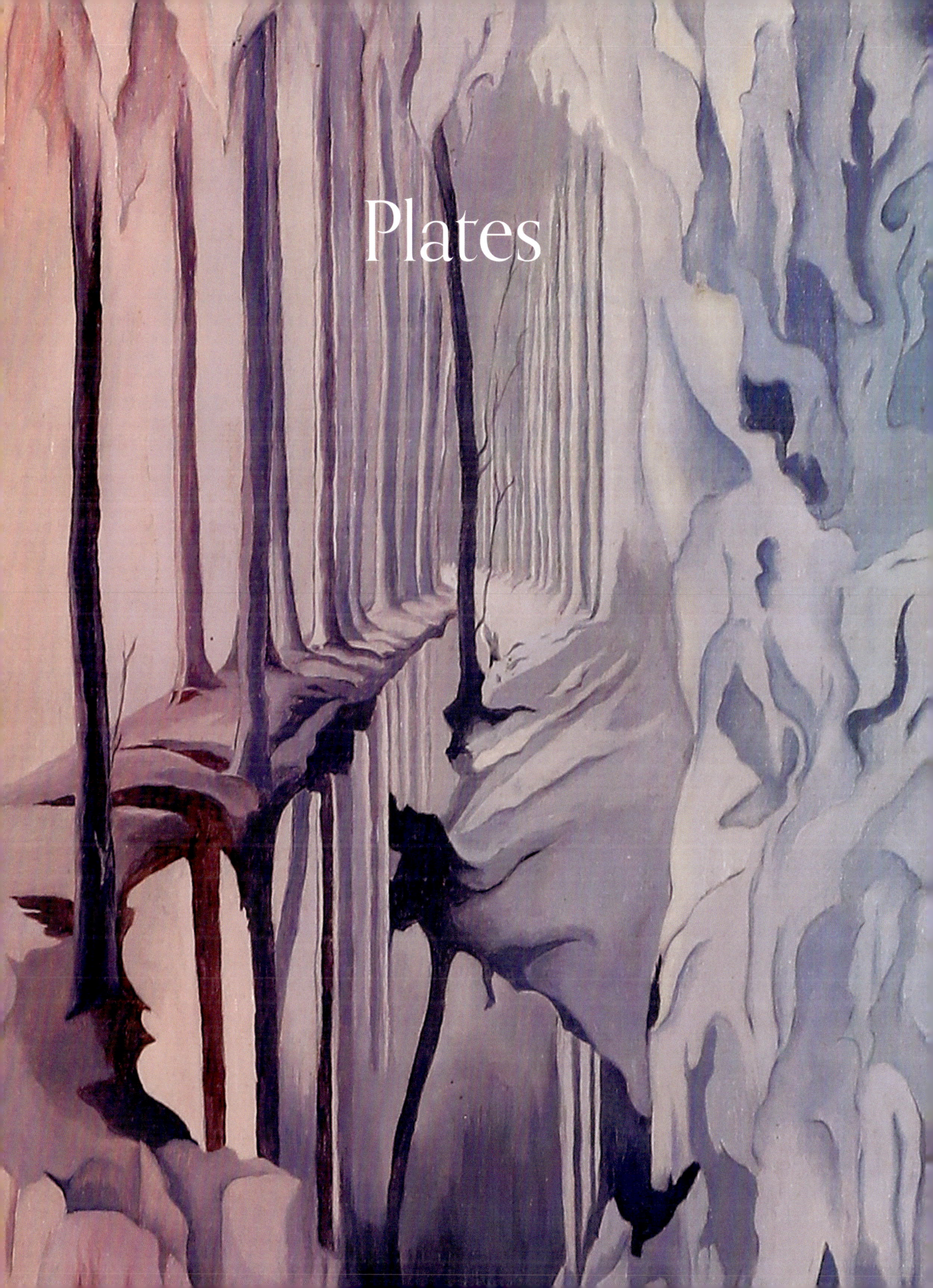

Plates

Elsa Thoresen (1906–1994), Untitled, 1935. Oil on canvas, 18⅛ × 15 in. (46 × 38 cm). Kunstsilo / The Tangen Collection. Photo courtesy of Bukowskis Auction, Stockholm.

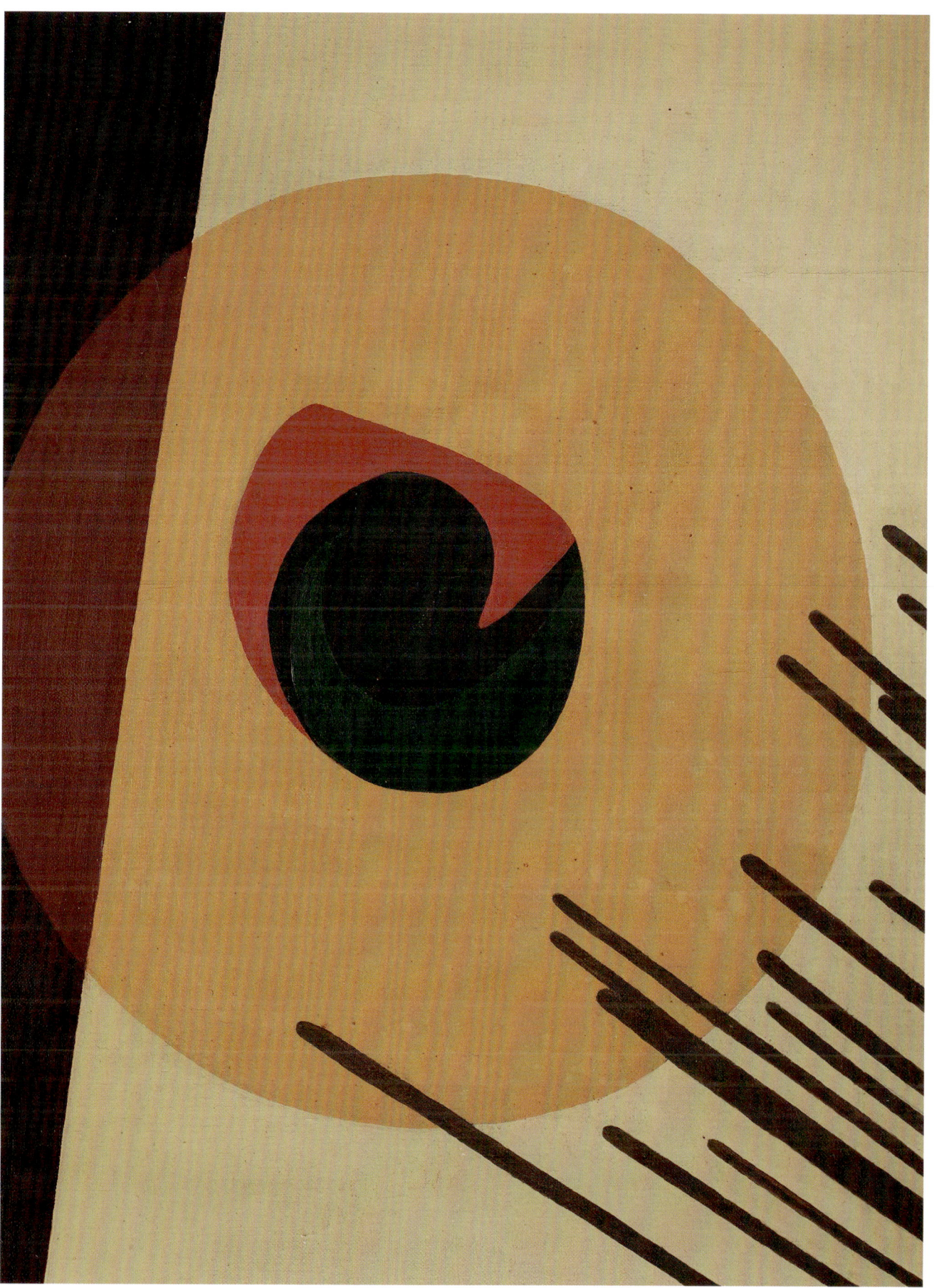

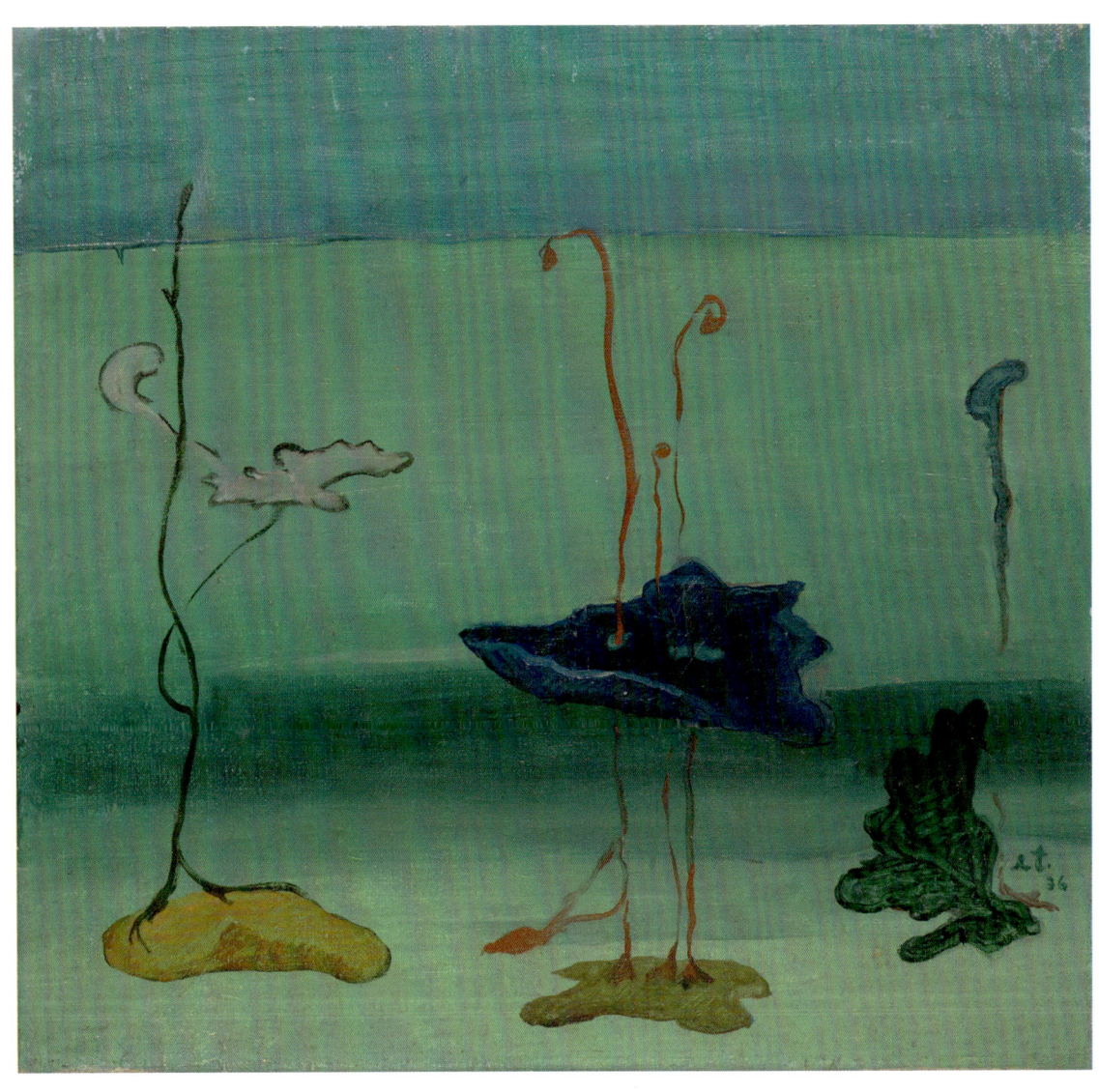

Elsa Thoresen (1906–1994), *Havbundens former* (The shapes of the seabed), 1936. Oil on canvas, 12 × 12½ in. (30.5 × 31.8 cm).

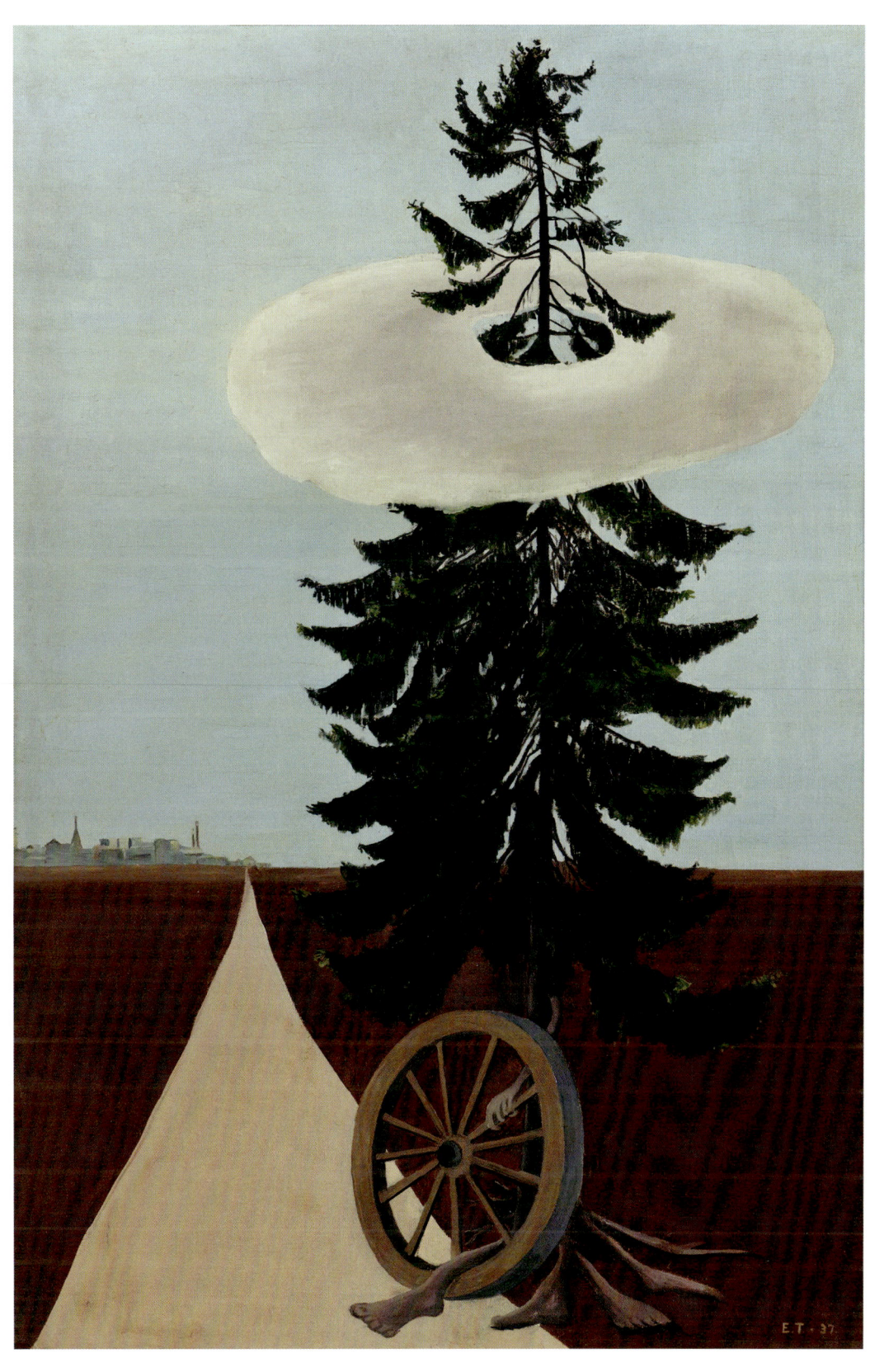

Elsa Thoresen (1906–1994), *Klassisk landskab* (Classic landscape), 1937. Oil on canvas,
30¾ × 20⅞ in. (78 × 53 cm). Museum Sønderjylland.

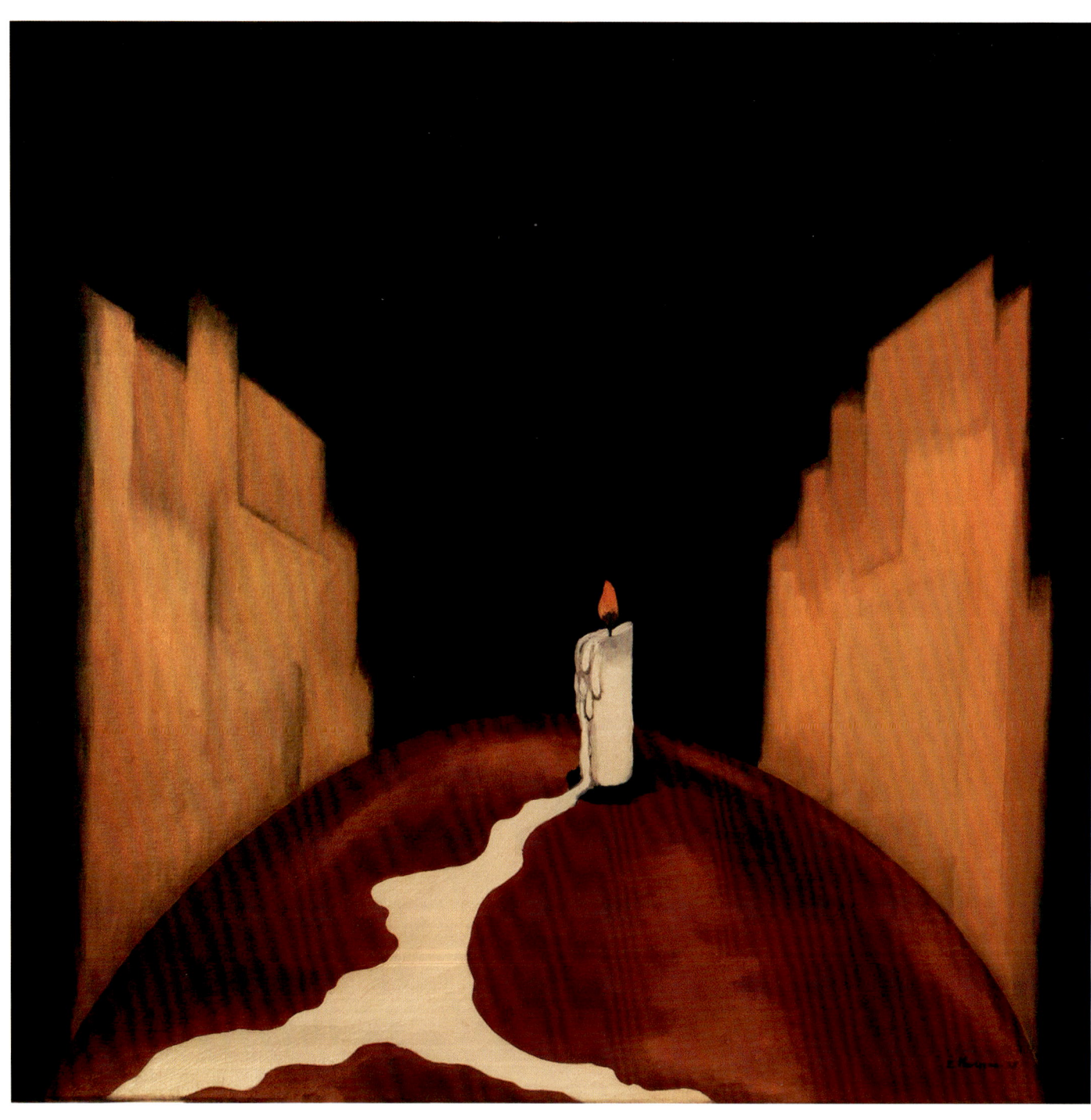

Elsa Thoresen (1906–1994), *Verdenslyset—lysets lys* (The light of the world—the light of light), 1938. Oil on canvas, 25¾ × 26¾ in. (65.5 × 68 cm). Fredrich Lovén Collection, Stockholm. Photo courtesy of Kent Belenius, Stockholm.

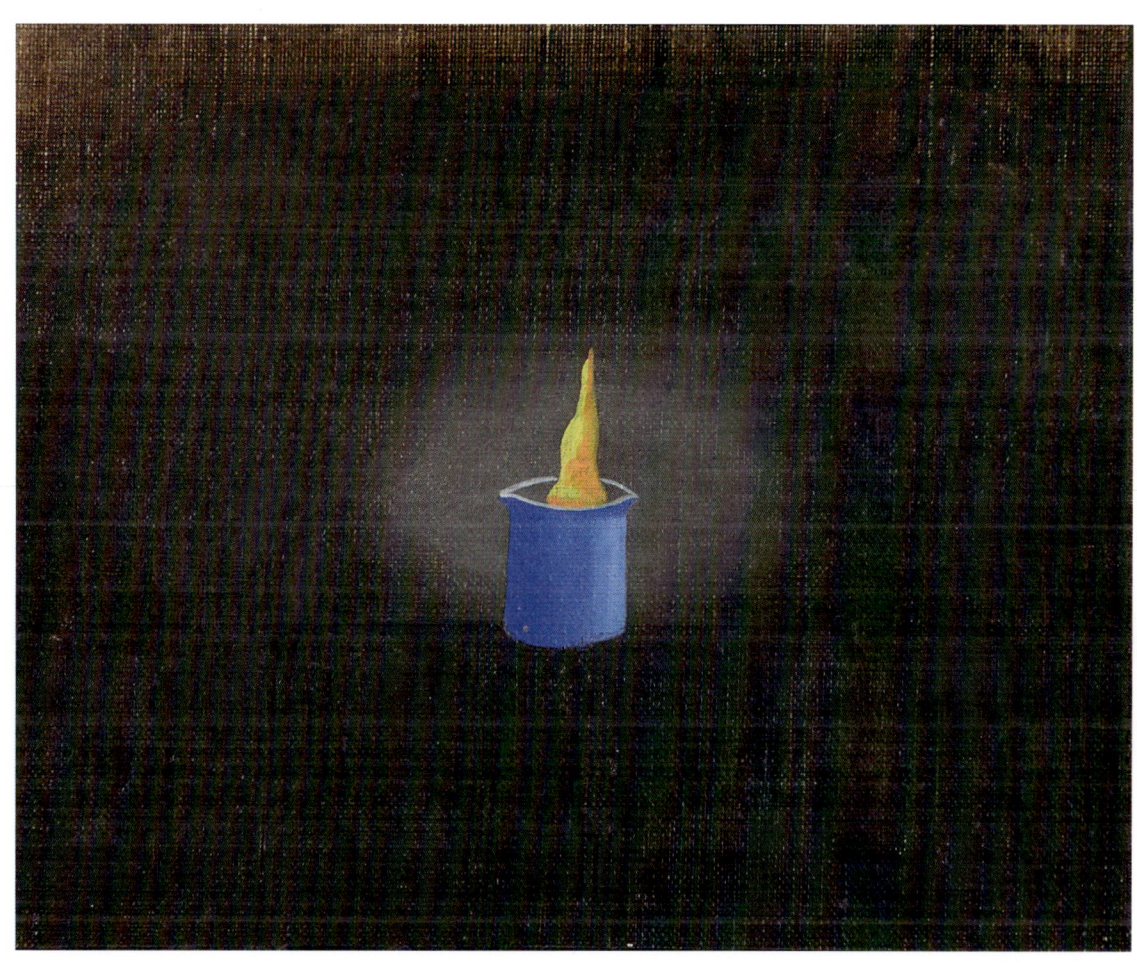

Elsa Thoresen (1906–1994), Untitled, circa 1938. Oil on board, 8⅝ × 10⅝ in. (21.9 × 27 cm).

Elsa Thoresen (1906–1994), Untitled, 1938. Oil on canvas, 18⅛ × 15 in. (46 × 38 cm).
Kunstsilo / The Tangen Collection. Photo courtesy of Bukowskis Auction, Stockholm.

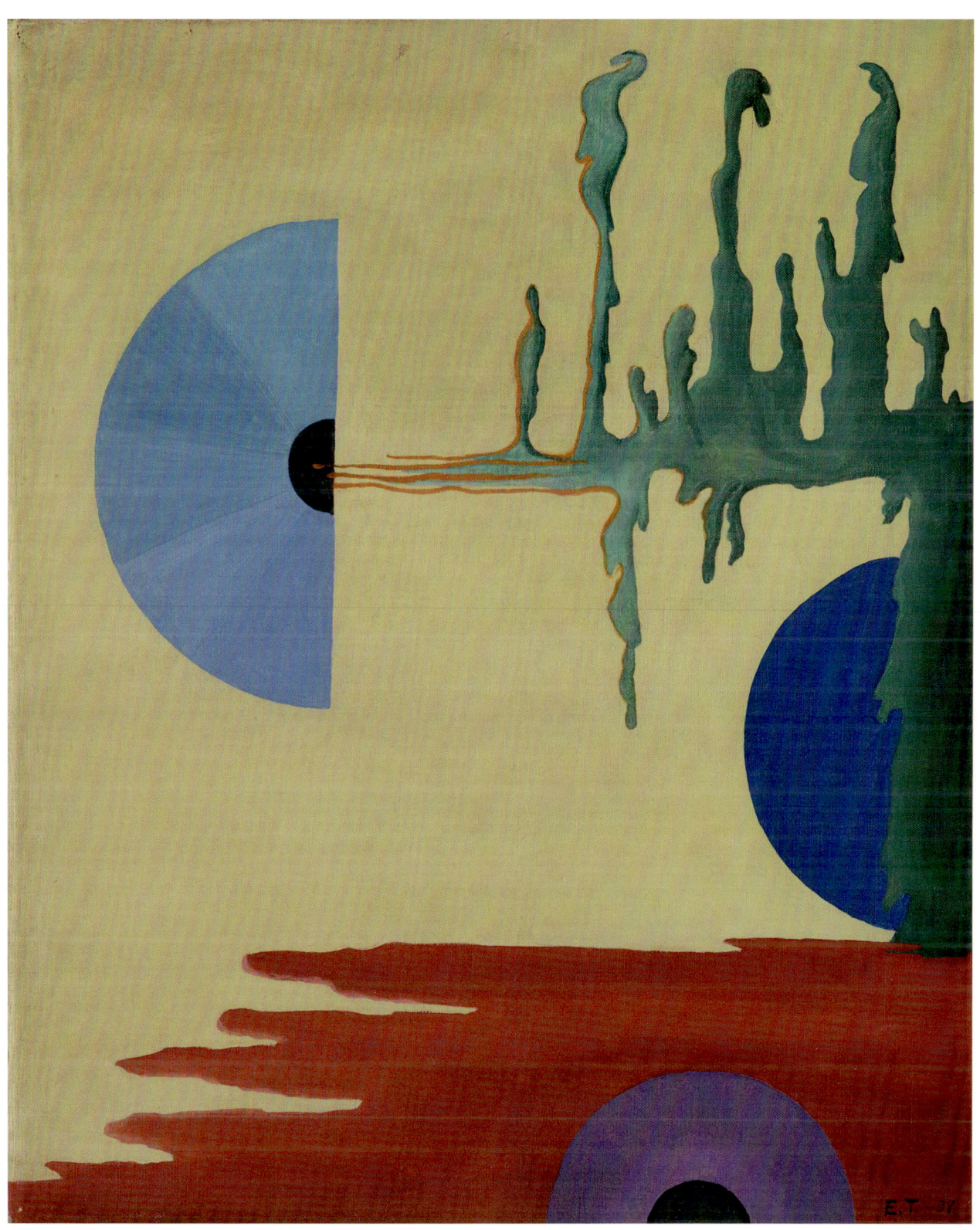

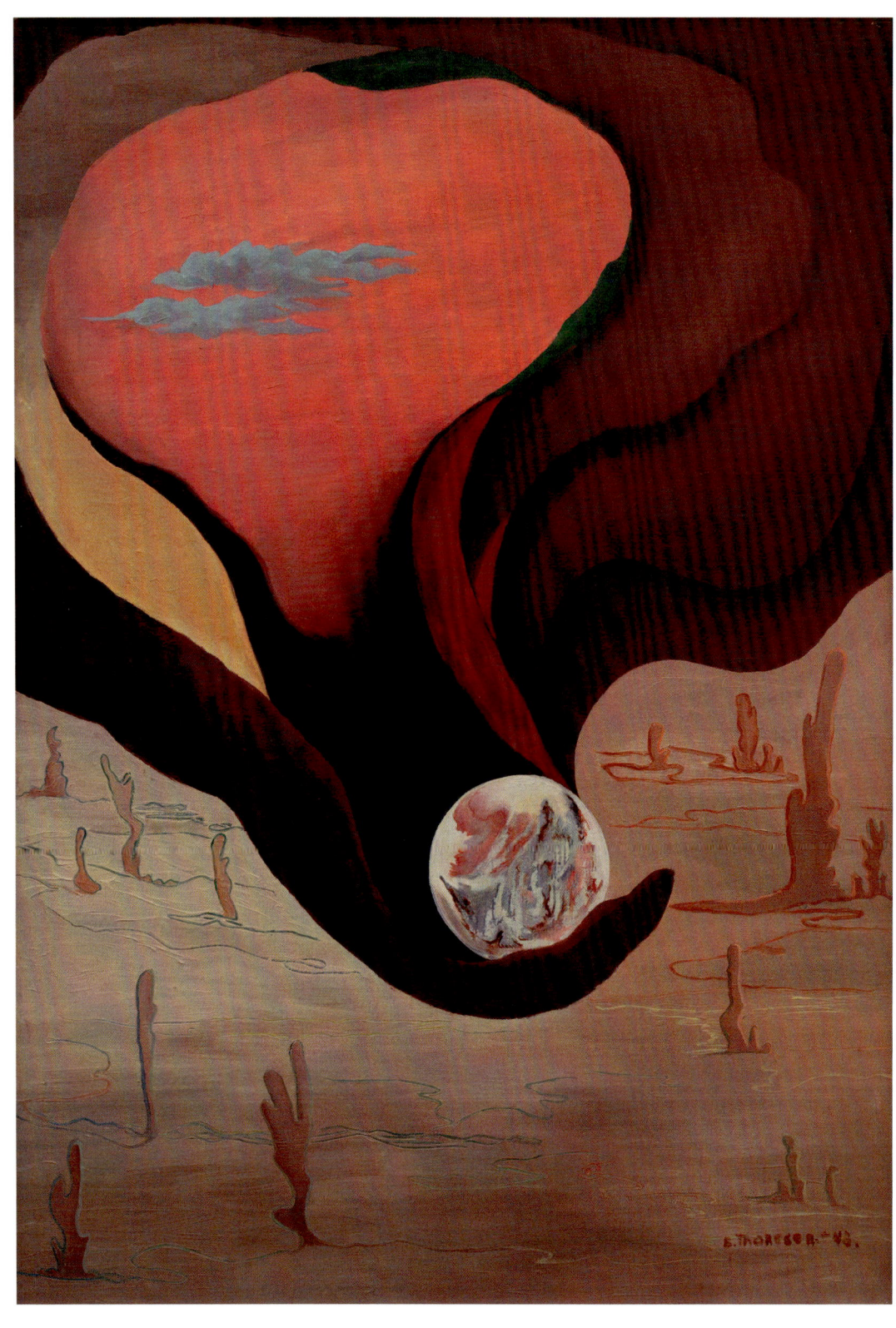

Elsa Thoresen (1906–1994), Untitled, 1943. Oil on canvas, 33⅛ × 23⅝ in. (84 × 60 cm).
Private collection, Sweden. Photo by Torben Eskerod.

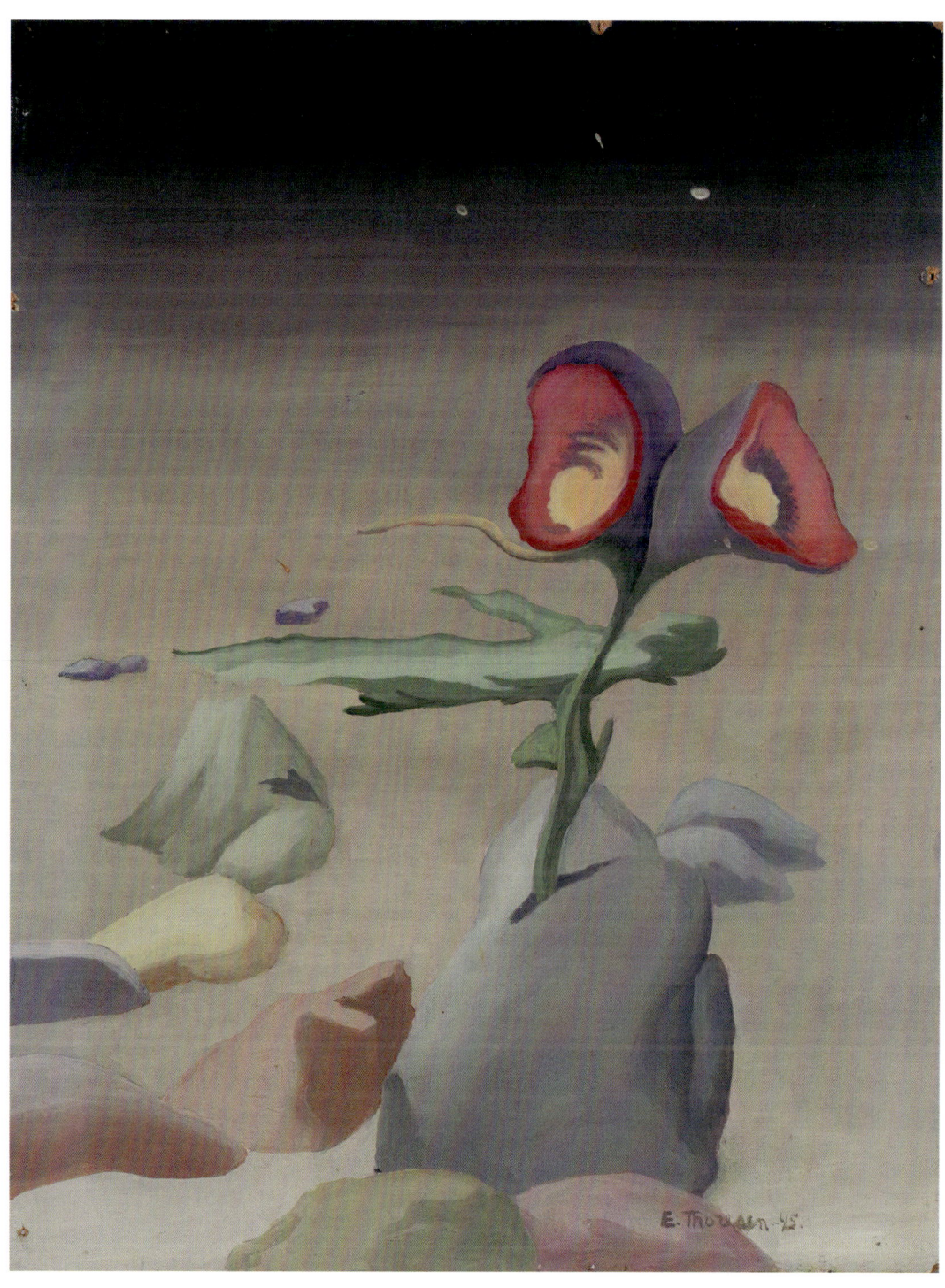

Elsa Thoresen (1906–1994), Untitled, 1945. Oil on board, 13⅞ × 10¾ in. (35.2 × 27.3 cm).

Elsa Thoresen (1906–1994), Untitled, 1945. Oil on board, 10½ × 13½ in. (26.7 × 34.3 cm).

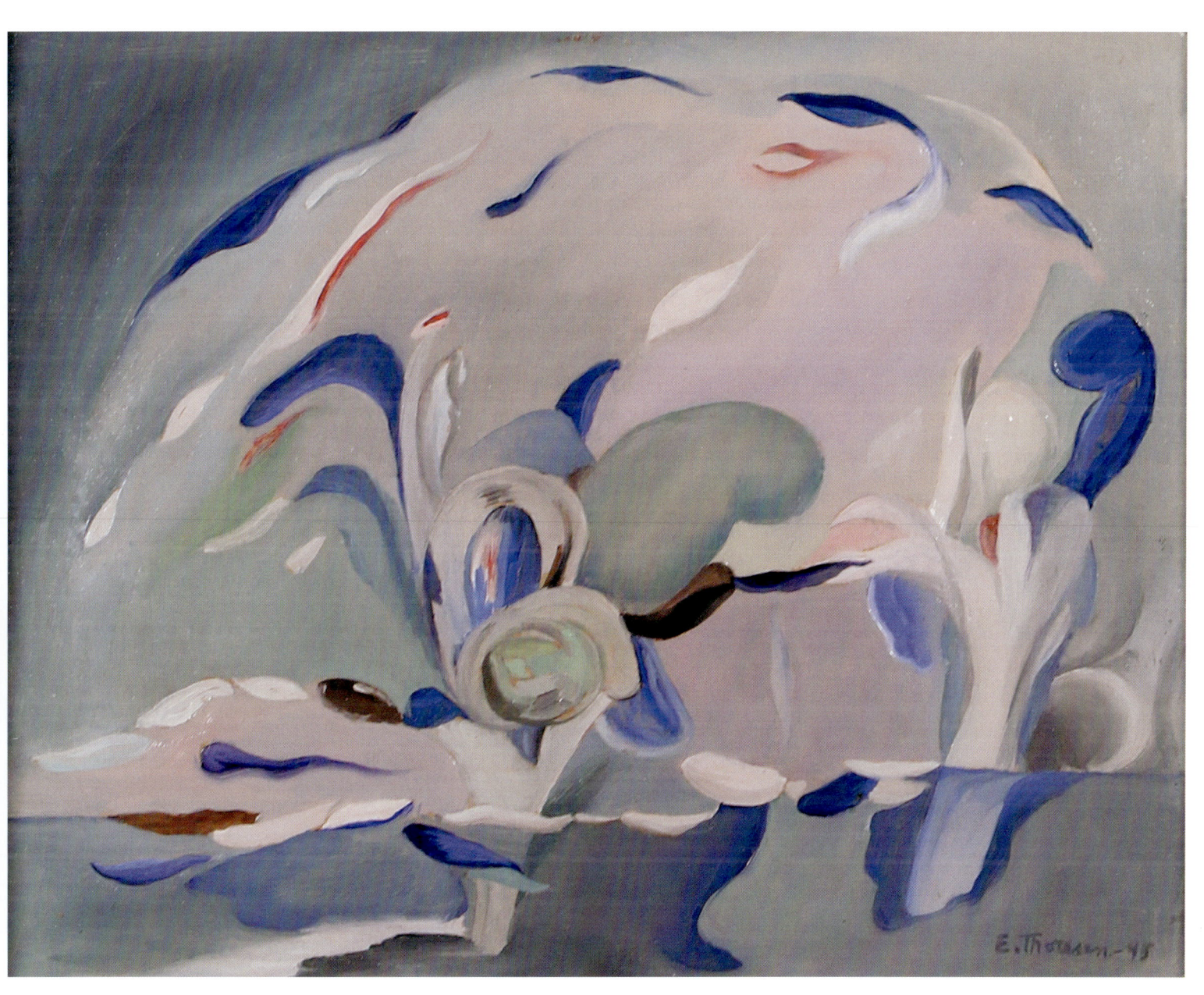

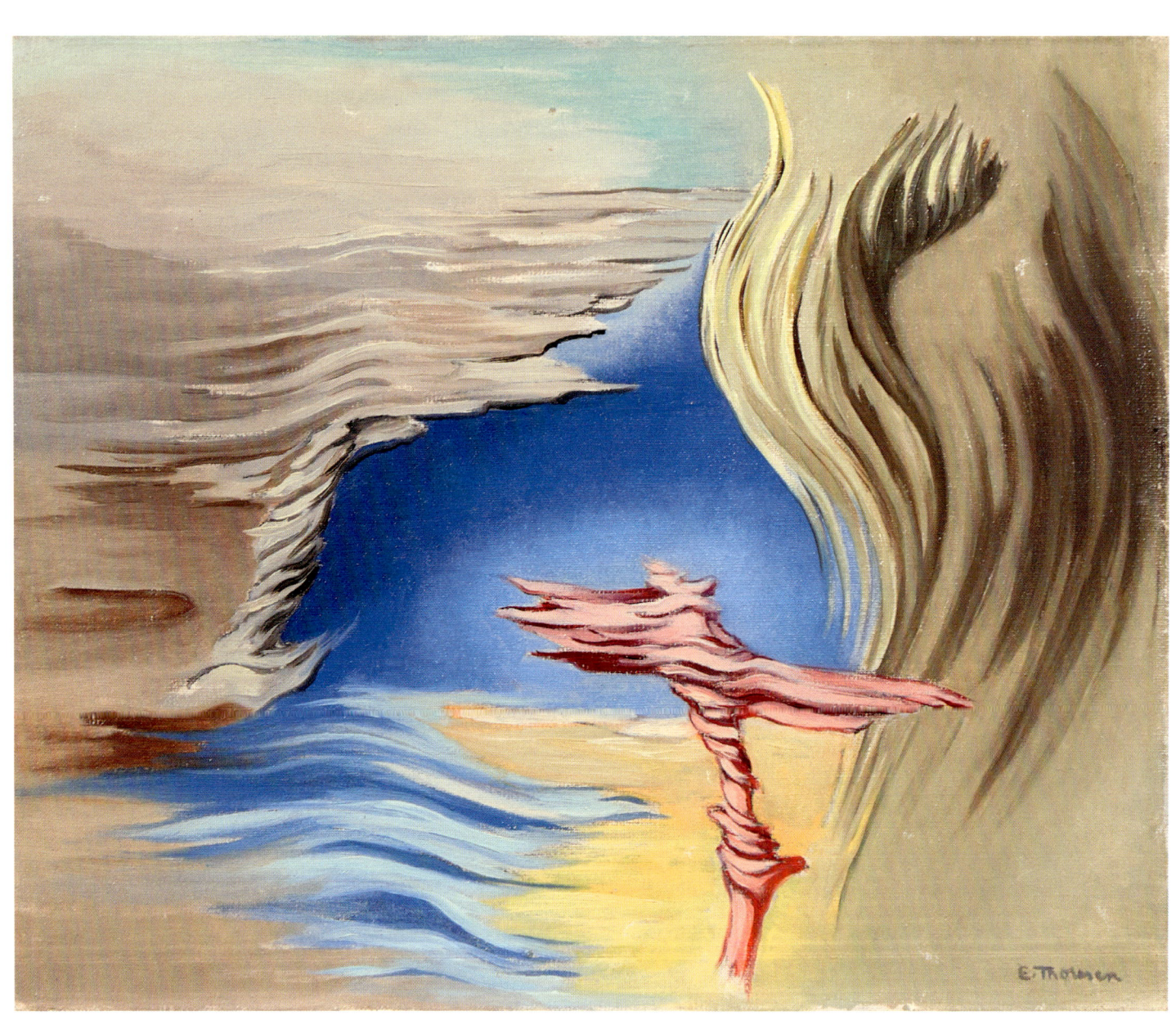

Elsa Thoresen (1906–1994), Untitled, 1945. Oil on canvas, 13 × 16 in. (33 × 40.6 cm).

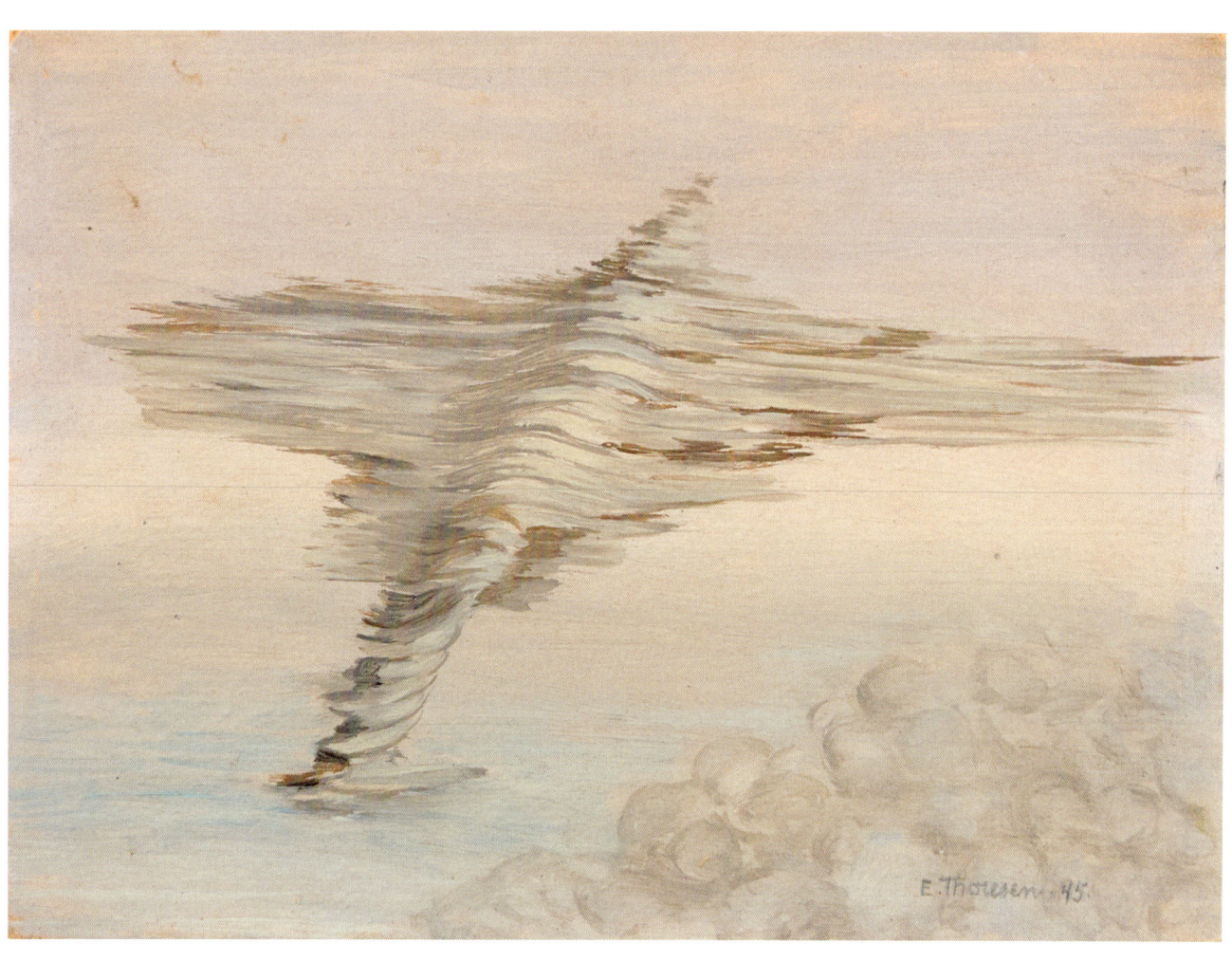

Elsa Thoresen (1906–1994), Untitled, 1945. Oil on board, 6¼ × 8⅝ in. (15.9 × 21.9 cm).

Elsa Thoresen (1906–1994), Untitled, circa 1945. Oil on canvas, 8¾ × 10⅝ in. (22.2 × 27 cm).

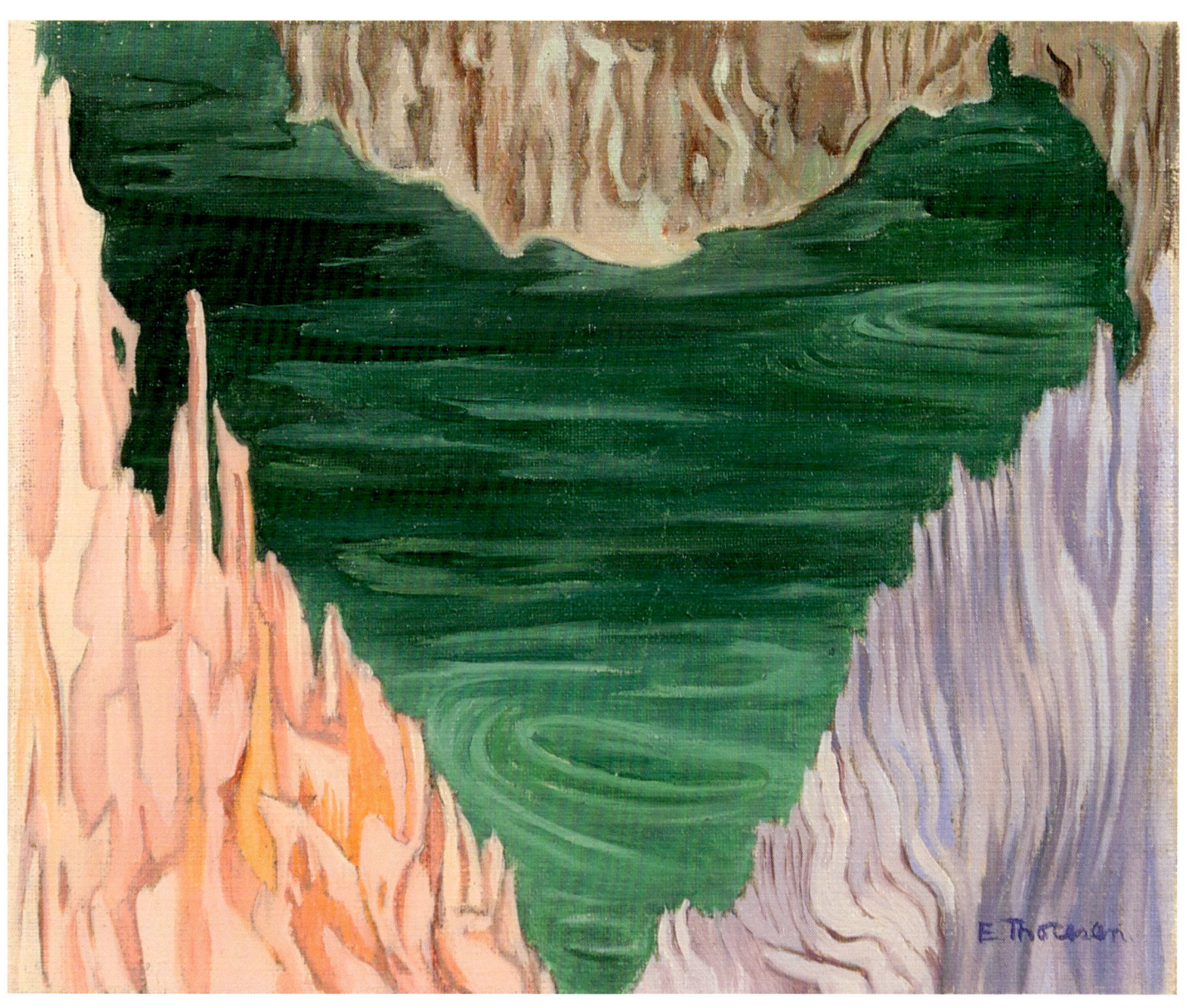

Elsa Thoresen (1906–1994), *Gjenstander til elementene* (Objects of the elements), 1945.
Oil on cardboard, 21⅝ × 18⅛ in. (55 × 46 cm). Museum Sønderjylland.

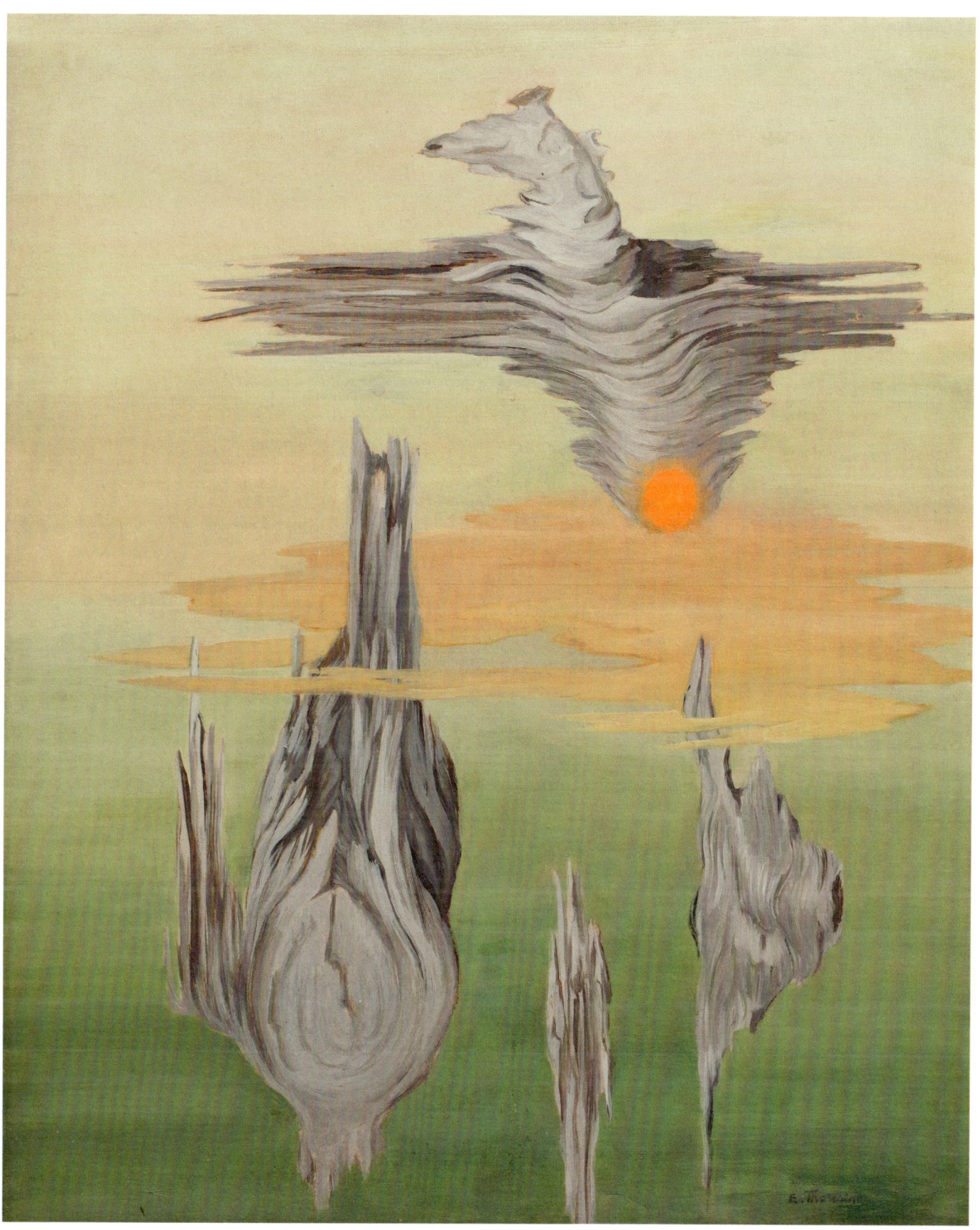

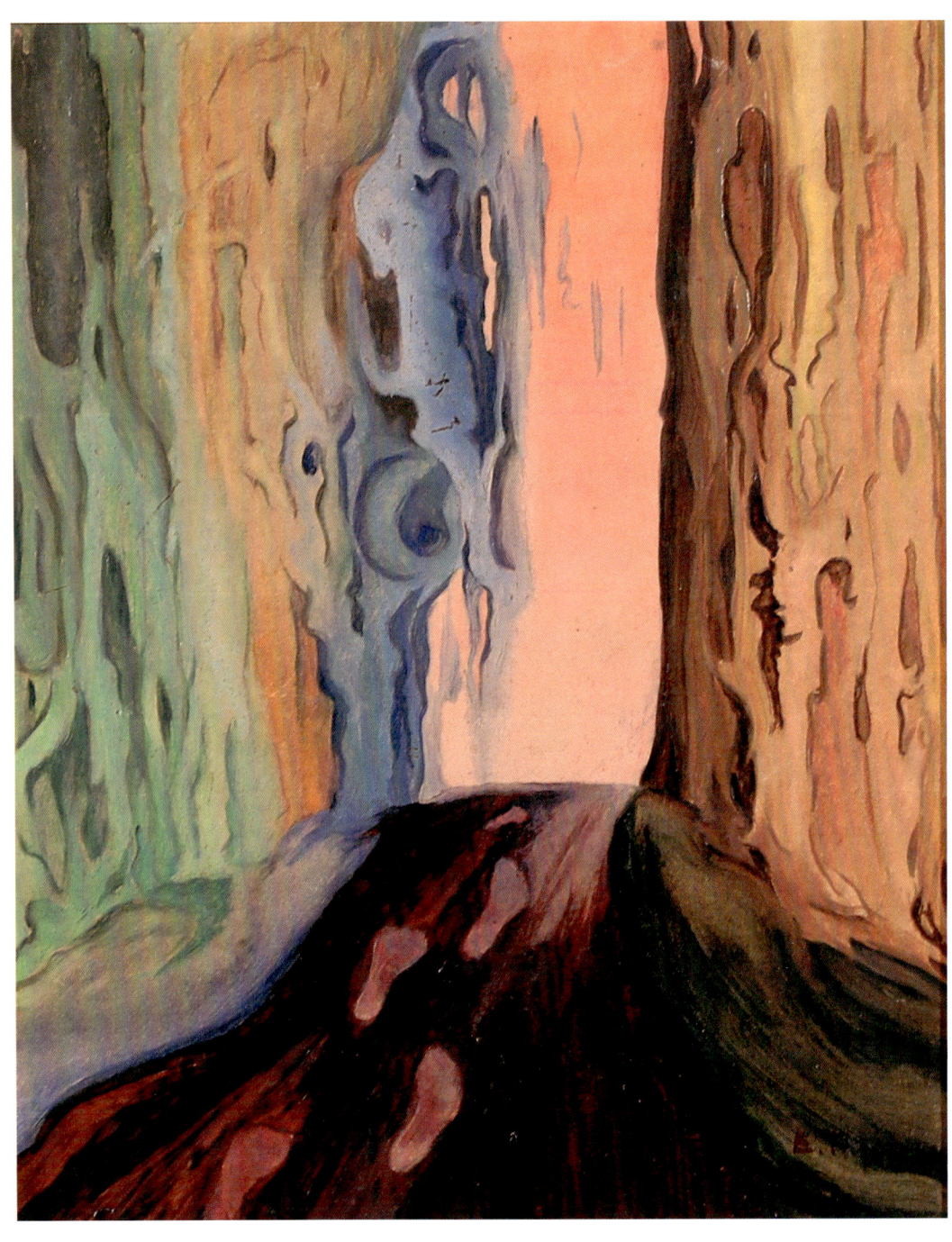

Elsa Thoresen (1906–1994), Untitled, circa 1945. Oil on board, 10 × 8½ in. (25.4 × 21.6 cm).

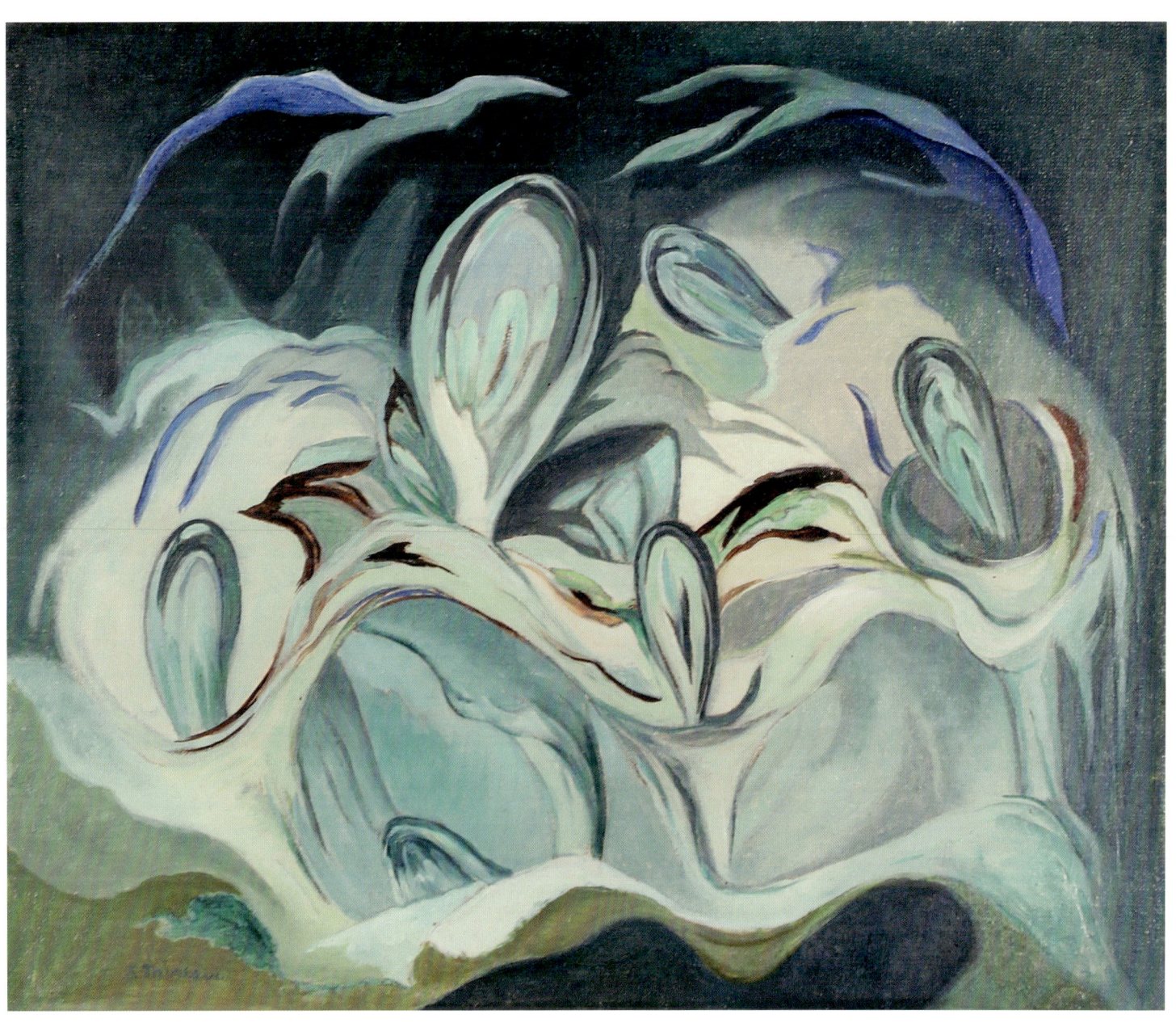

Elsa Thoresen (1906–1994), Untitled, circa 1945. Oil on canvas, 15 × 18⅛ in. (38 × 46 cm).

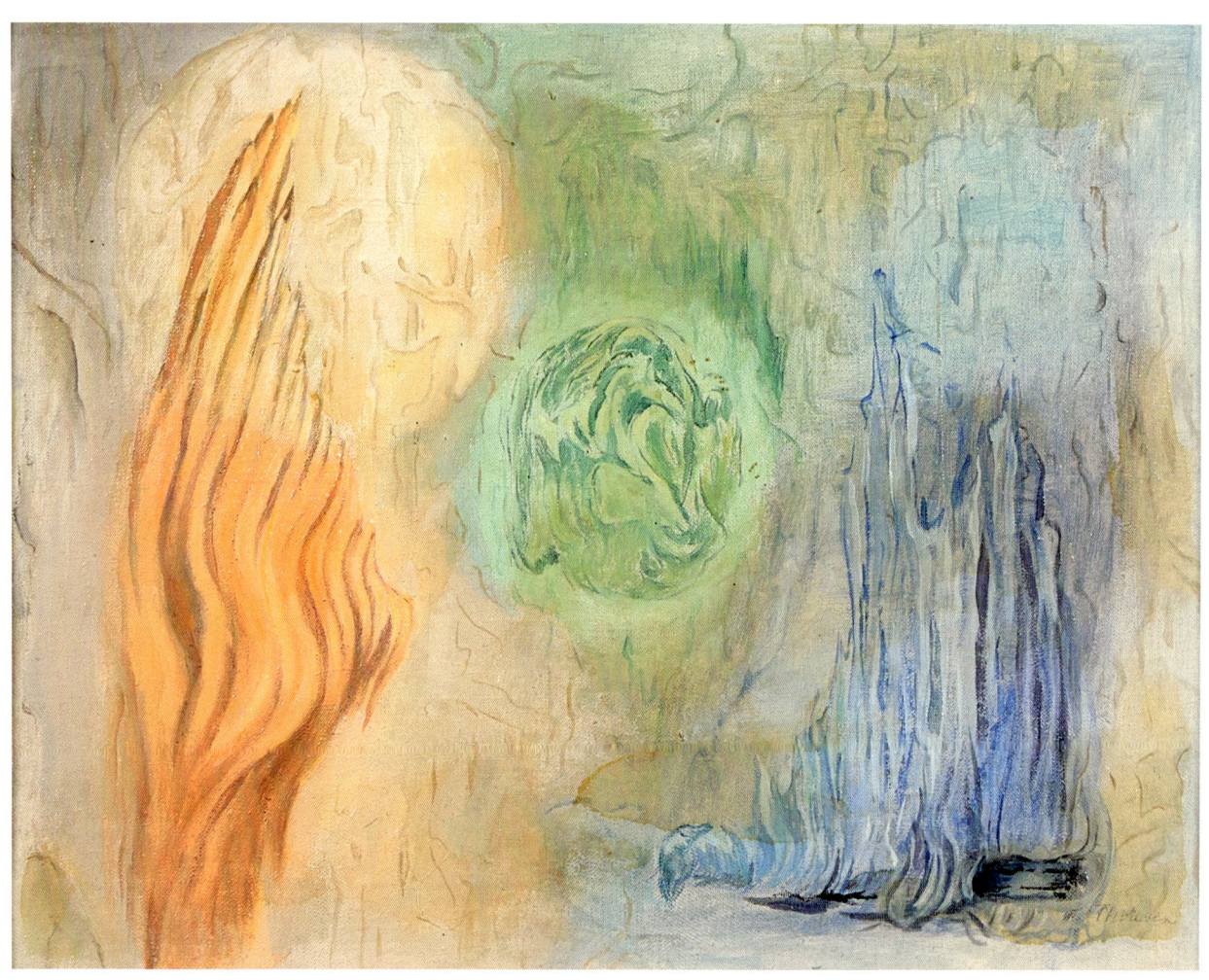

Elsa Thoresen (1906–1994), Untitled, circa 1946. Oil on canvas, 10¾ × 14 in. (27.3 × 35.6 cm).

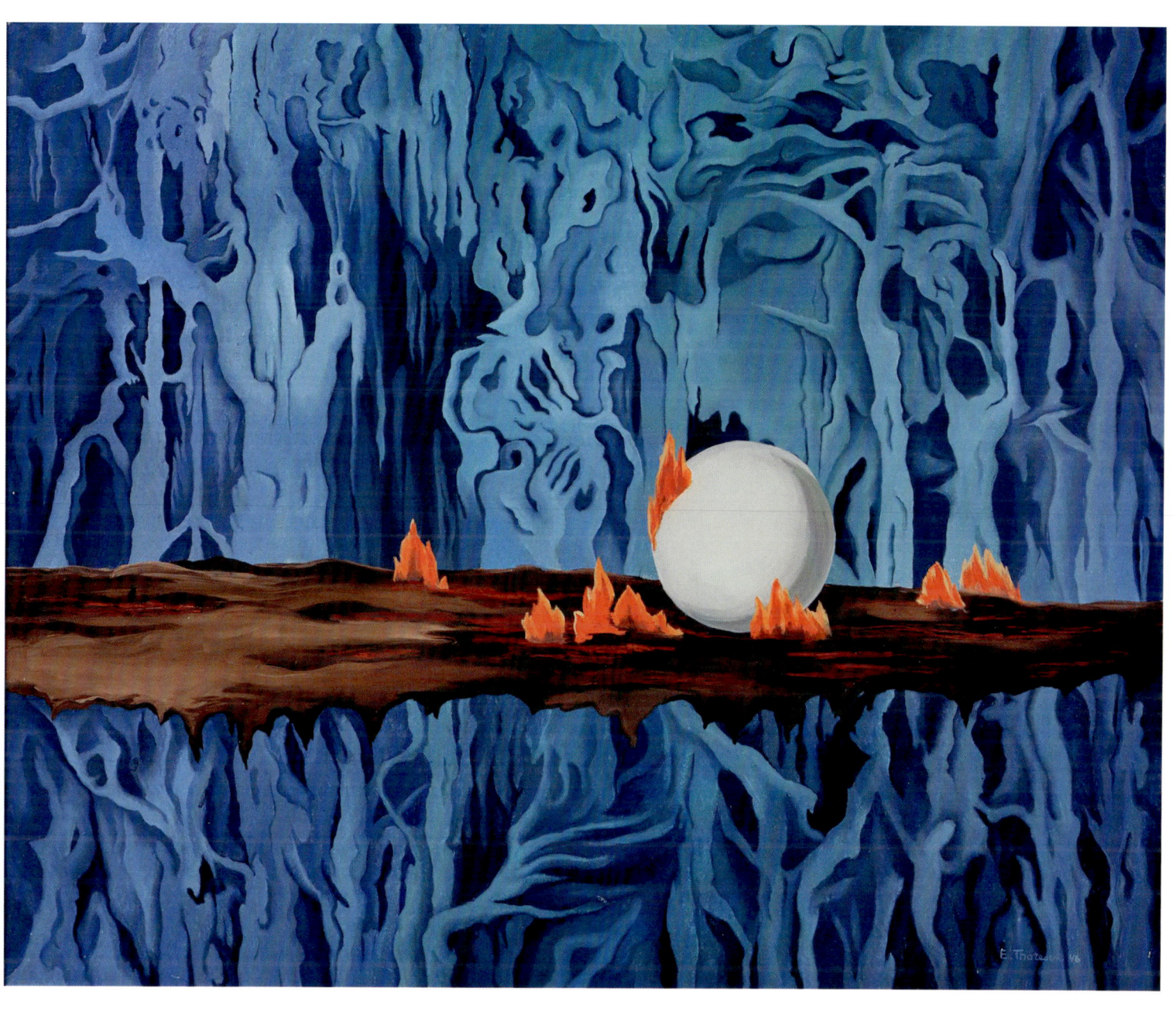

Elsa Thoresen (1906–1994), *Brinnande jord III* (Burning Earth III), 1946. Oil on canvas,
31⅞ × 39⅝ in. (81 × 100.5 cm). Private collection.
Photo courtesy of Bukowskis Auction, Stockholm.

Elsa Thoresen (1906–1994), *Berget i natten* (The mountain at night), circa 1946. Oil on board, 13 × 16¼ in. (33 × 41.3 cm).

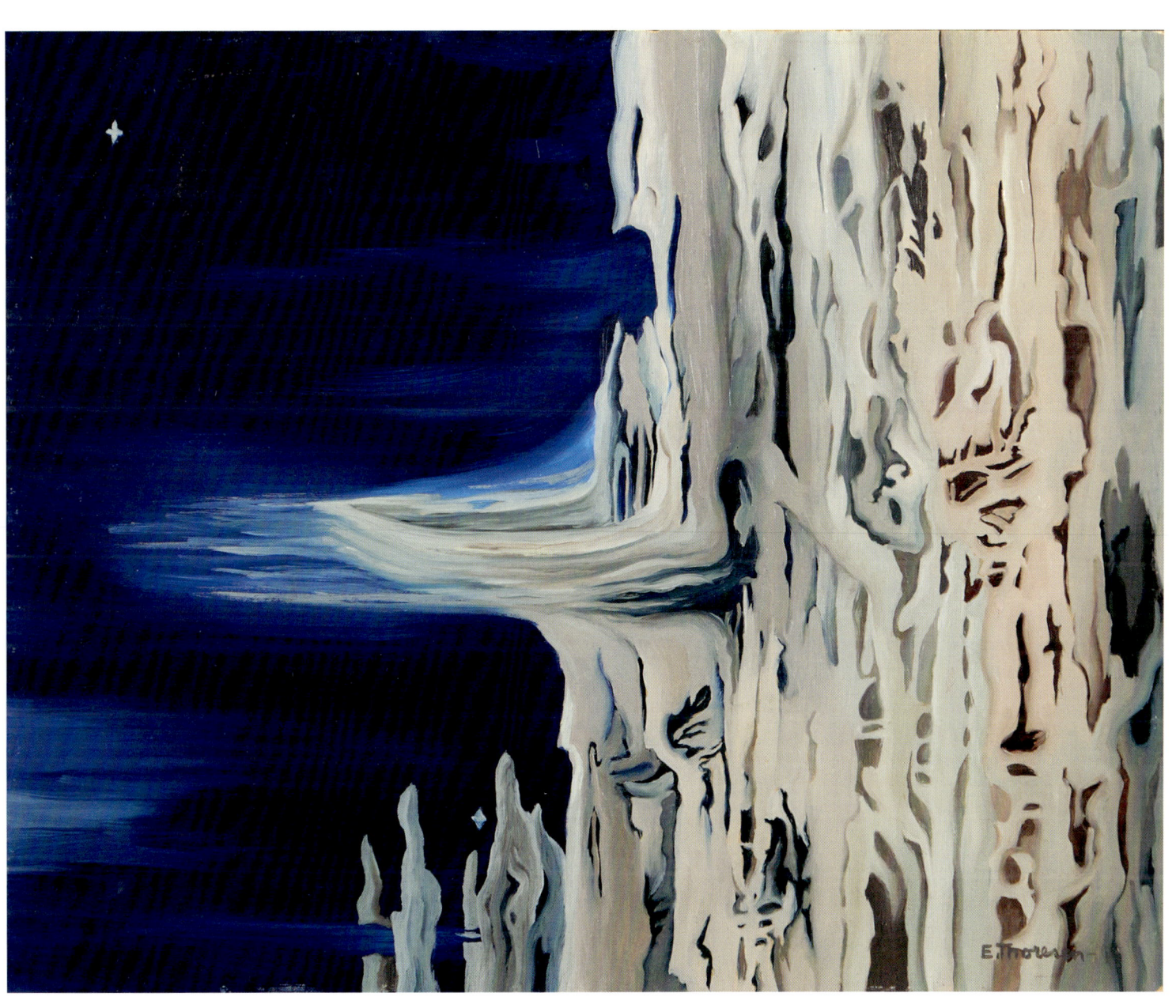

Elsa Thoresen (1906–1994), *Skovens poesi* (The poetry of the forest), 1947. Oil on panel, 20⅞ × 30¾ in. (53 × 78 cm). Museum Sønderjylland.

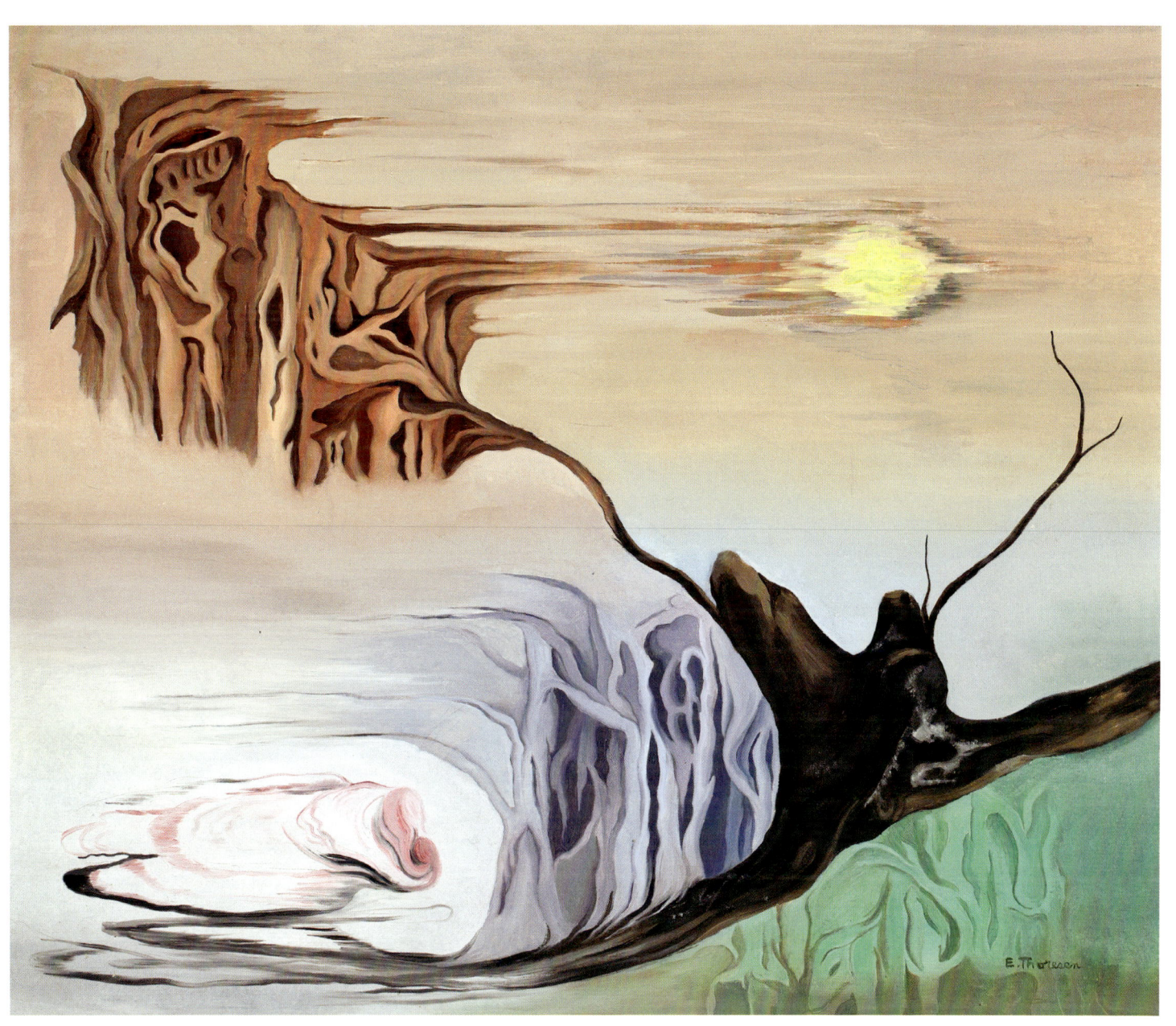

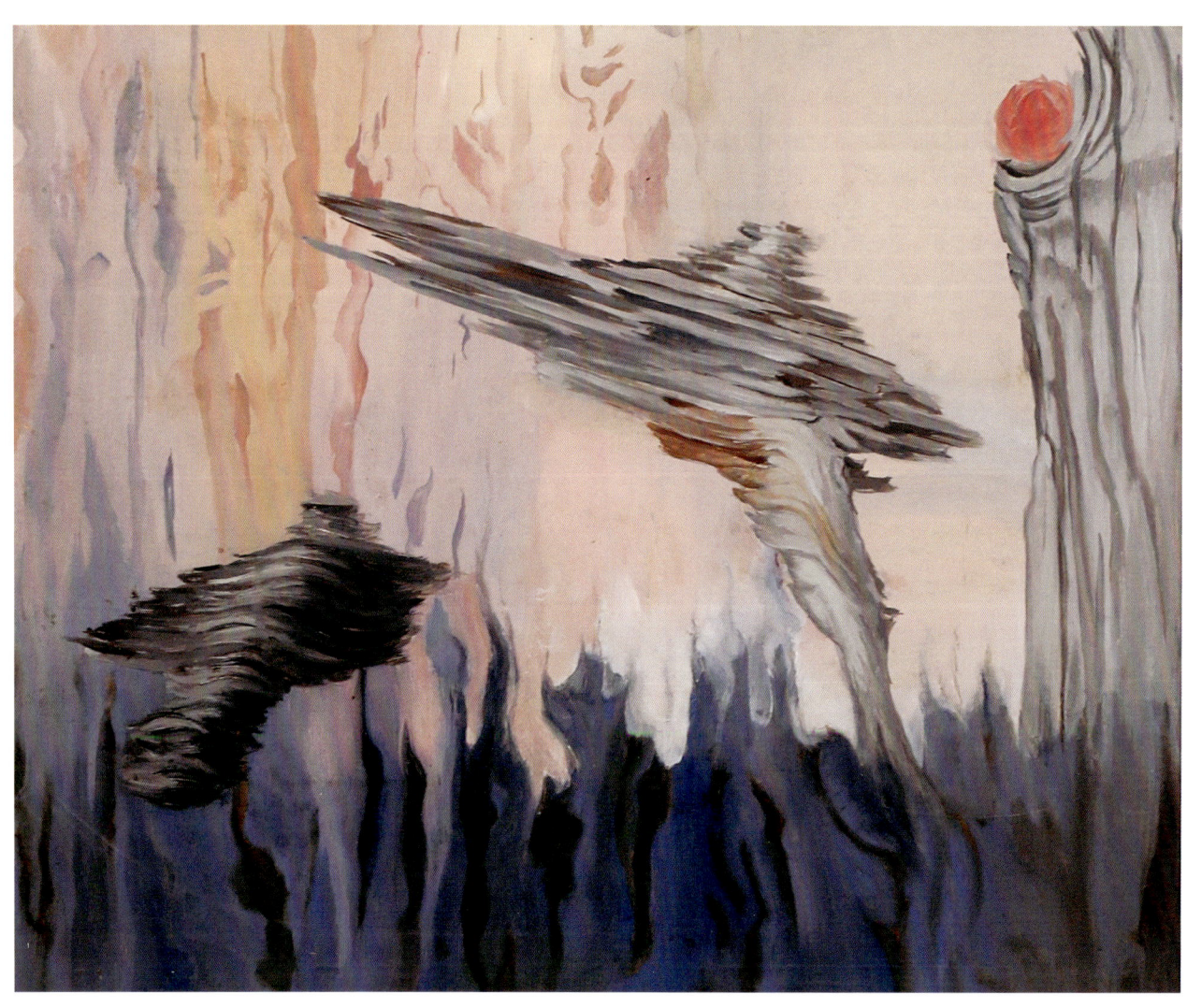

Elsa Thoresen (1906–1994), Untitled, circa 1948. Oil on board, 13 × 16 in. (33 × 40.6 cm).

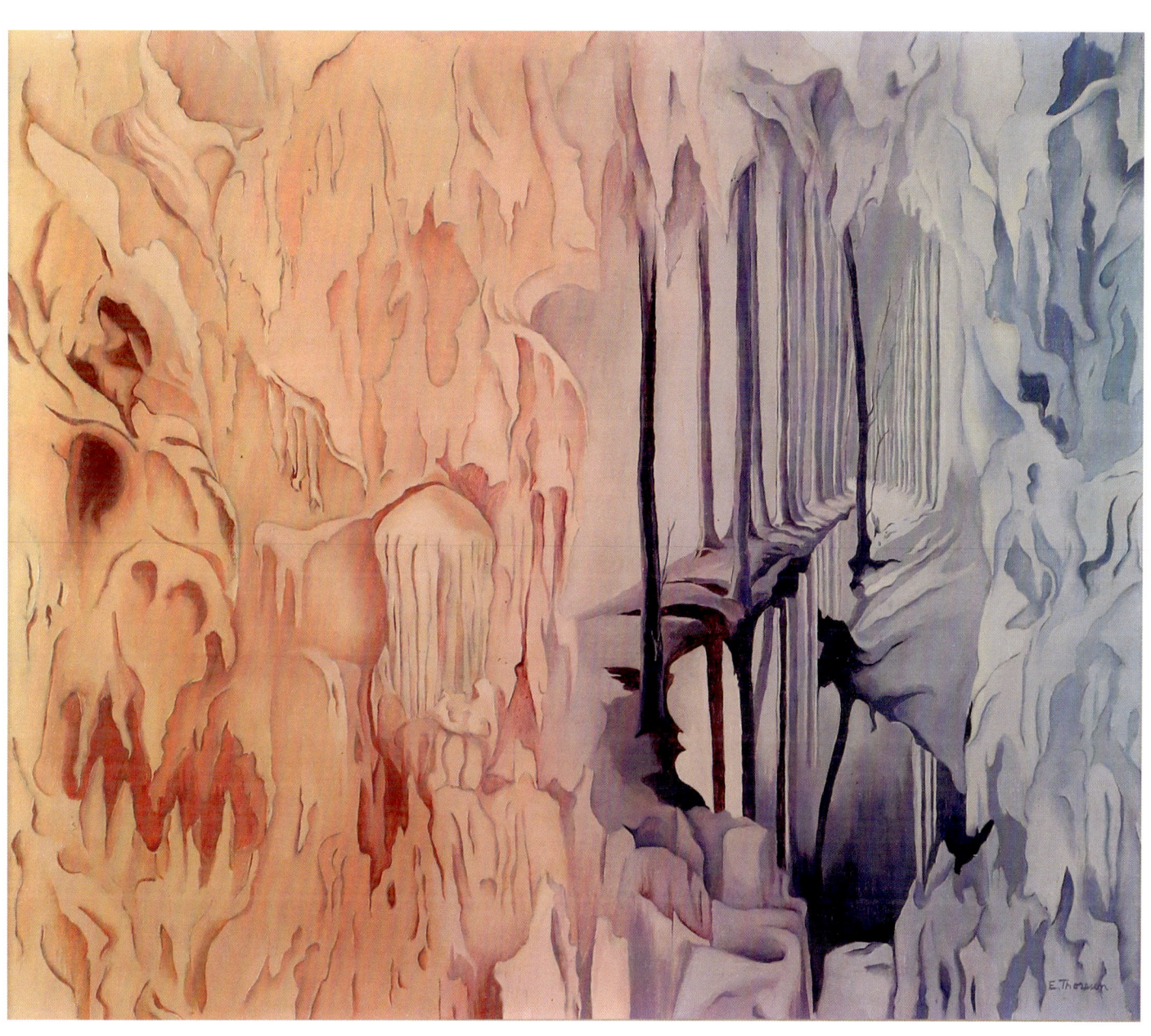

Elsa Thoresen (1906–1994), Untitled, circa 1948. Oil on canvas, 21 × 25 in. (53.3 × 63.5 cm).

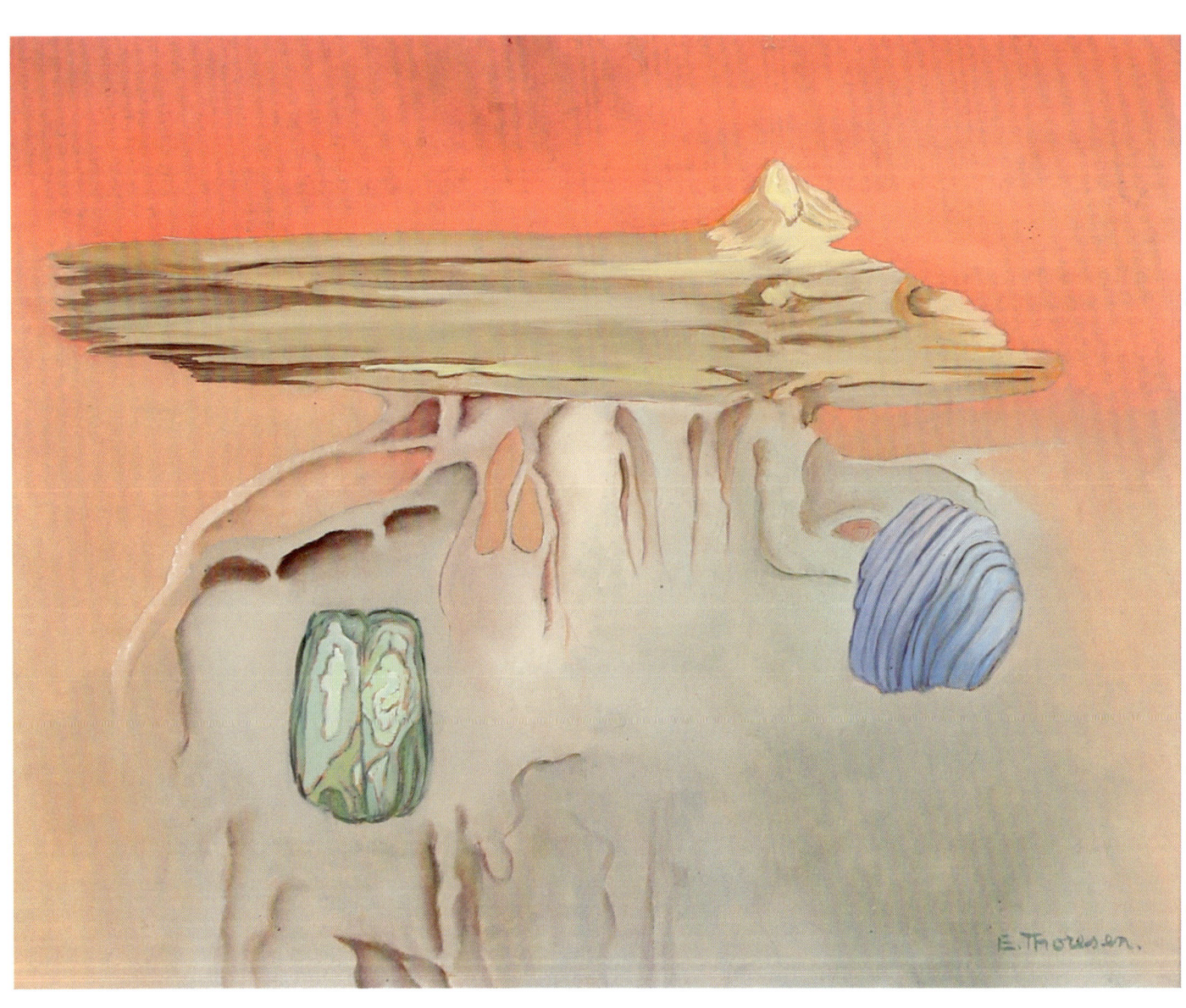

Elsa Thoresen (1906–1994), Untitled, 1948. Oil on board, 10¾ × 13⅞ in. (27.3 × 35.2 cm).

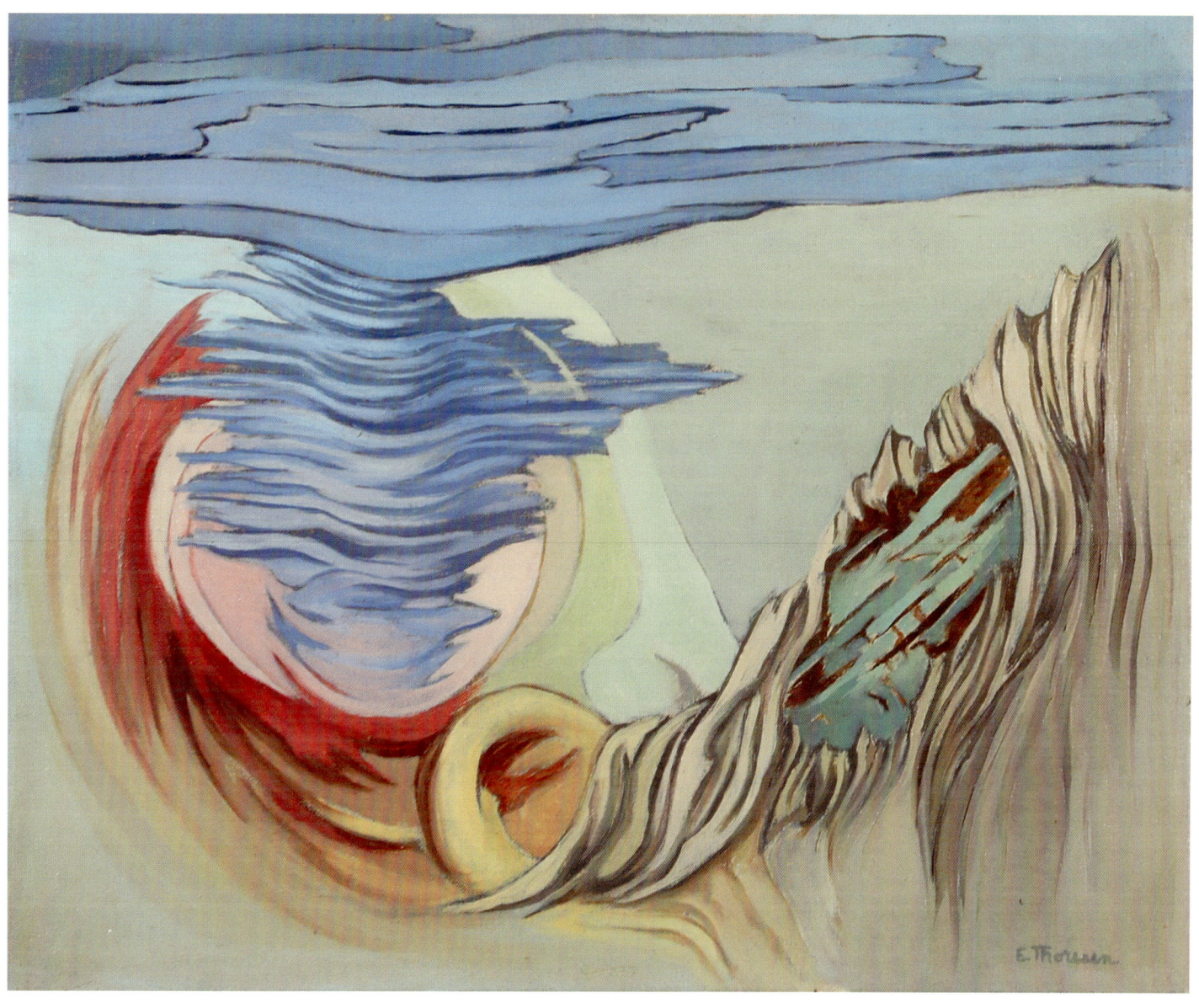

Elsa Thoresen (1906–1994), *Skogens, havets och luftens poetiska object* (The poetic objects of the forest, the sea and the air), circa 1948. Oil on canvas, 13 × 16¼ in. (33 × 41.3 cm).

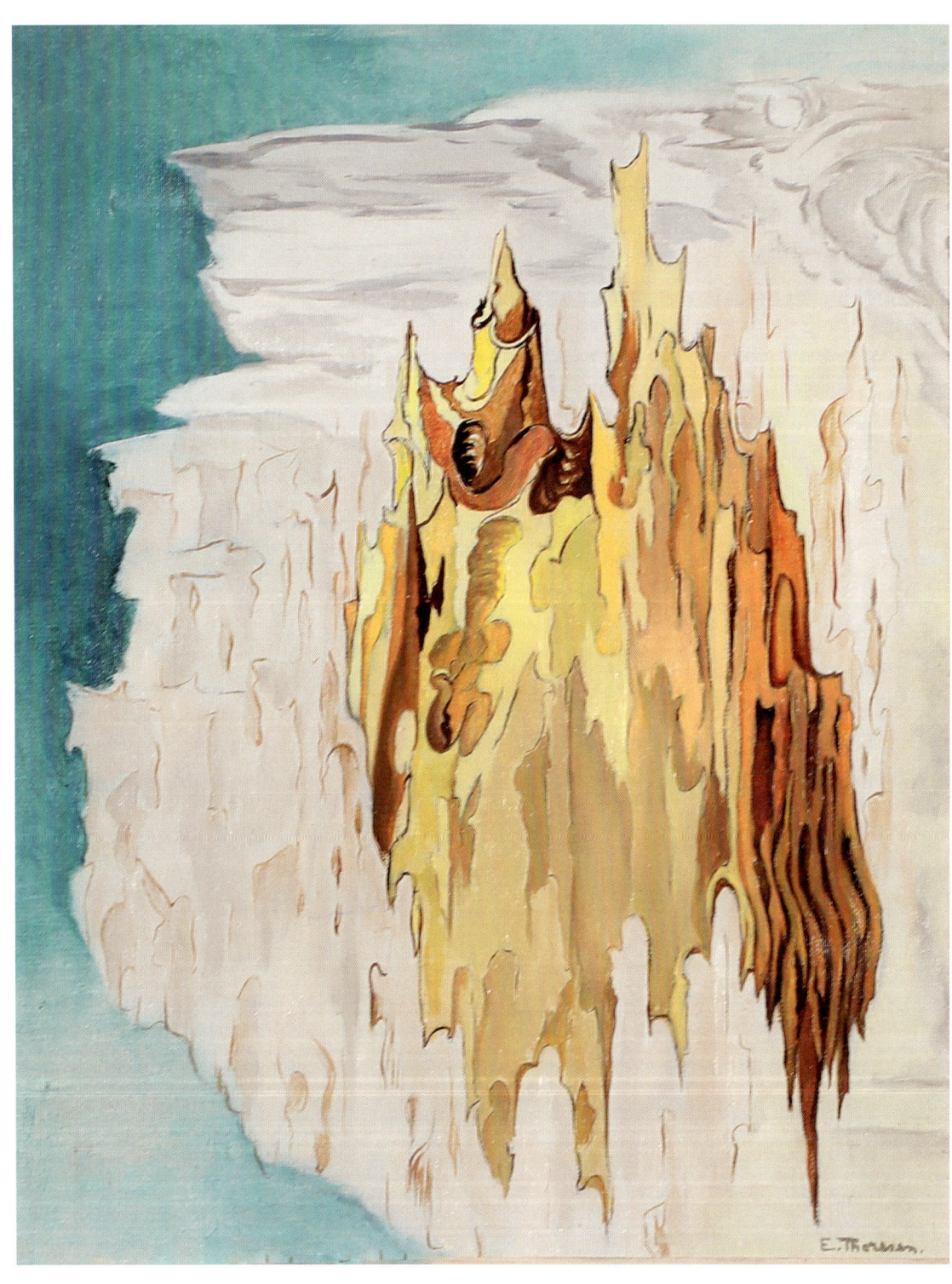

Elsa Thoresen (1906–1994), Untitled, 1949. Oil on canvas, 16 × 13 in. (40.6 × 33 cm).

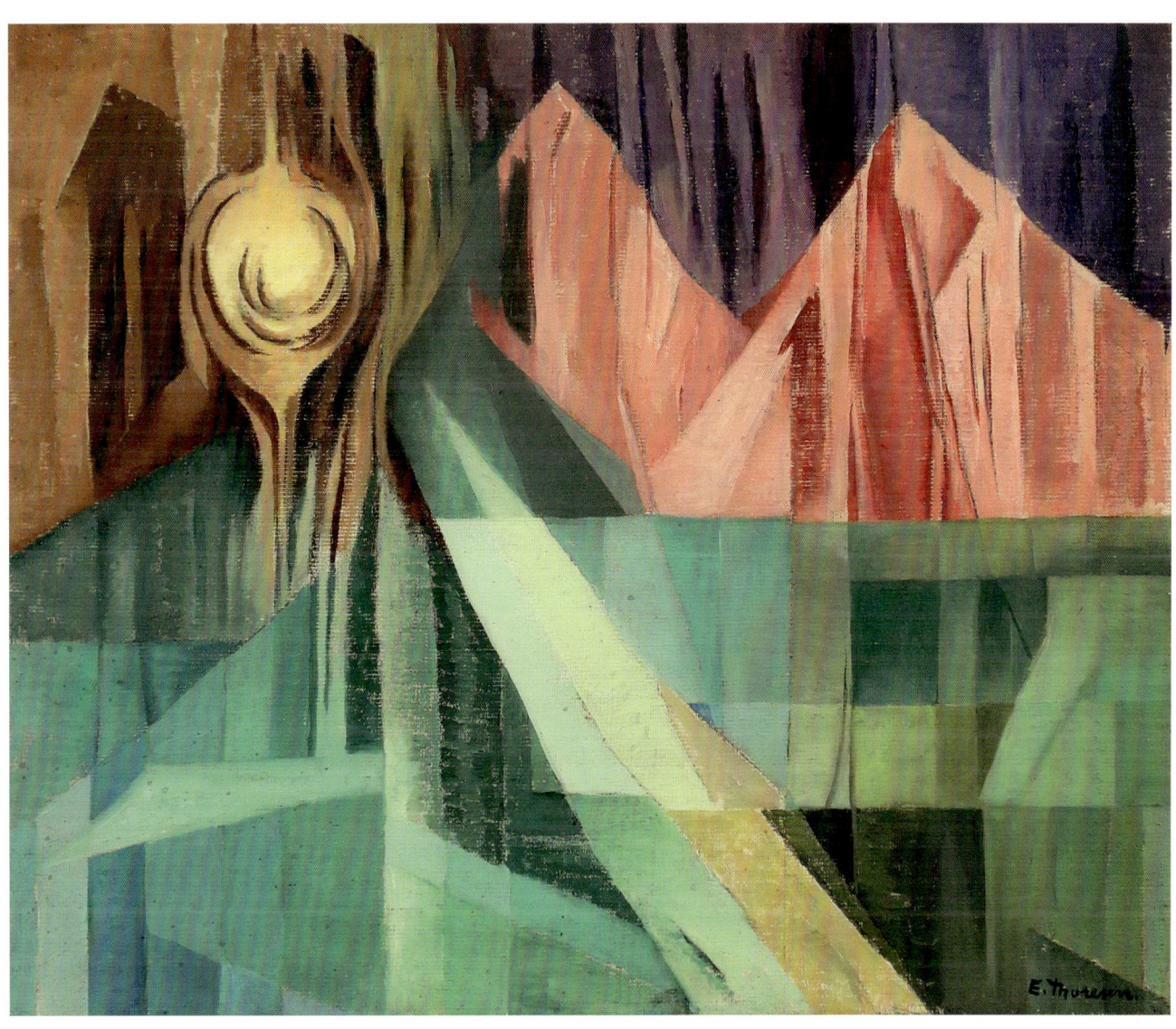

Elsa Thoresen (1906–1994), Untitled, circa 1949. Oil on canvas, 15 × 18⅛ in. (38 × 46 cm).

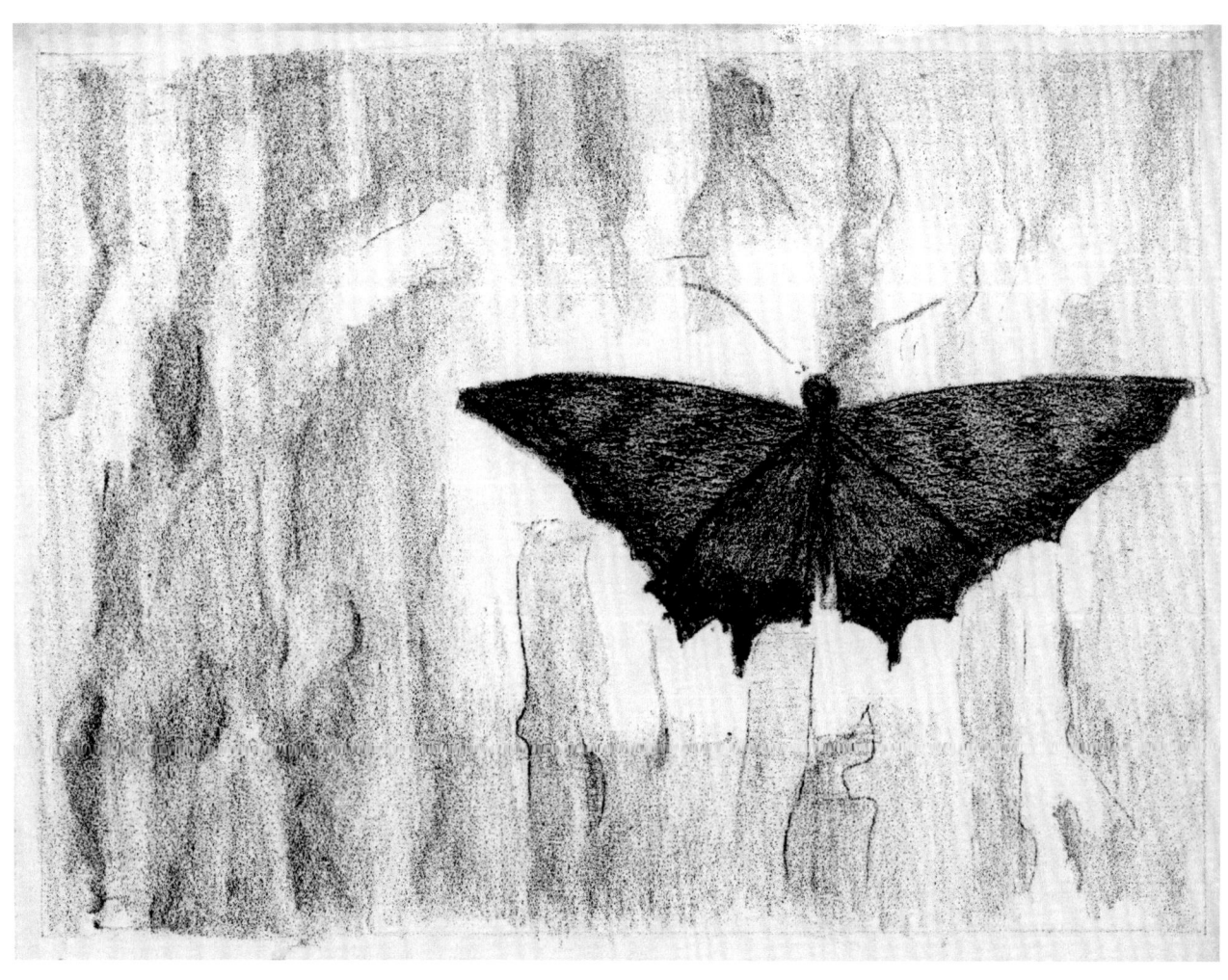

Elsa Thoresen (1906–1994), Untitled, 1950. Lithograph, 5 × 6⅝ in. (12.7 × 16.8 cm).

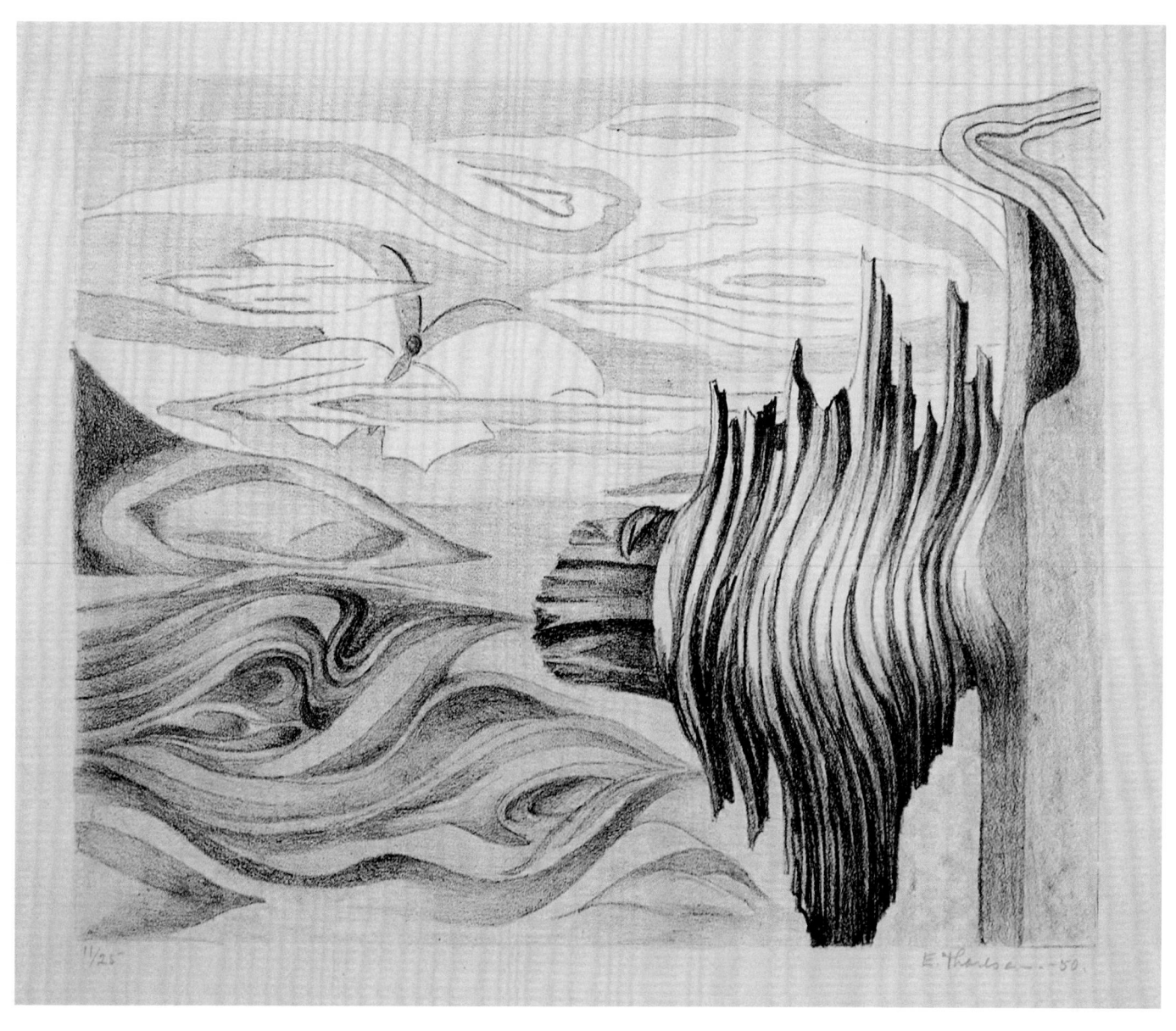

Elsa Thoresen (1906–1994), Untitled, 1950. Lithograph, 8¾ × 10¾ in. (22.2 × 27.3 cm).

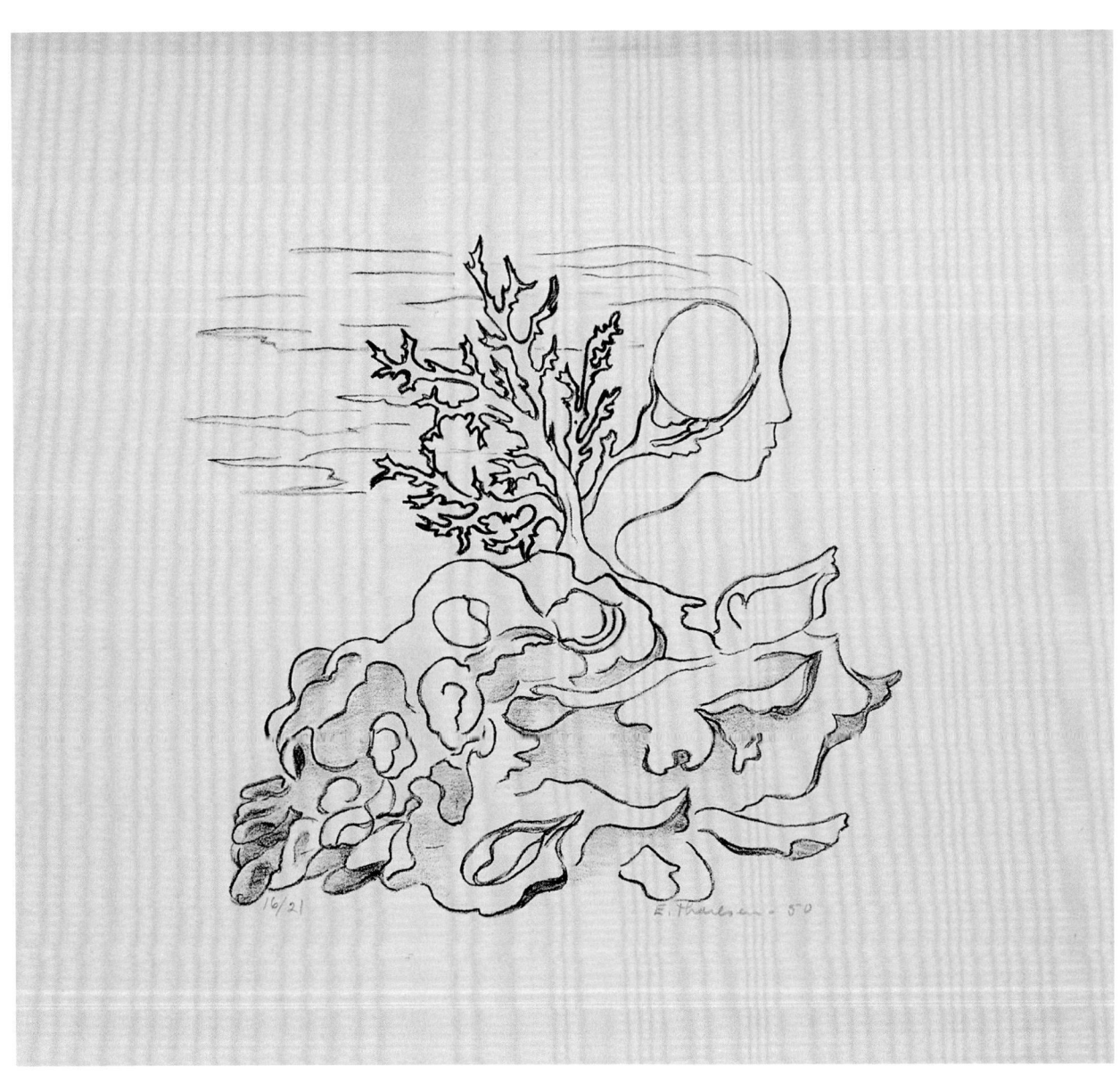

Elsa Thoresen (1906–1994), Untitled, 1950. Lithograph, 7½ × 8½ in. (19.1 × 21.6 cm).

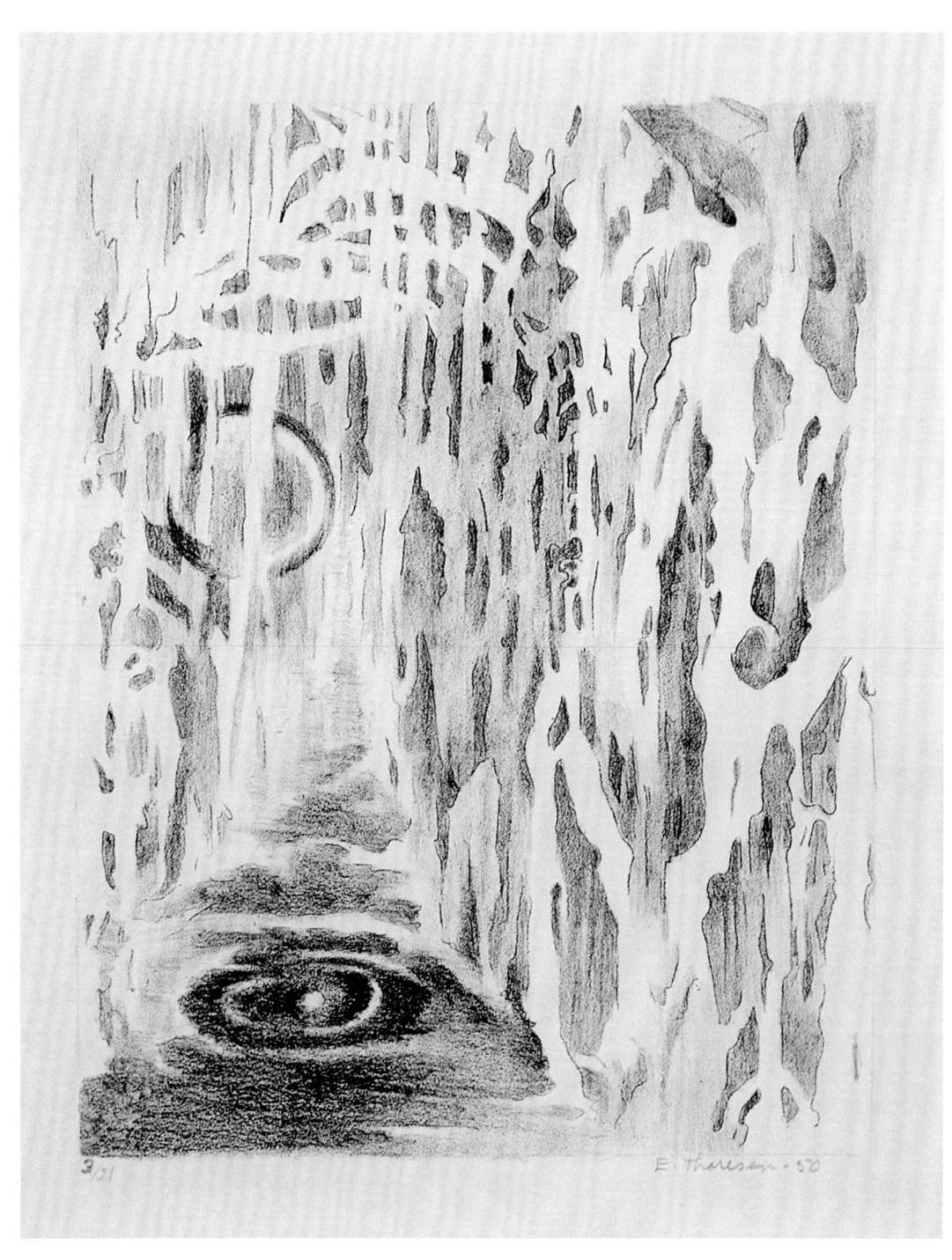

Elsa Thoresen (1906–1994), Untitled, 1950. Lithograph, 9¾ × 7½ in. (24.8 × 19.1 cm).

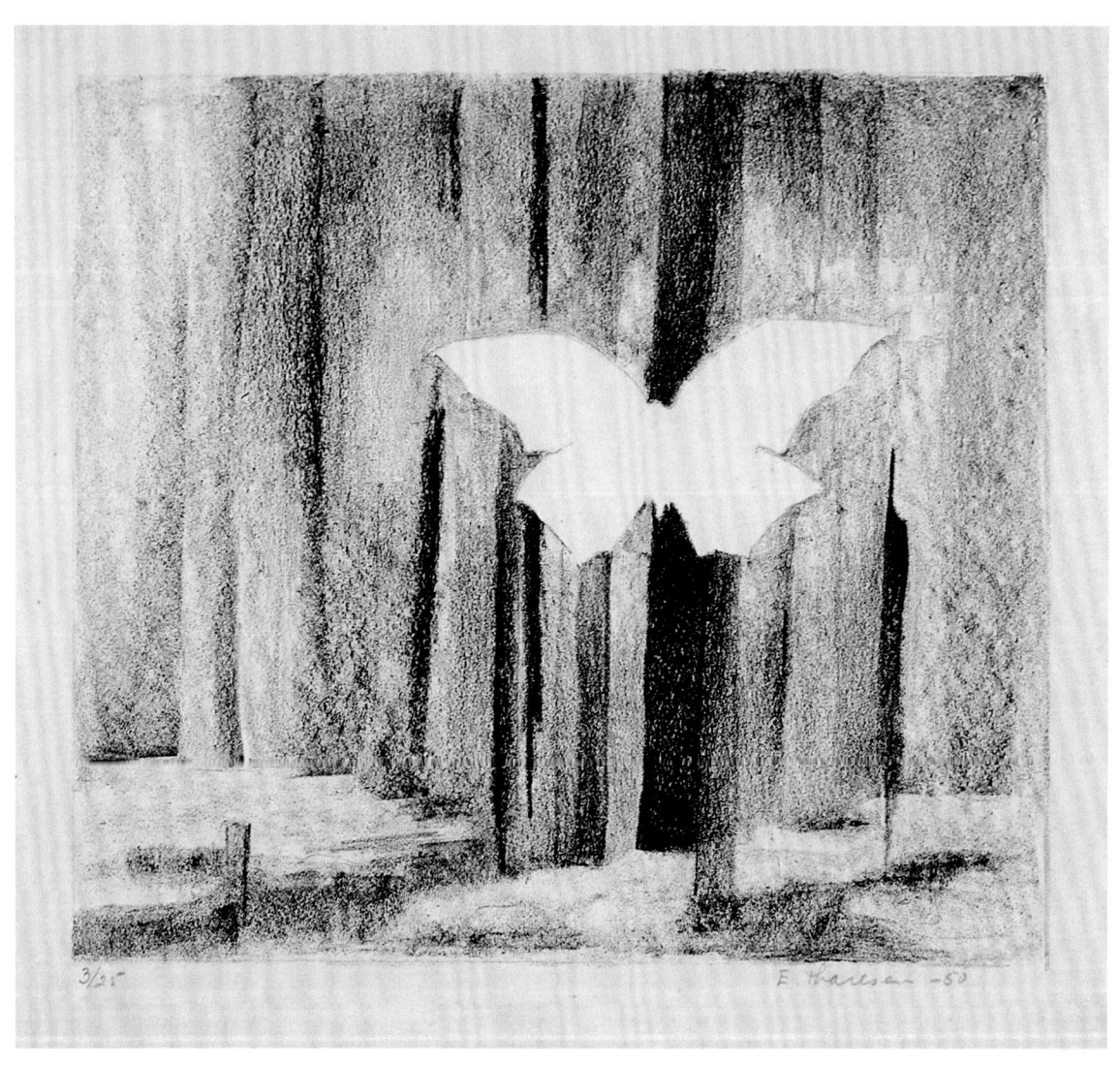

Elsa Thoresen (1906–1994), Untitled, 1950. Lithograph, 7½ × 8½ in. (19.1 × 21.6 cm).

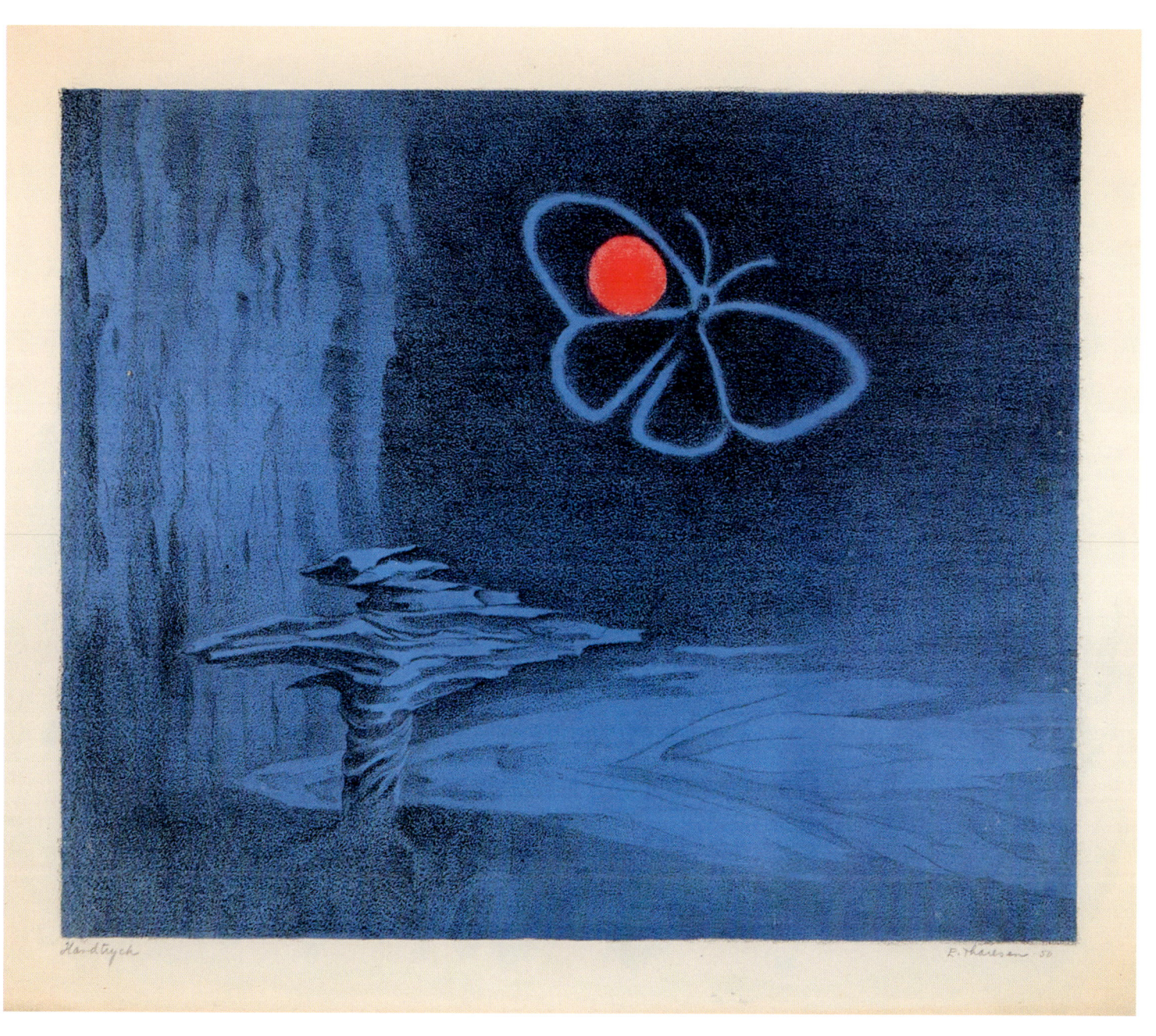

Handtych   E. Thoresen - 50

Elsa Thoresen (1906–1994), Untitled, 1950. Color lithograph, 13 × 16 in. (33 × 40.6 cm).

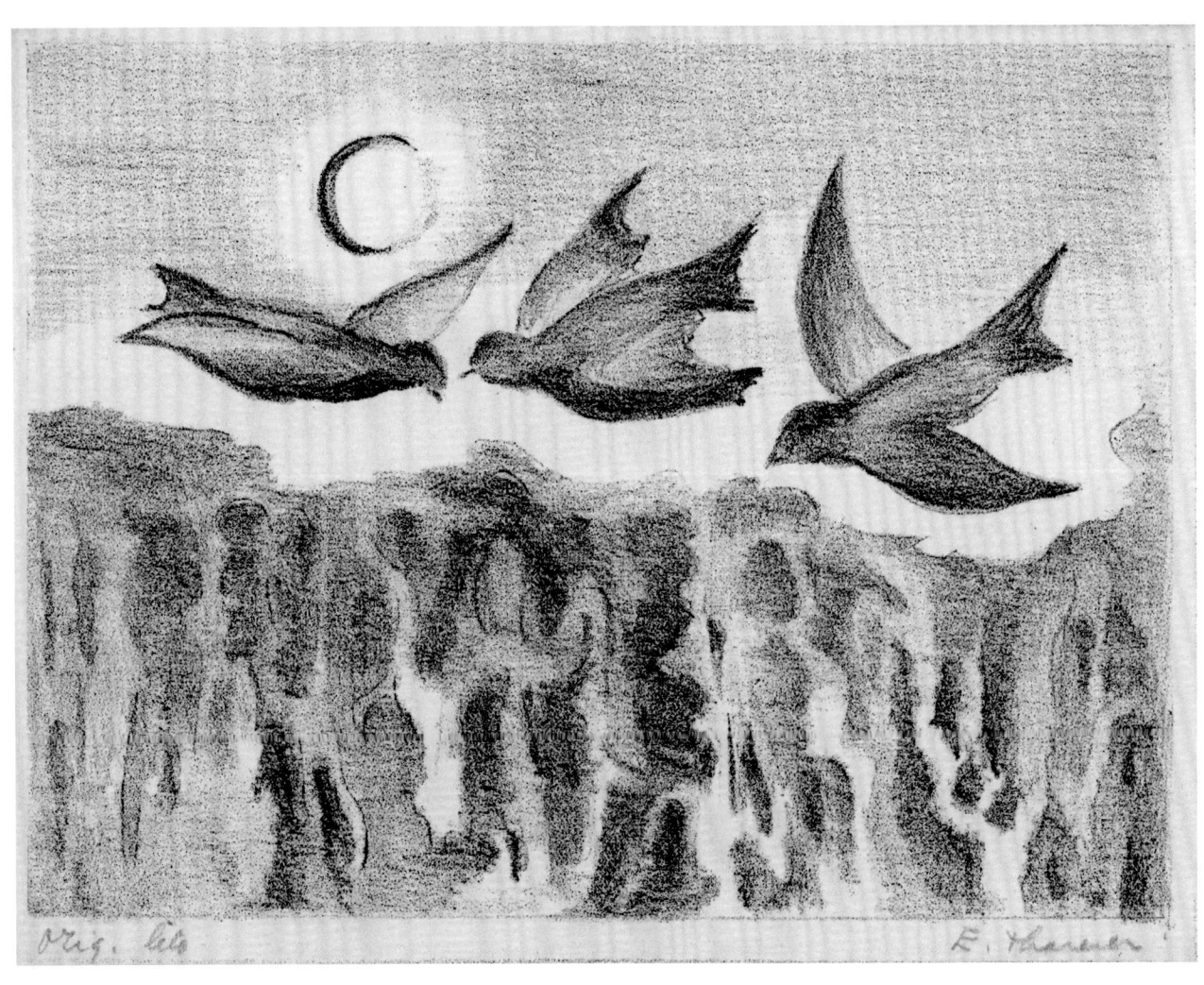

Elsa Thoresen (1906–1994), Untitled, 1950. Lithograph, 5½ × 6⅝ in. (14 × 16.8 cm).

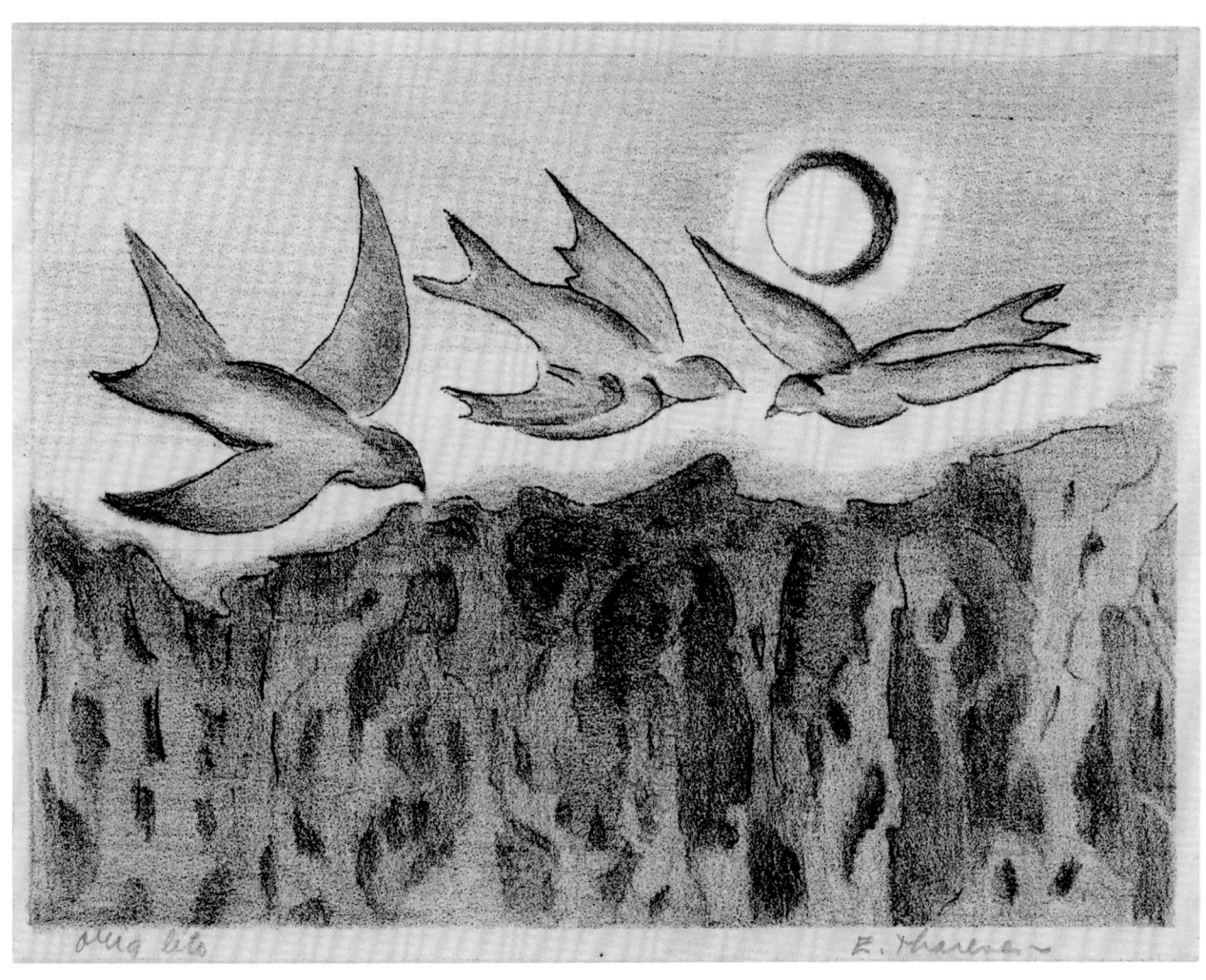

Elsa Thoresen (1906–1994), Untitled, 1950. Lithograph, 5½ × 6⅝ in. (14 × 16.8 cm).

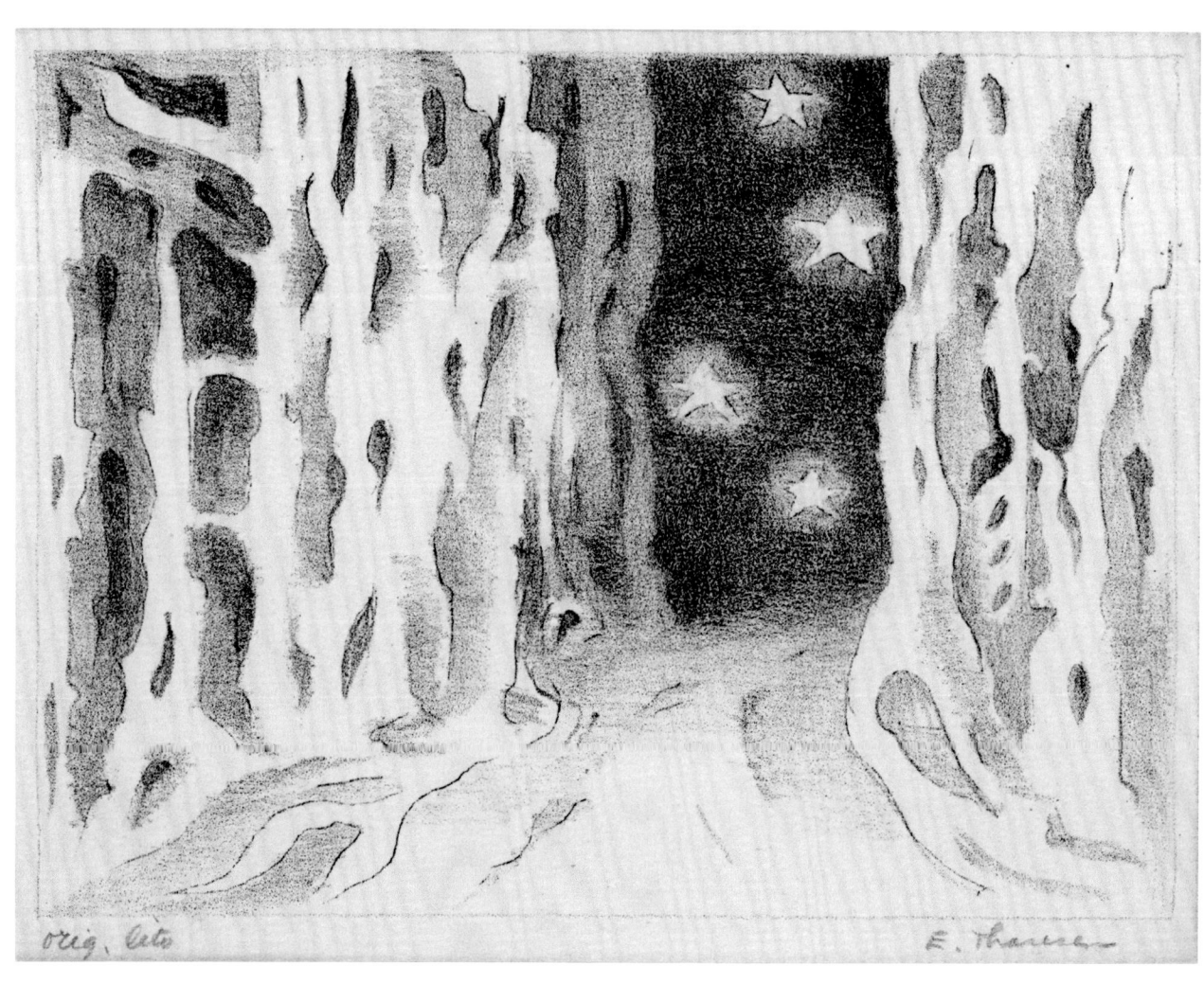

orig. lito   E. Thoresen

Elsa Thoresen (1906–1994), Untitled, 1950. Lithograph, 5 × 6⅝ in. (12.7 × 16.8 cm).

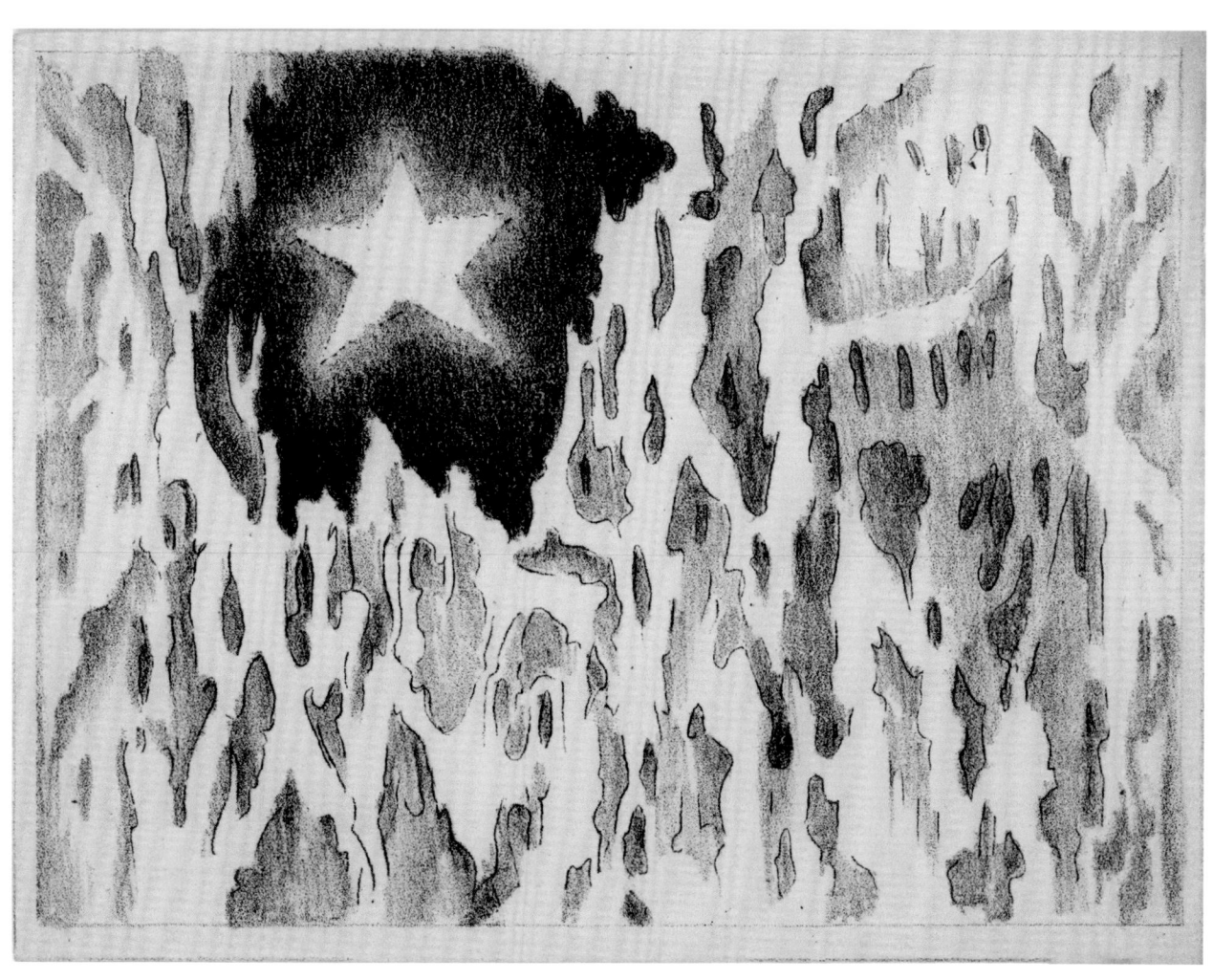

Elsa Thoresen (1906–1994), Untitled, 1950. Lithograph, 5 × 6⅝ in. (12.7 × 16.8 cm).

Elsa Thoresen (1906–1994), Untitled, circa 1950. Oil on paper, 3 × 4¼ in. (7.6 × 10.8 cm).
Mount: 7⅛ × 8⅜ in. (18.1 × 21.3 cm).

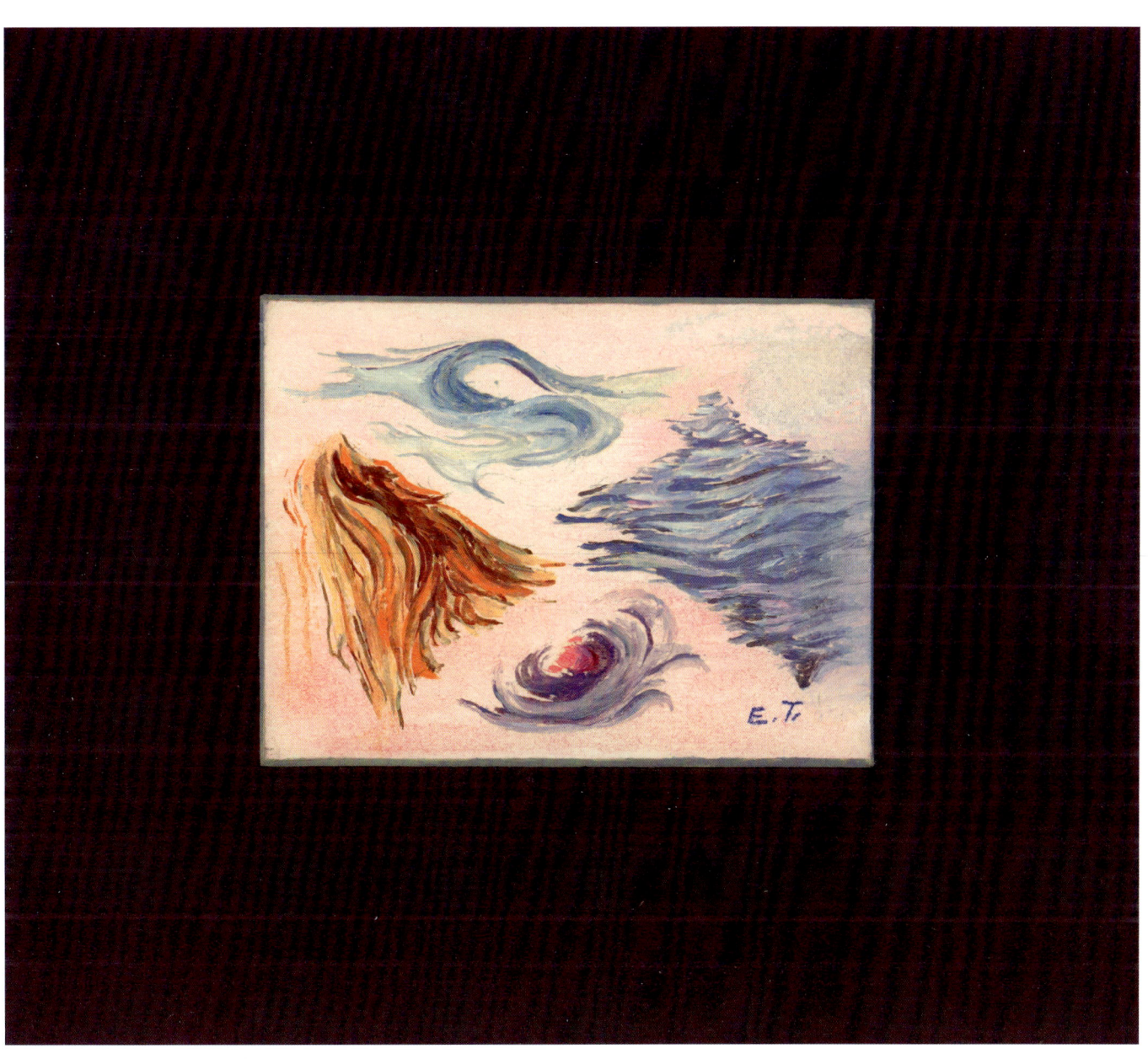

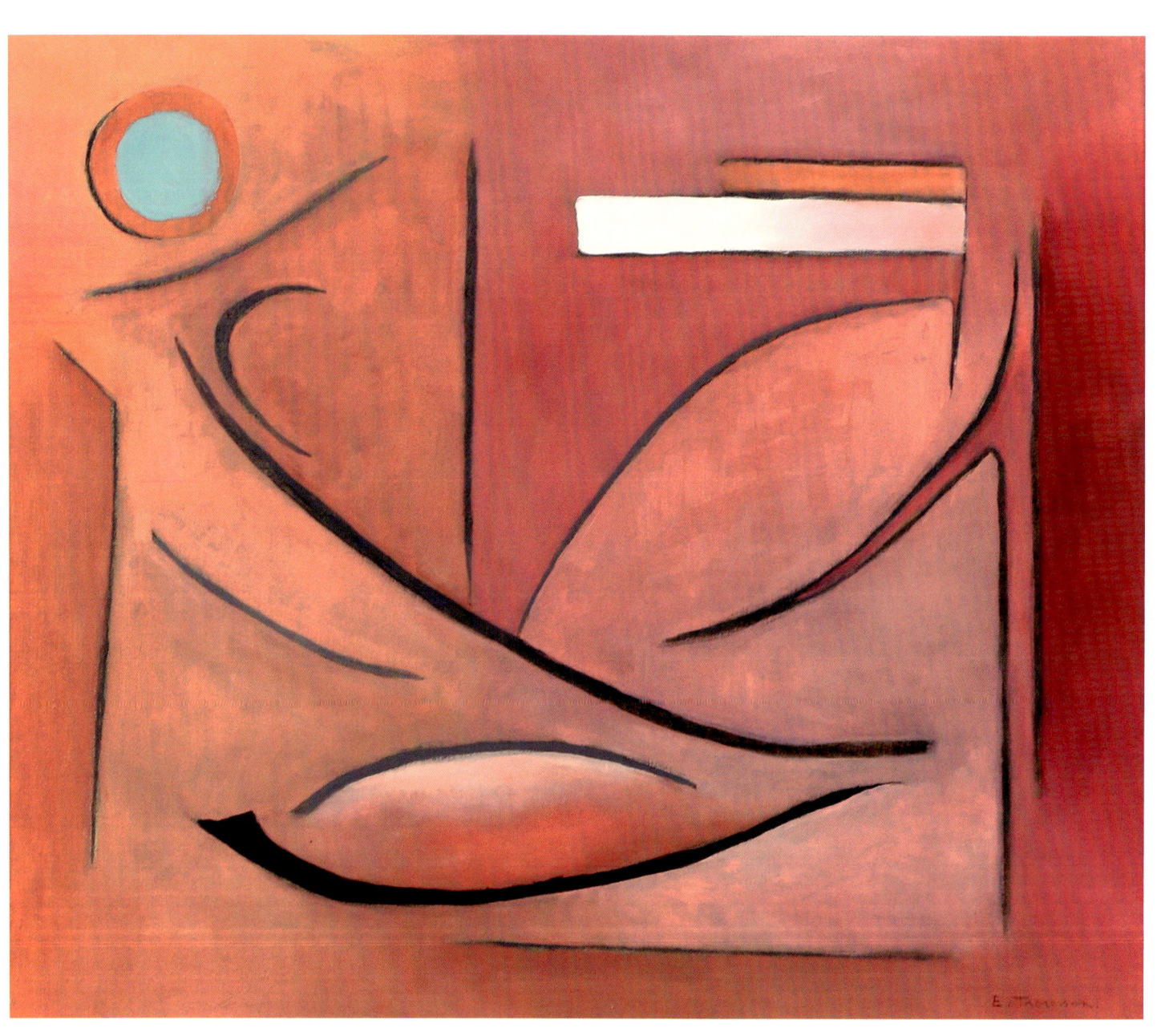

Elsa Thoresen (1906–1994), Untitled, circa 1958. Oil on canvas, 20 × 24 in. (50.8 × 61 cm).

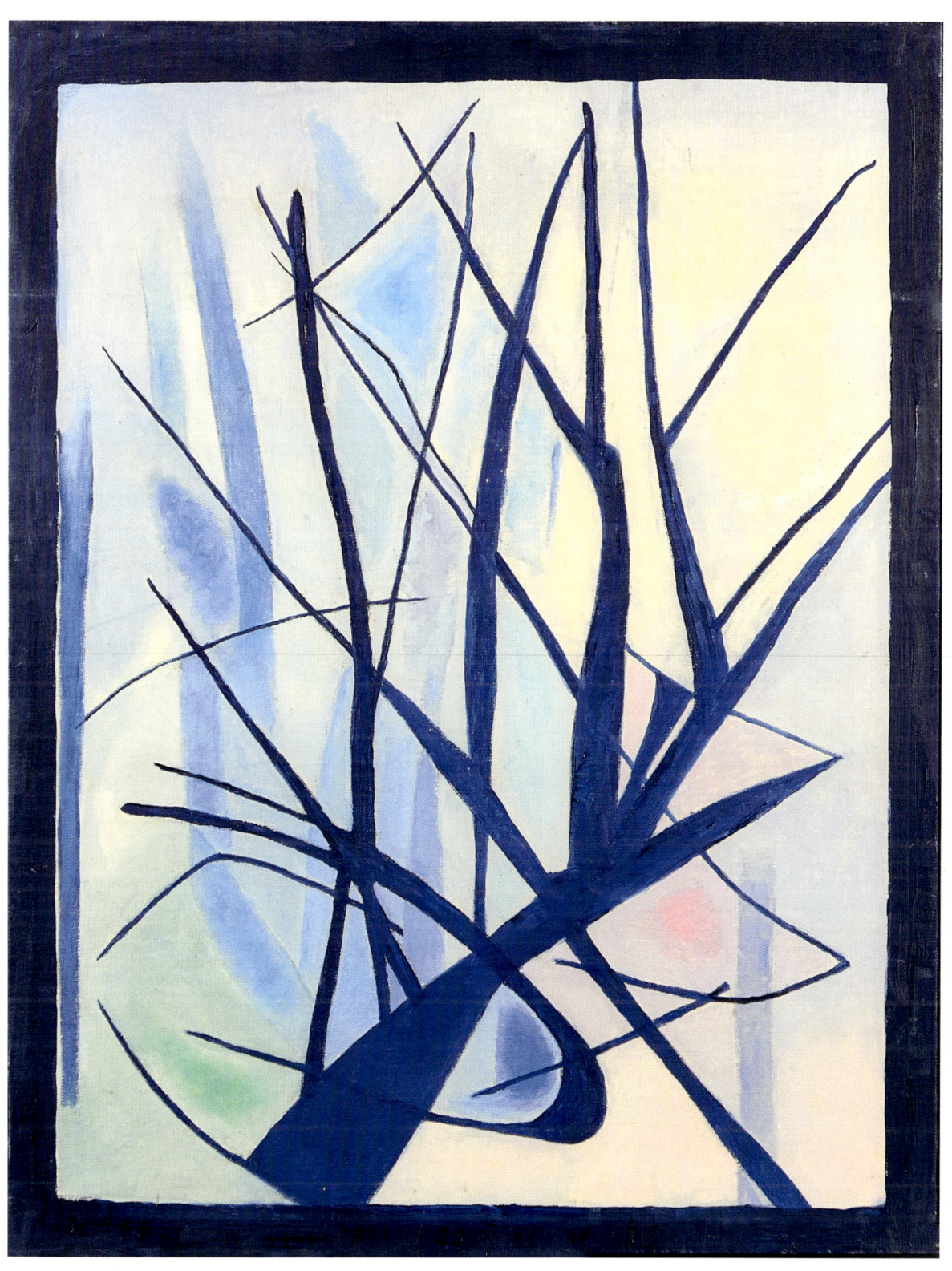

Elsa Thoresen (1906–1994), Untitled, circa 1958. Oil on board, 28 × 21⅞ in. (71.1 × 55.6 cm).

Elsa Thoresen (1906–1994), *Green World*, 1960. Oil on canvas, 18¼ × 24 in. (46.4 × 61 cm).

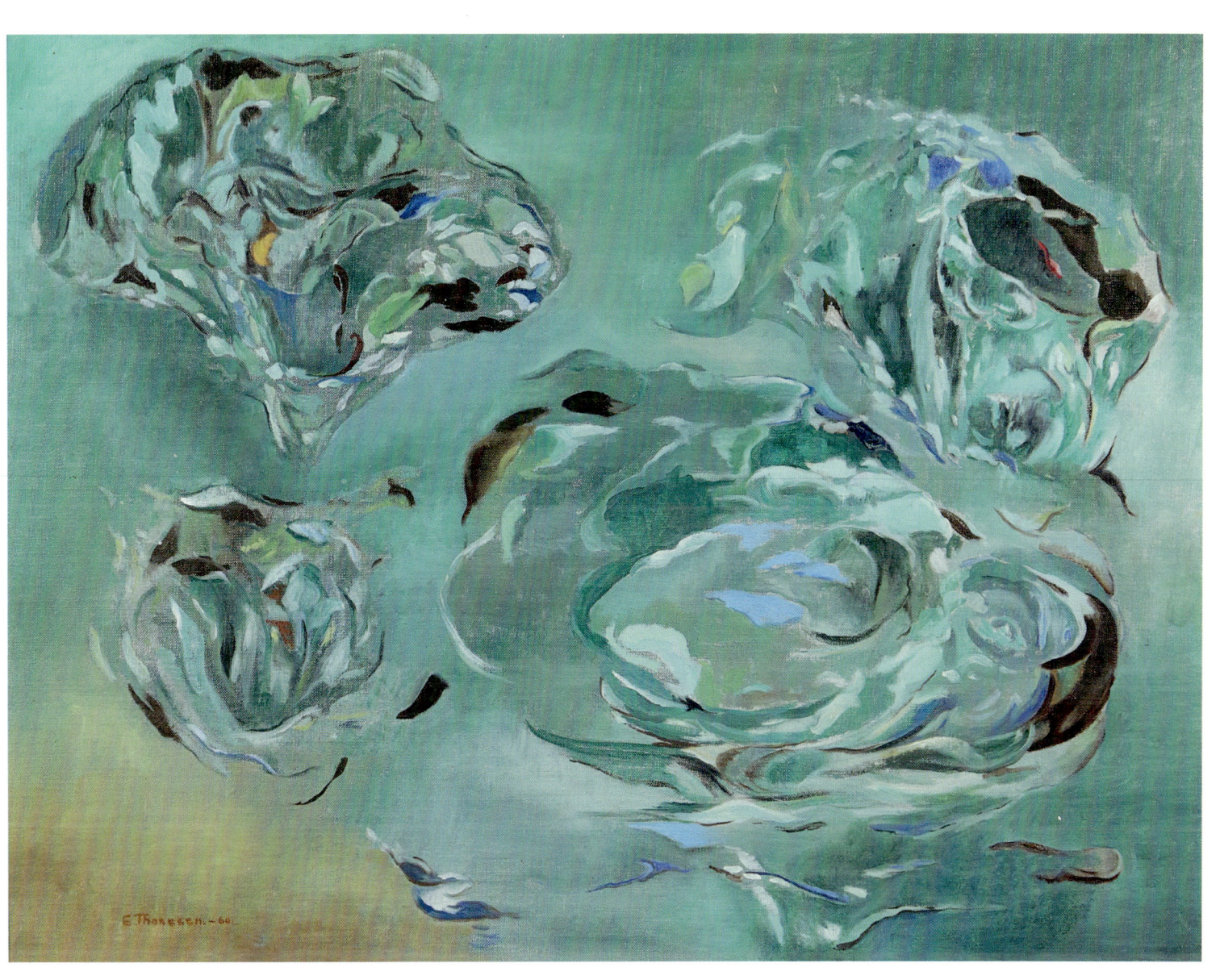

Elsa Thoresen (1906–1994), Untitled, circa 1960. Oil on canvas, 24 × 30 in. (61 × 76.2 cm).

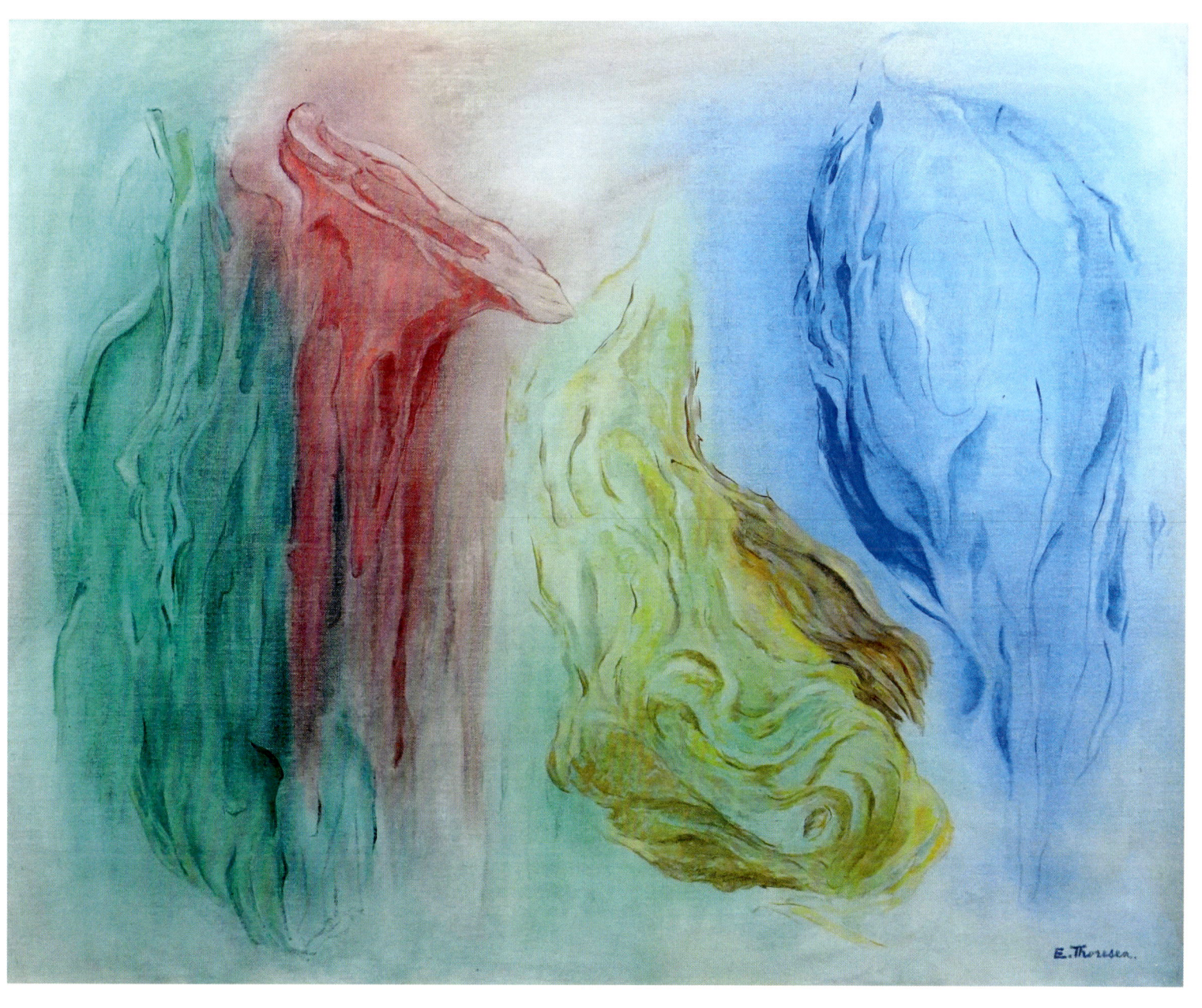

Elsa Thoresen (1906–1994), Untitled, circa 1960. Oil on canvas, 36 × 24 in. (91.4 × 61 cm).

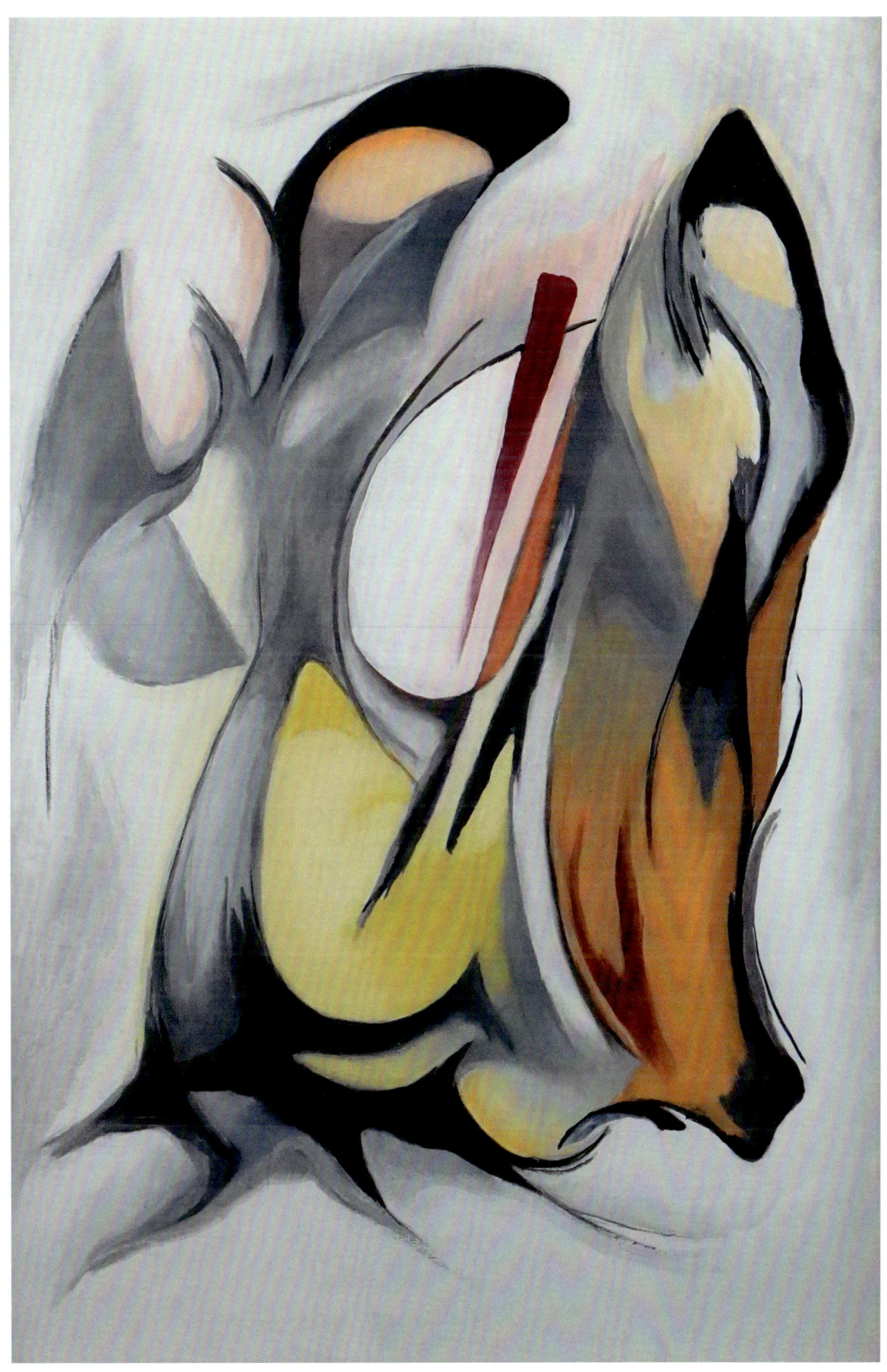

Elsa Thoresen (1906–1994), Untitled, circa 1960. Oil on canvas, 40 × 30 in. (101.6 × 76.2 cm).

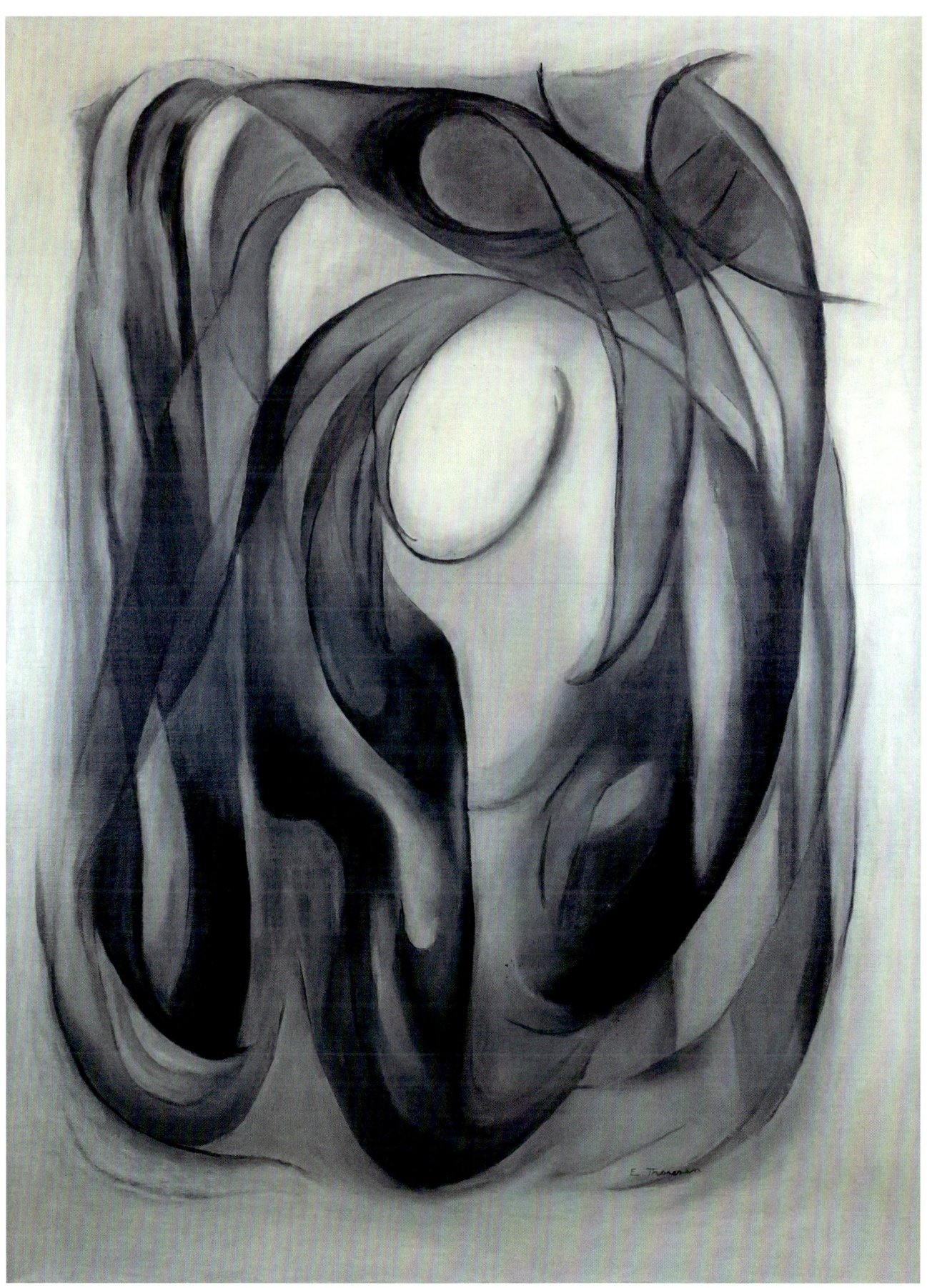

Elsa Thoresen (1906–1994), Untitled, 1962. Oil on canvas, 13½ × 16⅛ in. (34.3 × 41 cm).

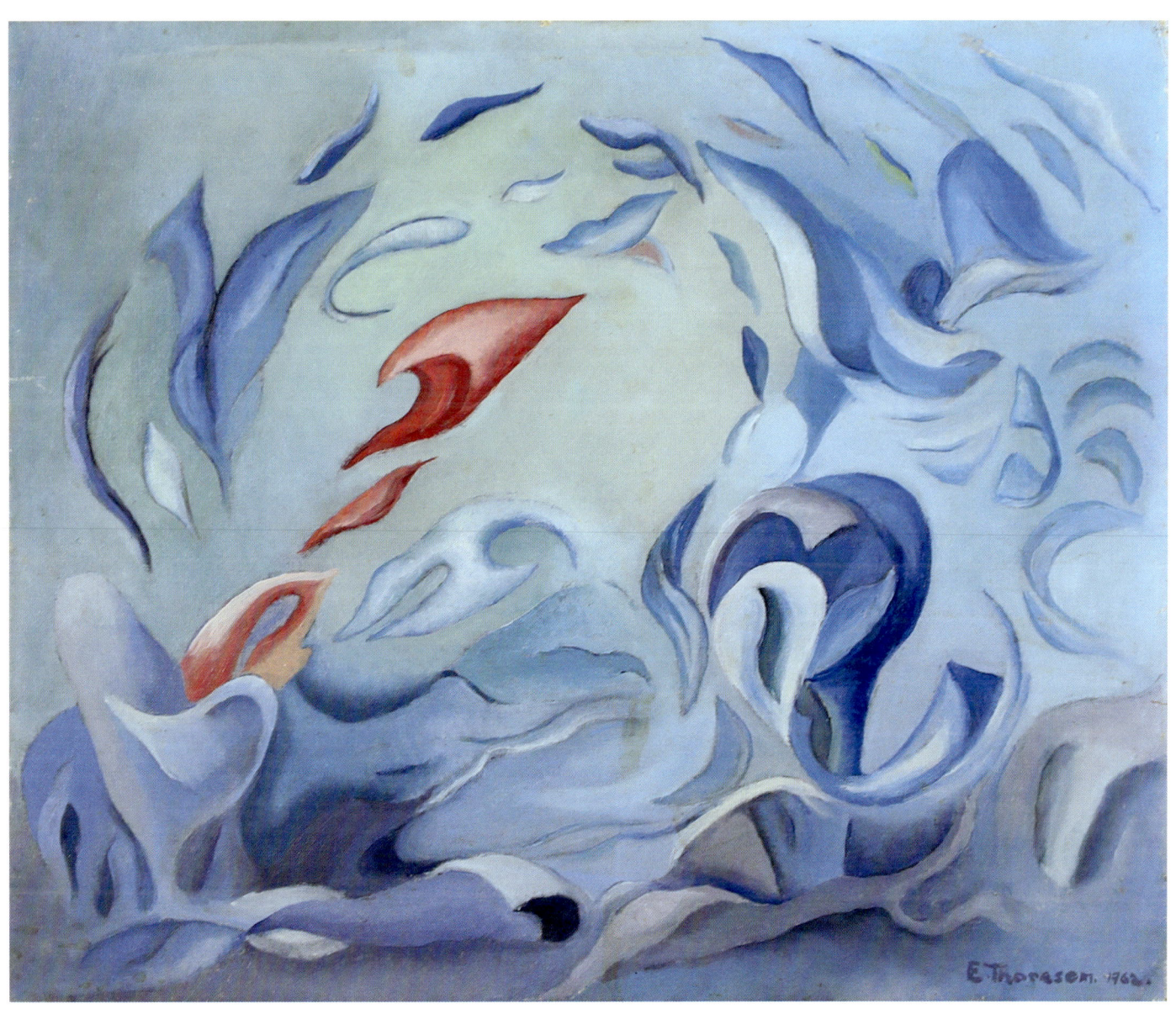

Elsa Thoresen (1906–1994), Untitled, circa 1962. Oil on canvas, 30 × 40 in. (76.2 × 101.6 cm).

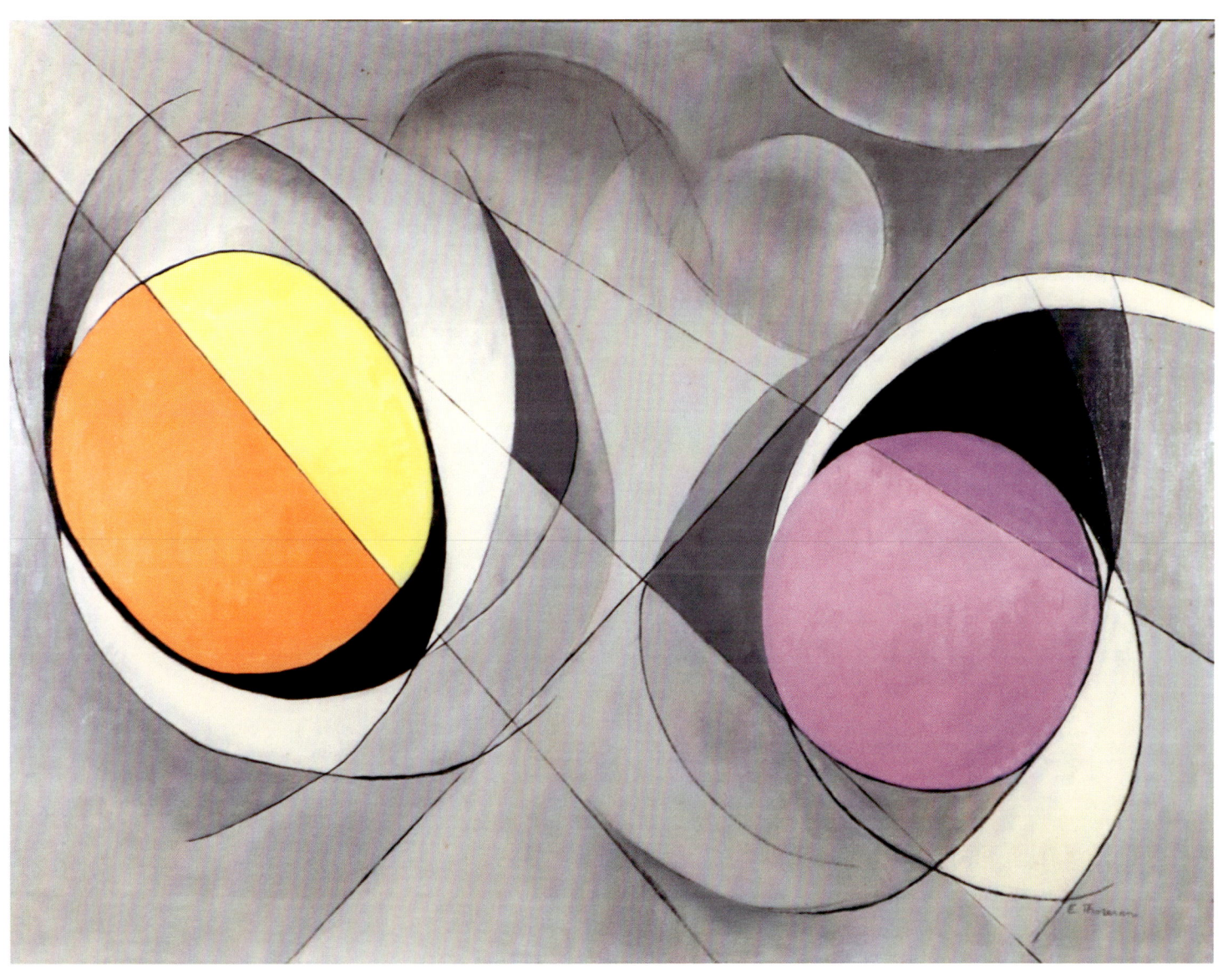

Elsa Thoresen (1906–1994), Untitled, circa 1962. Oil on canvas, 48 × 29⅞ in. (122 × 75.9 cm).

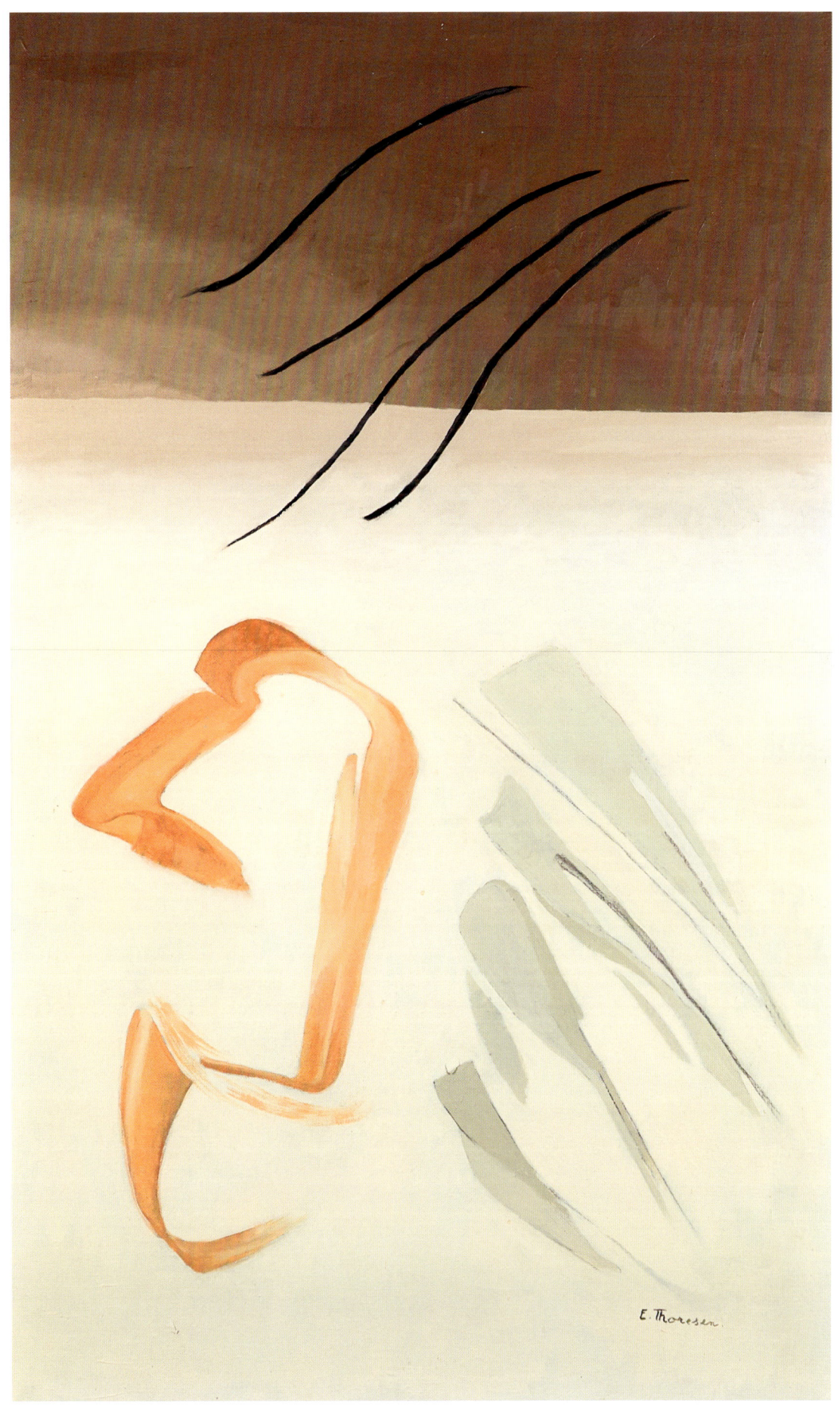

Elsa Thoresen (1906–1994), Untitled, circa 1962. Oil on board, 16 × 20 in. (40.6 × 50.8 cm).

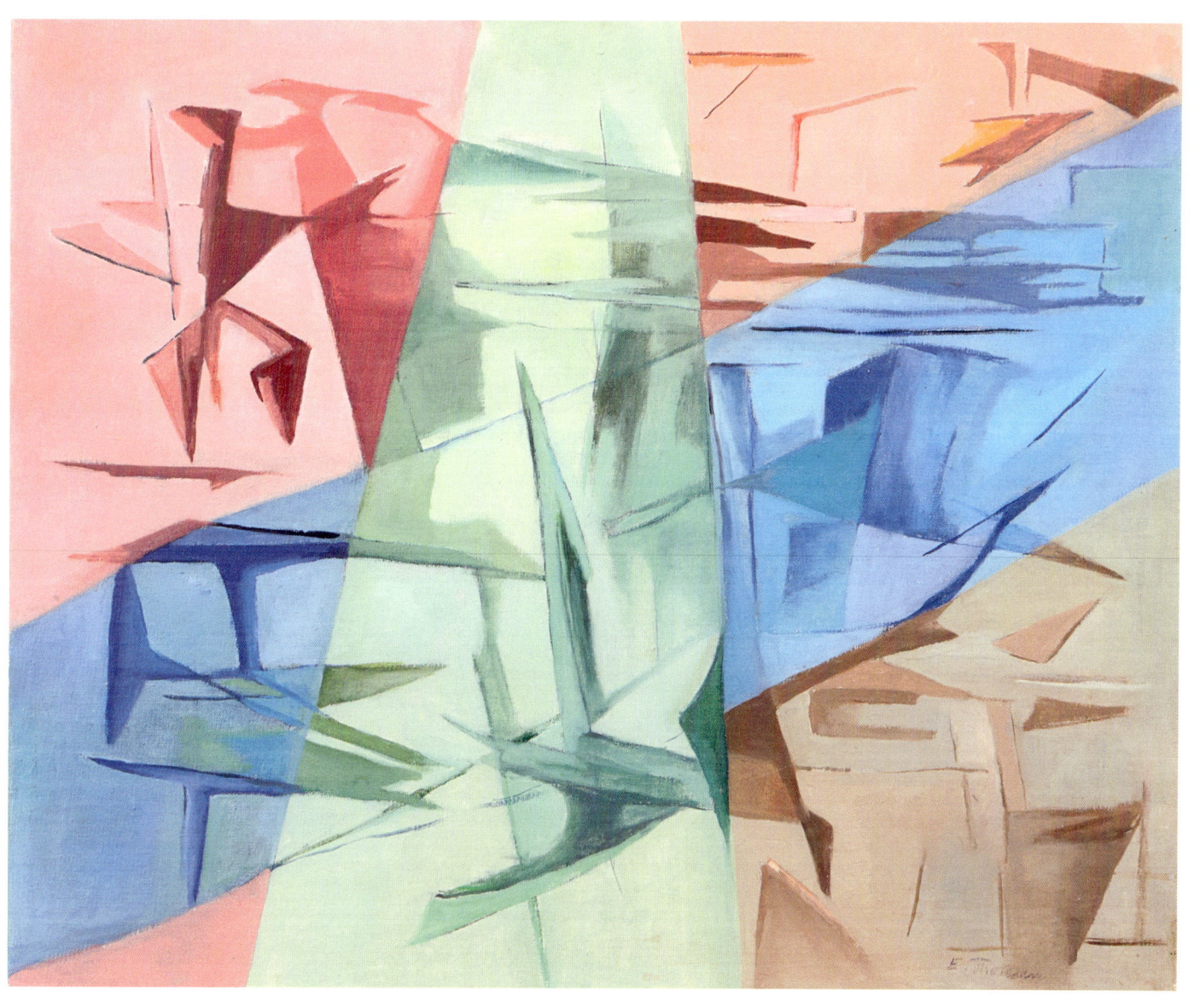

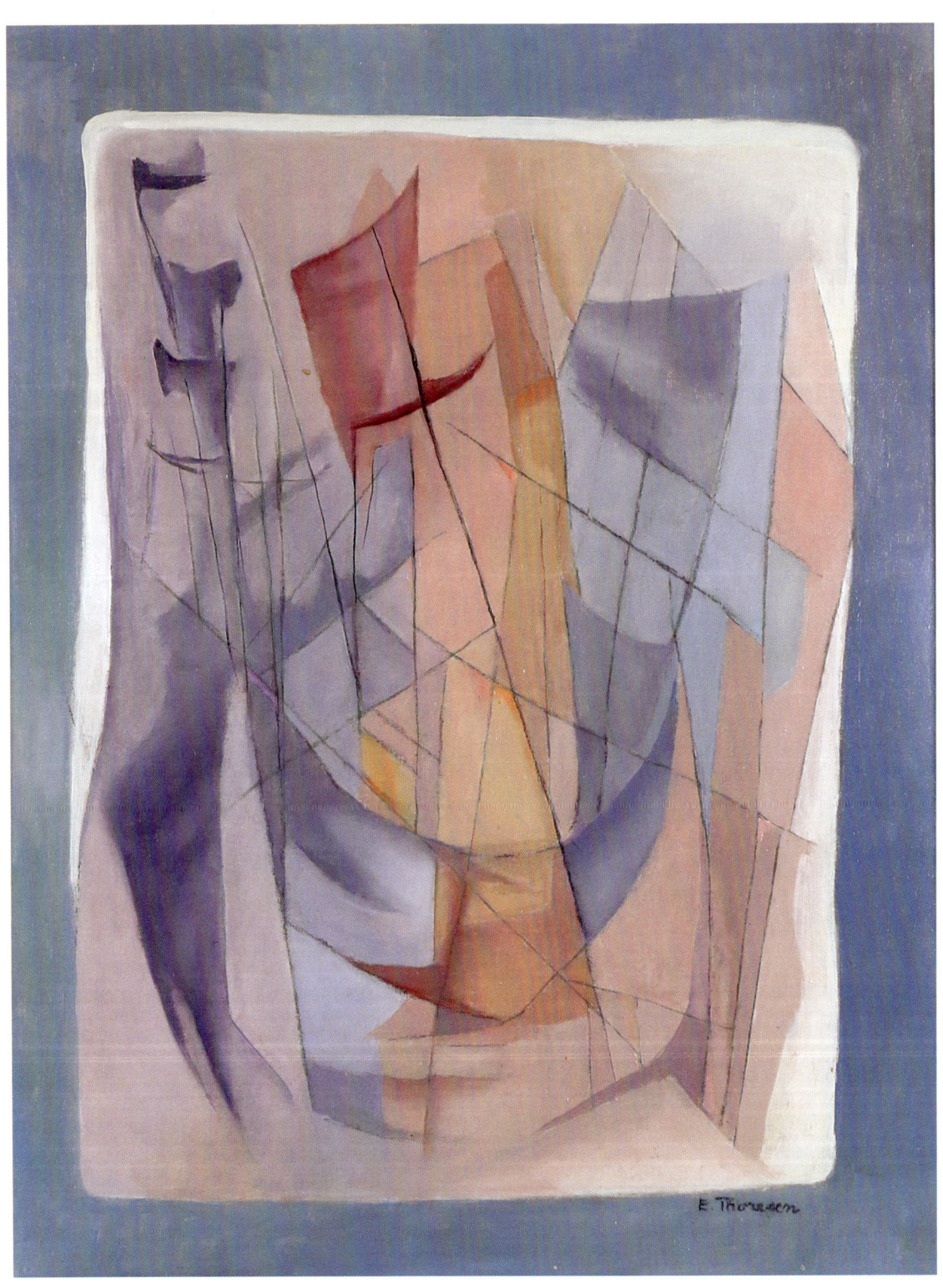

Elsa Thoresen (1906–1994), Untitled, circa 1965. Oil on canvas, 28 × 22 in. (71.1 × 55.9 cm).

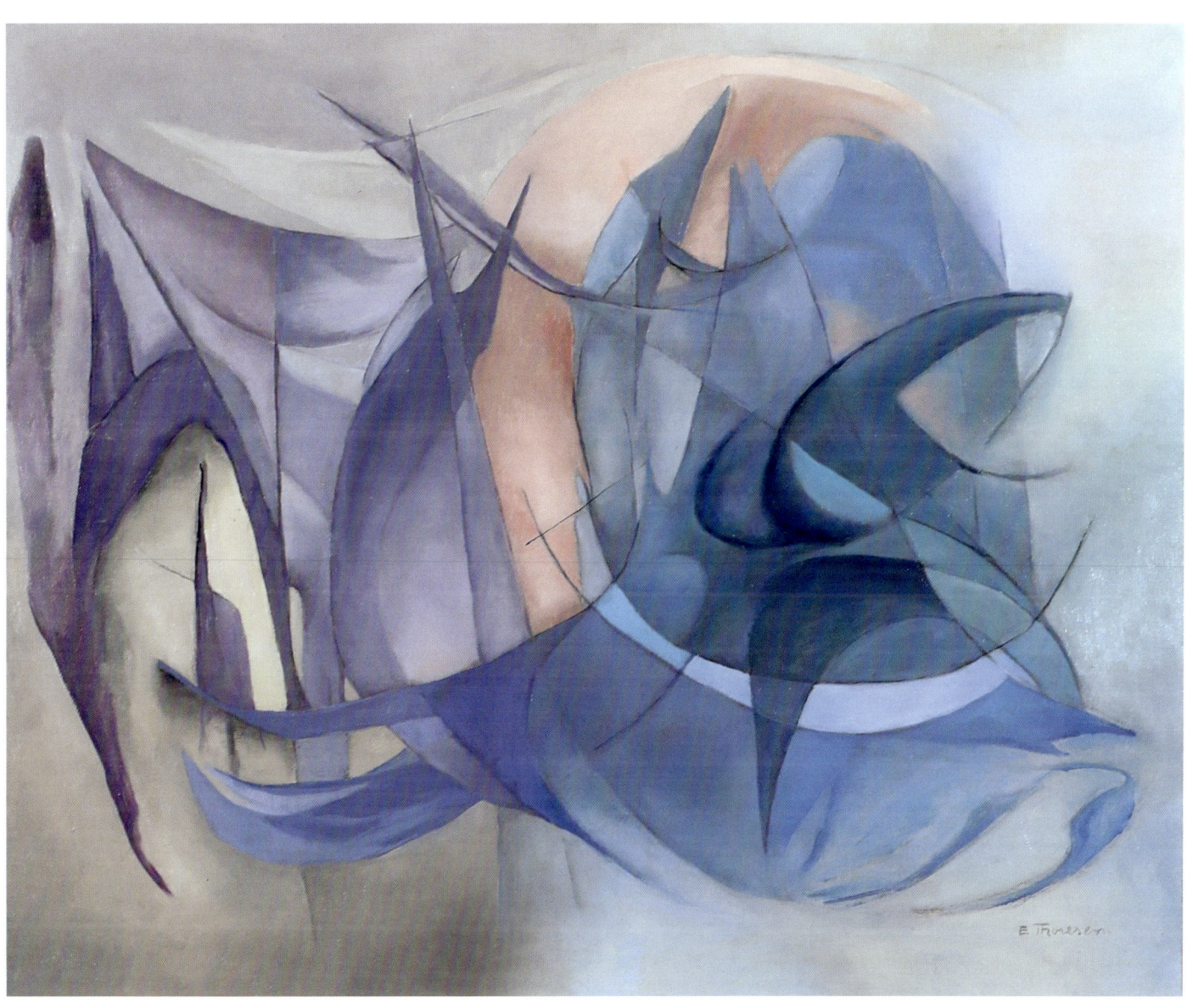

Elsa Thoresen (1906–1994), Untitled, circa 1965. Oil on canvas, 24 × 30 in. (61 × 76.2 cm).

Elsa Thoresen (1906–1994), Untitled, circa 1970. Oil on canvas, 24 × 40 in. (61 × 101.6 cm).

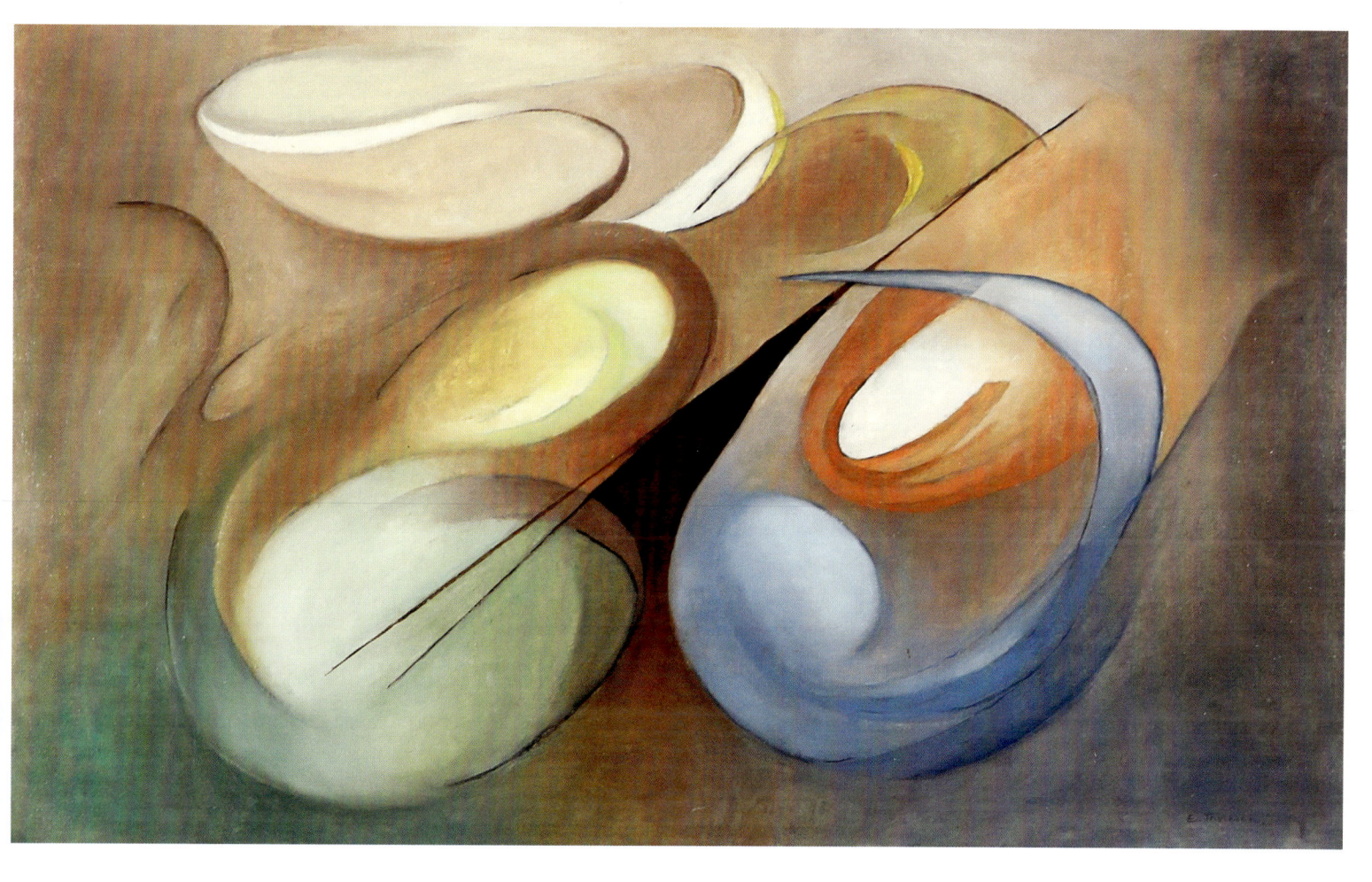

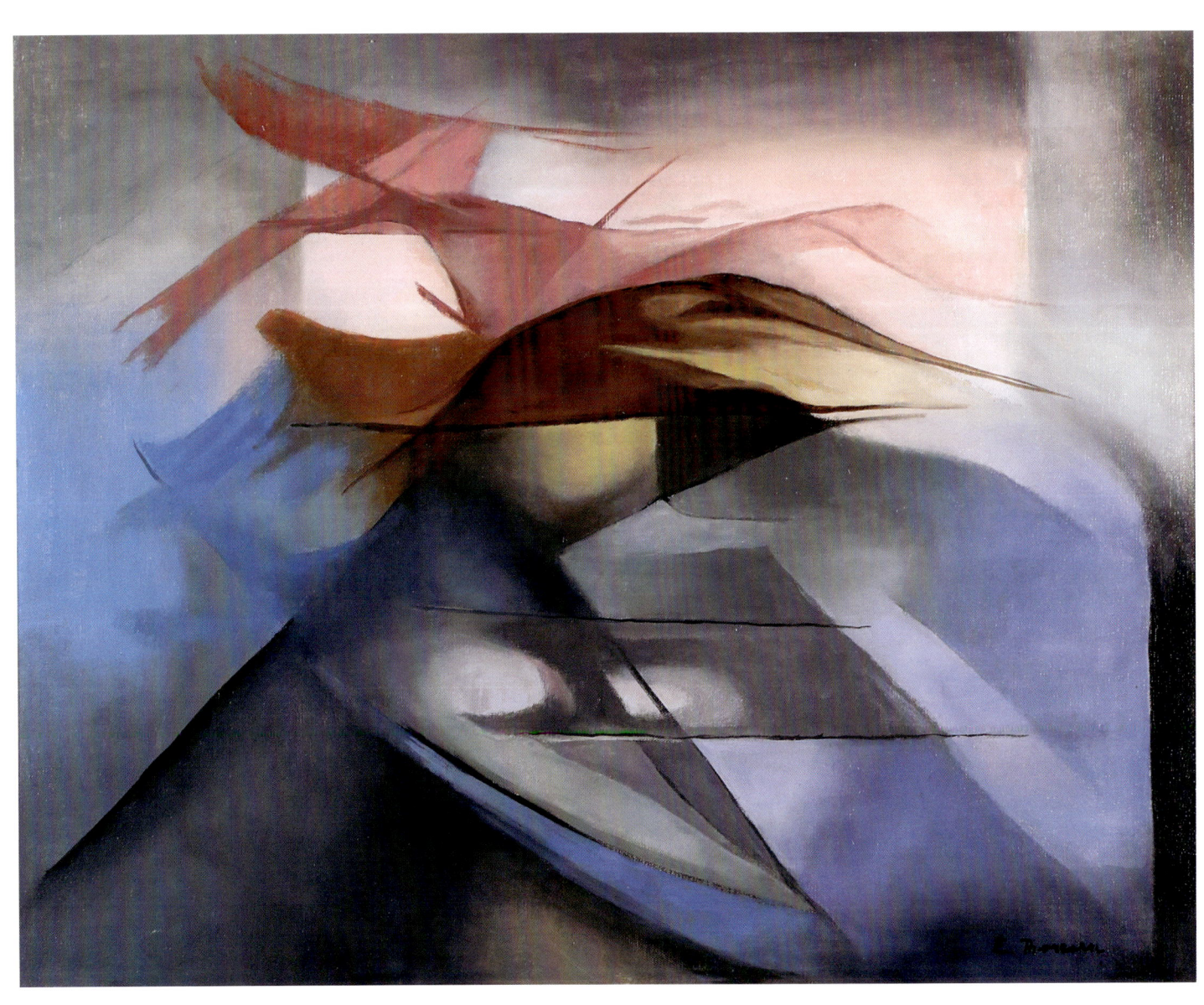

Elsa Thoresen (1906–1994), Untitled, circa 1970. Oil on canvas, 22 × 28 in. (55.9 × 71.1 cm).

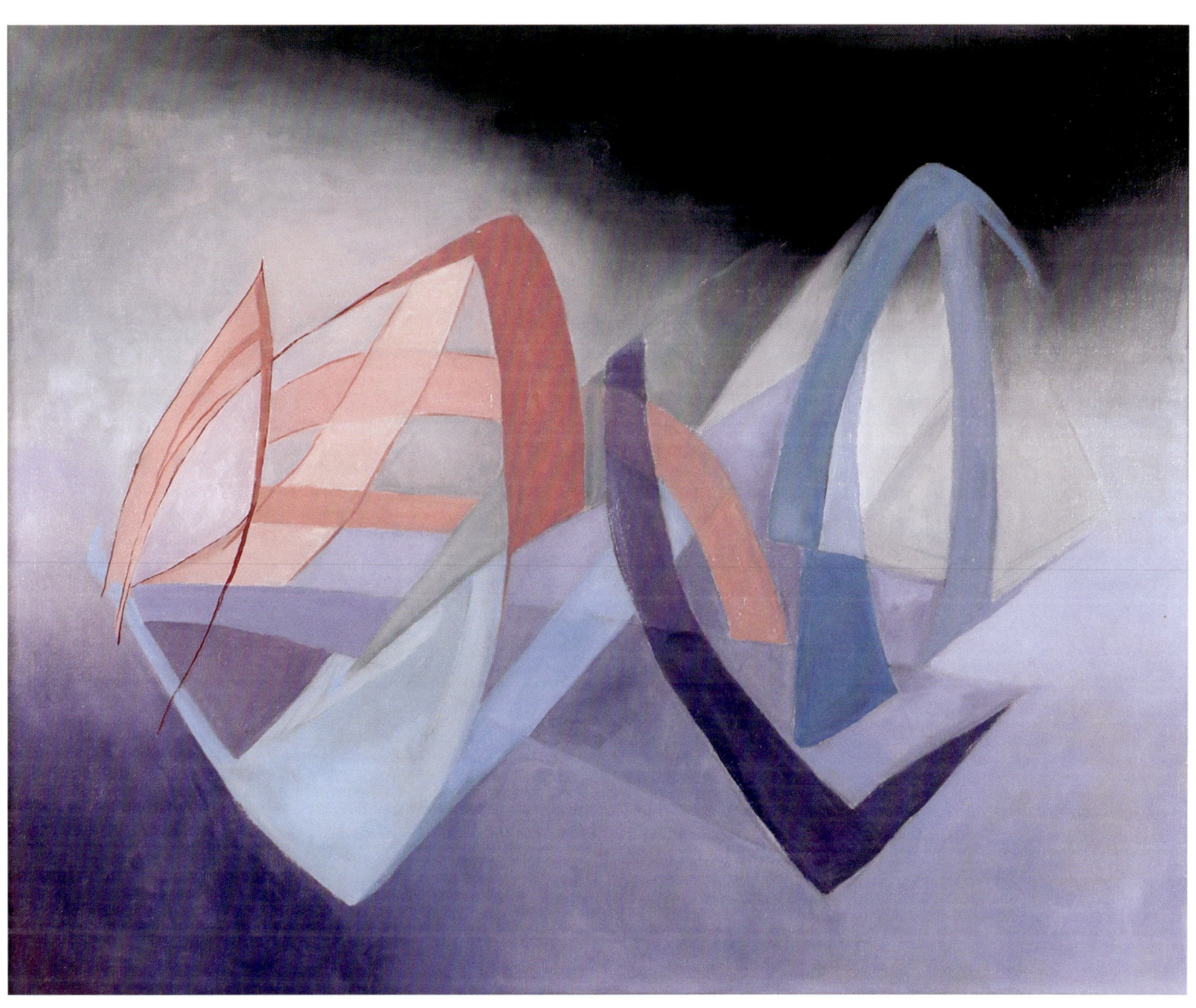

Elsa Thoresen (1906–1994), Untitled, circa 1970. Oil on canvas, 24 × 30 in. (61 × 76.2 cm).

Elsa Thoresen (1906–1994), Untitled, circa 1970. Oil on canvas, 24 × 30 in. (61 × 76.2 cm).

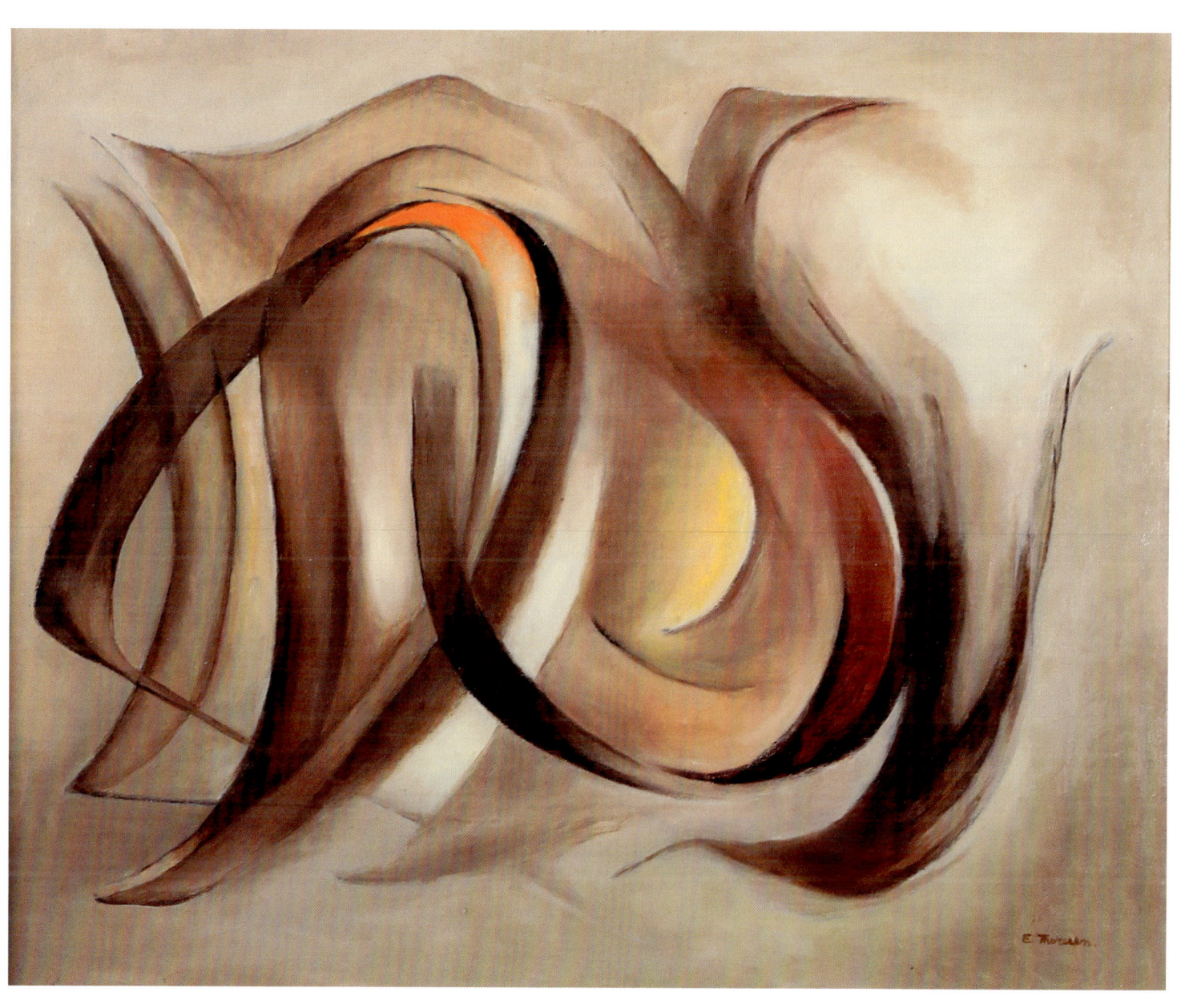

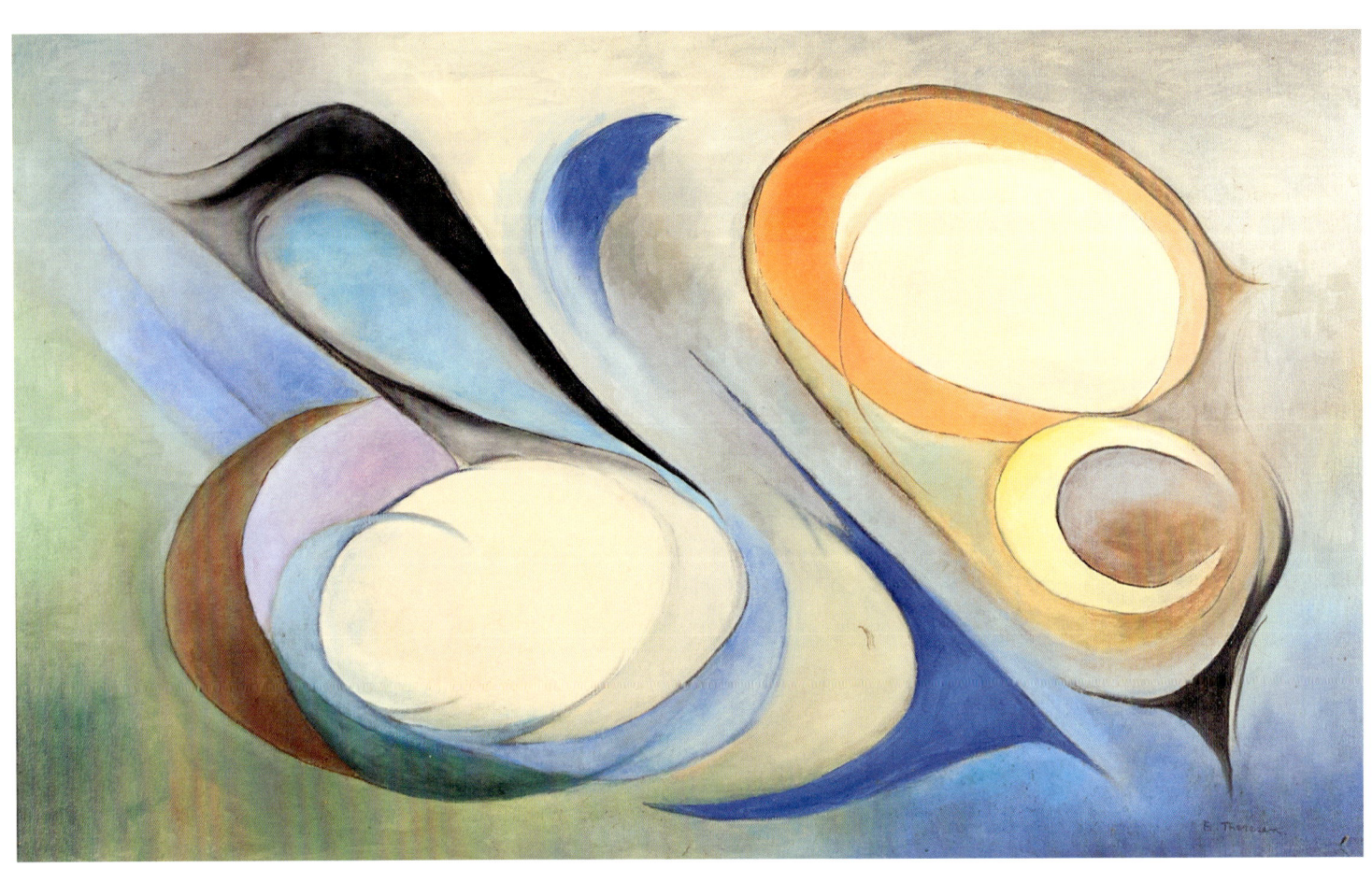

Elsa Thoresen (1906–1994), Untitled, circa 1970. Oil on canvas, 24 × 40 in. (61 × 101.6 cm).

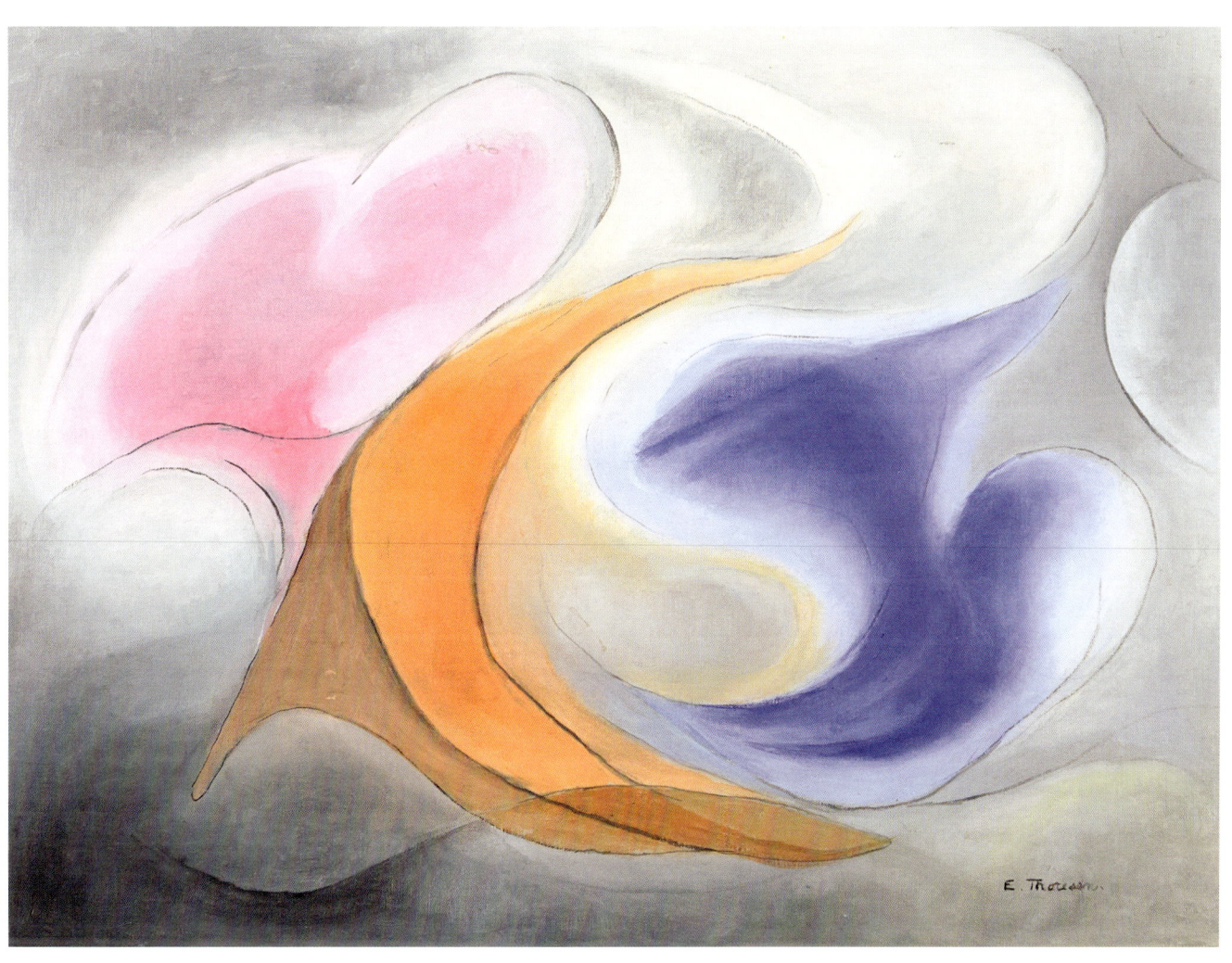

Elsa Thoresen (1906–1994), Untitled, circa 1970. Oil on canvas, 22 × 30 in. (55.9 × 76.2 cm).

Elsa Thoresen (1906–1994), Untitled, circa 1970. Oil on board, 30 × 24 in. (76.2 × 61 cm).

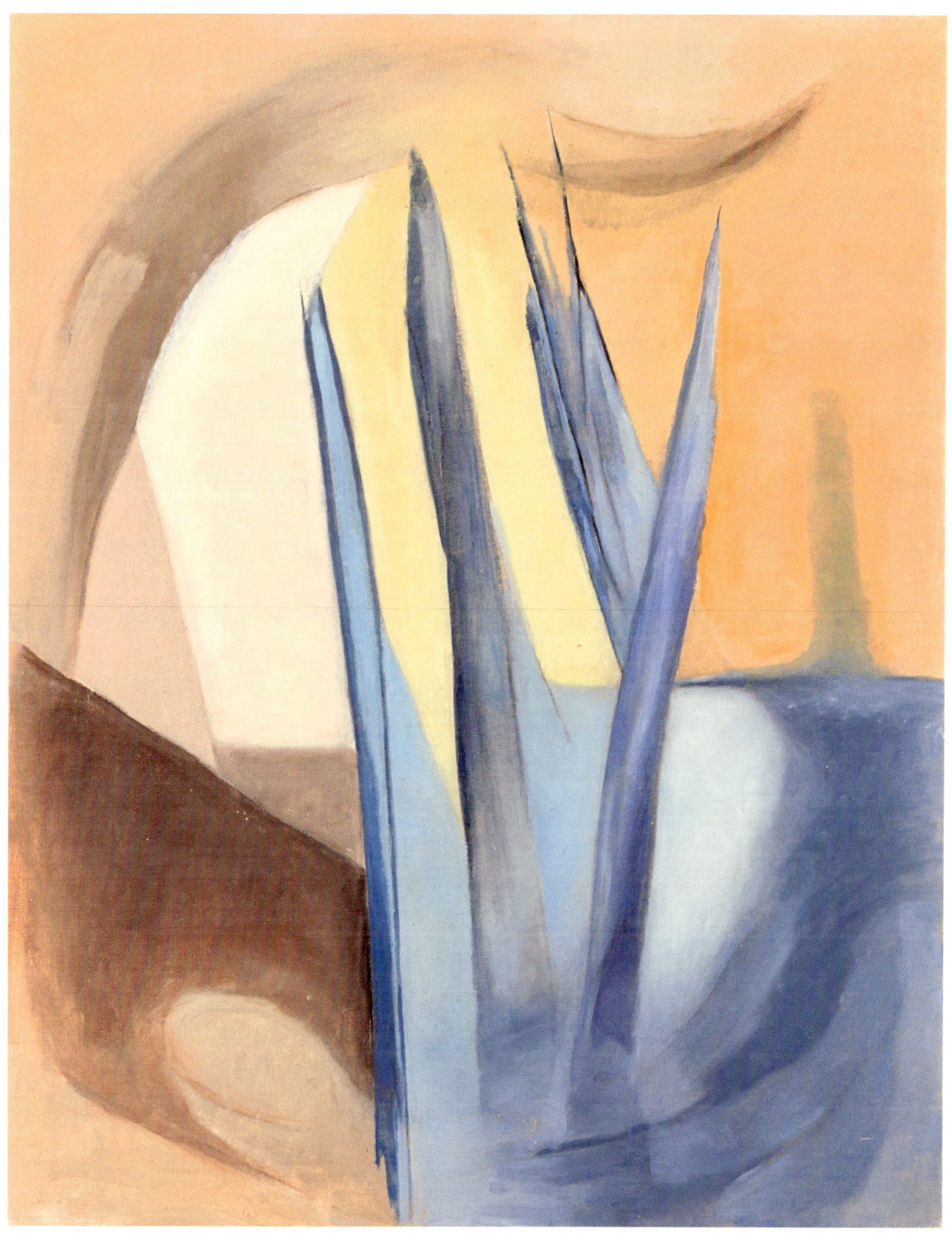

Elsa Thoresen (1906–1994), Untitled, circa 1970. Oil on canvas, 20 × 24 in. (50.8 × 61 cm).

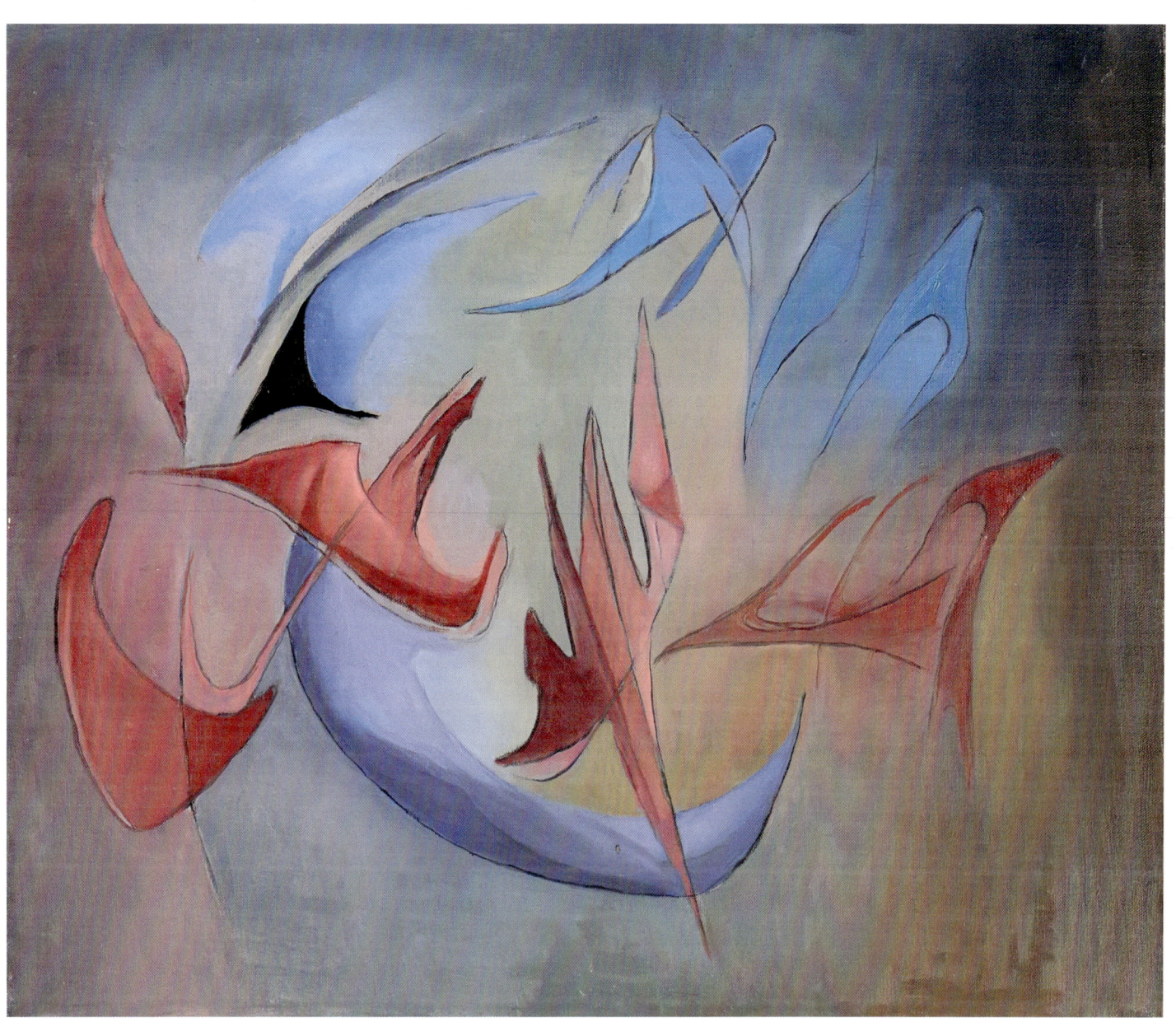

Elsa Thoresen (1906–1994), Untitled, 1973. Oil on canvas, 24 × 12 in. (61 × 30.5 cm).

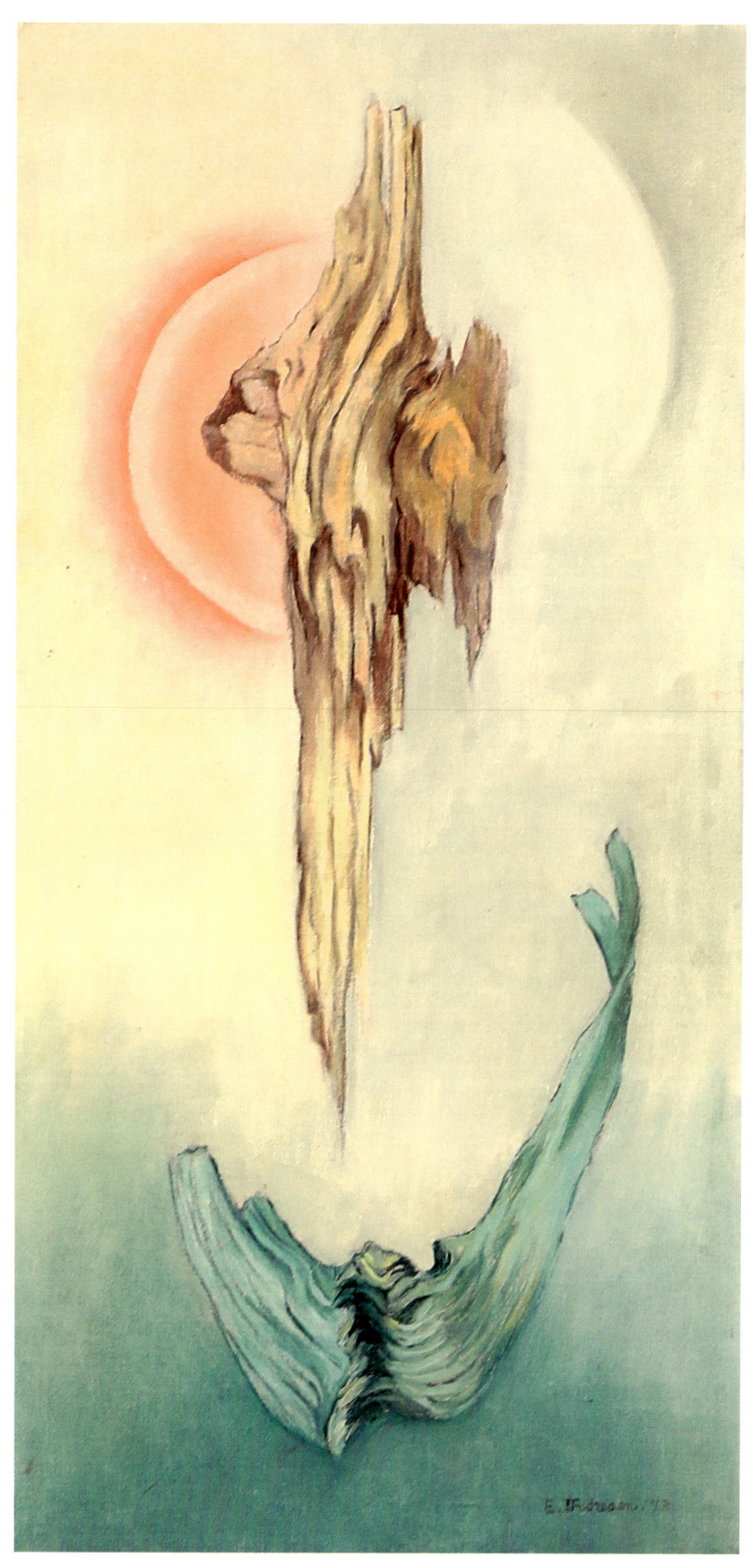

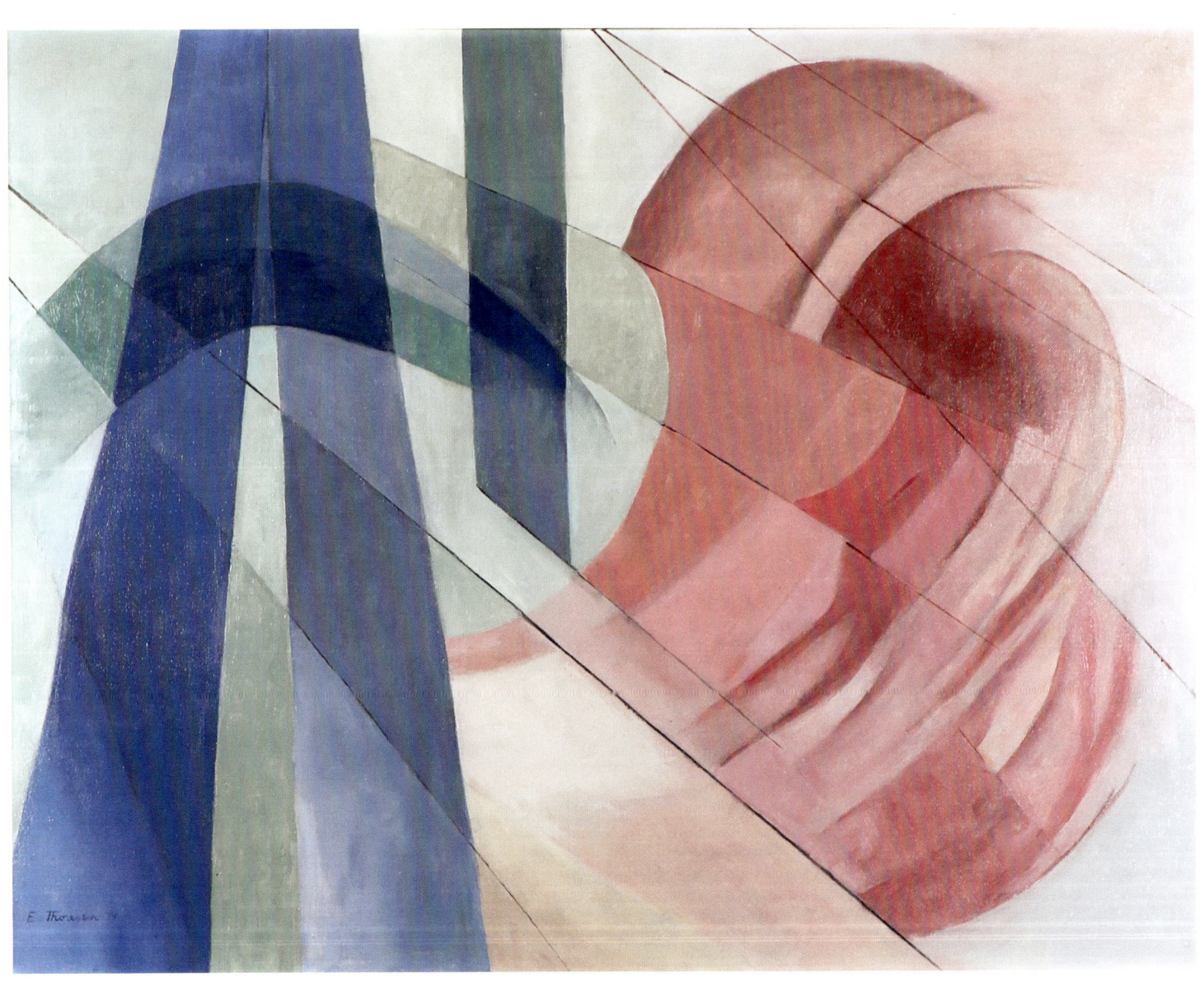

Elsa Thoresen (1906–1994), Untitled, 1974. Oil on canvas, 30 × 40½ in. (76.2 × 102.9 cm).

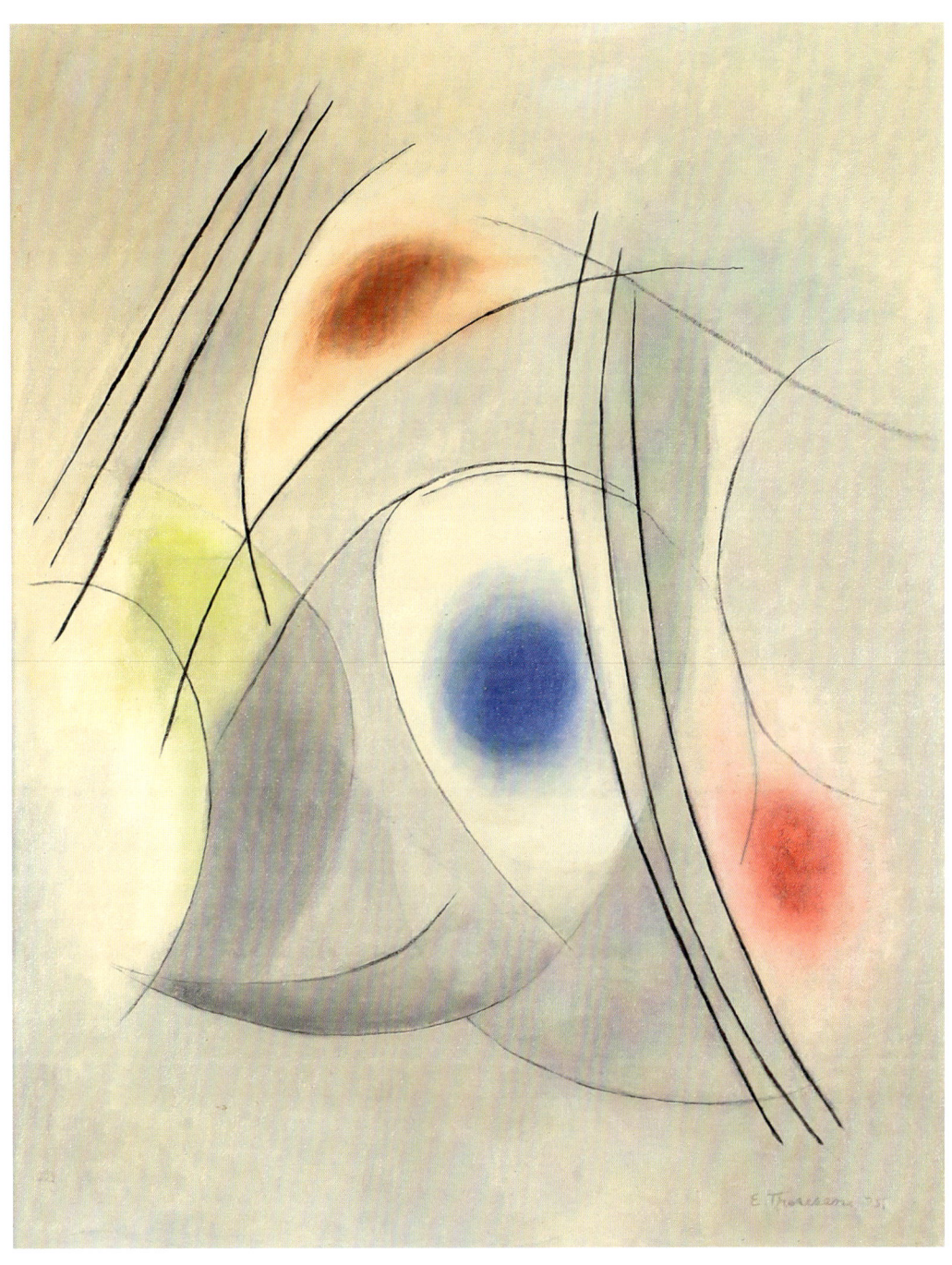

Elsa Thoresen (1906–1994), Untitled, 1975. Oil on board, 24 × 30 in. (61 × 76.2 cm).

Elsa Thoresen (1906–1994), Untitled, 1975. Oil on board, 30 × 24 in. (76.2 × 61 cm).

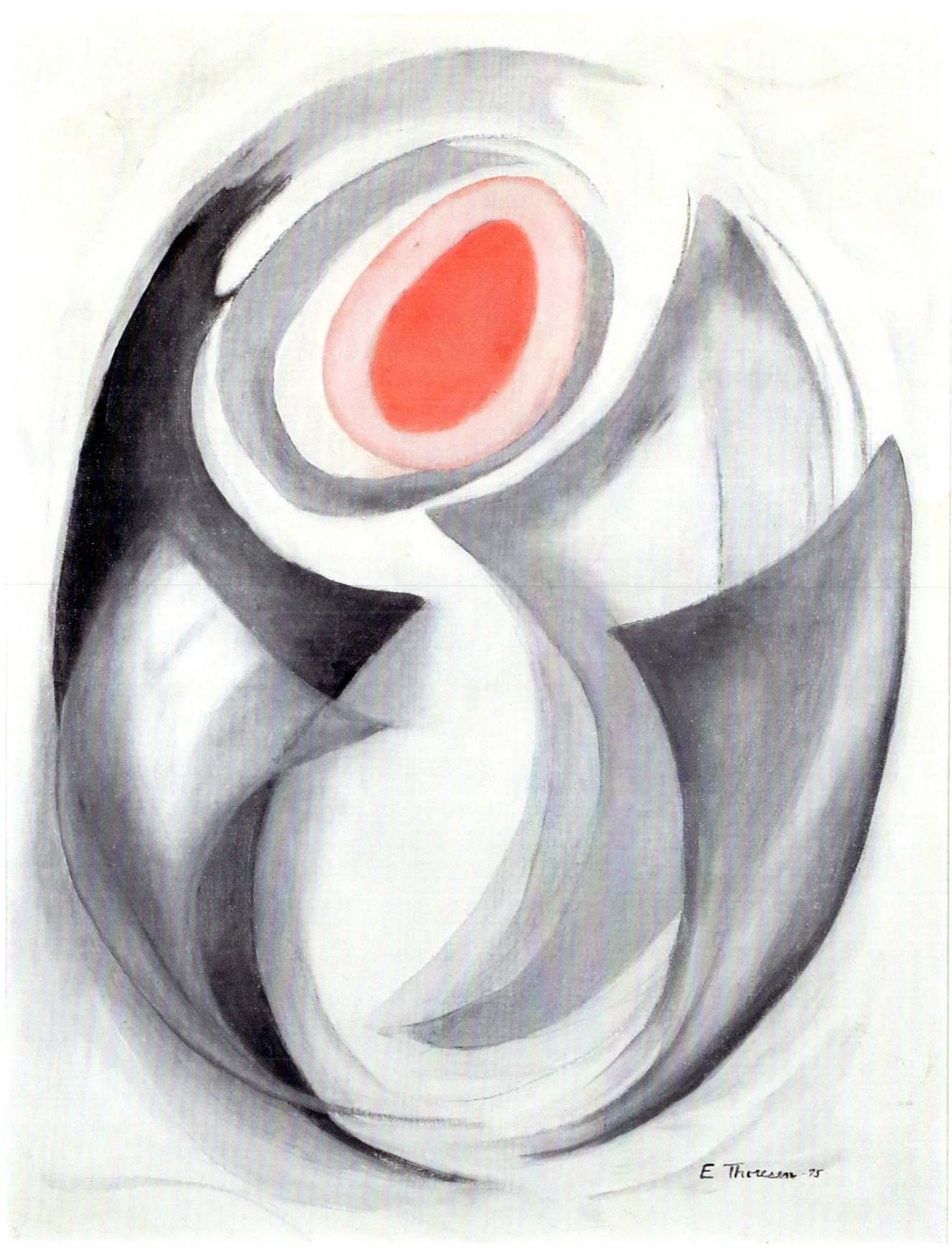

Elsa Thoresen (1906–1994), Untitled, 1975. Oil on canvas, 36 × 48 in. (91.4 × 122 cm).

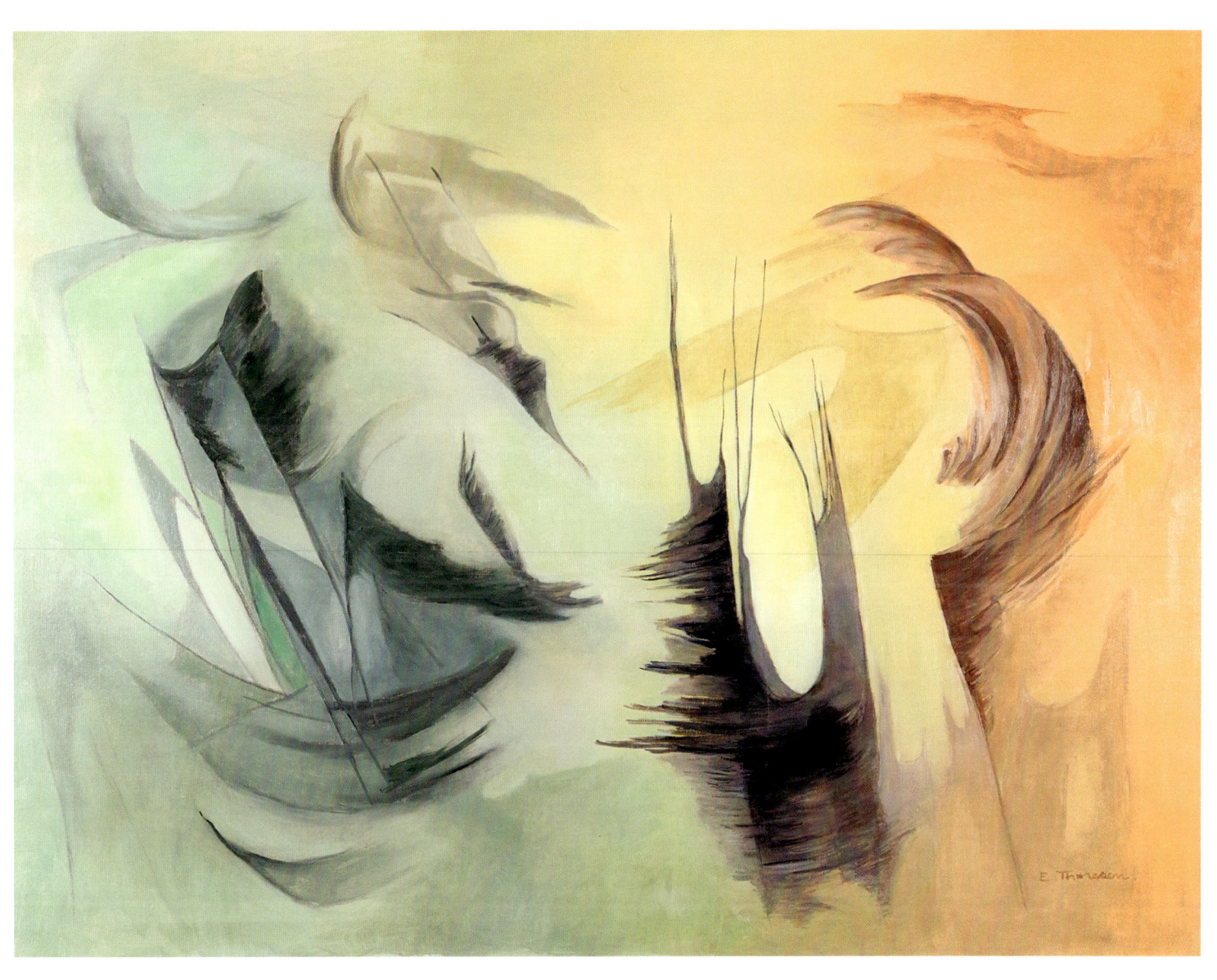

Elsa Thoresen (1906–1994), Untitled, circa 1978. Oil on canvas, 24 × 20 in. (61 × 50.8 cm).

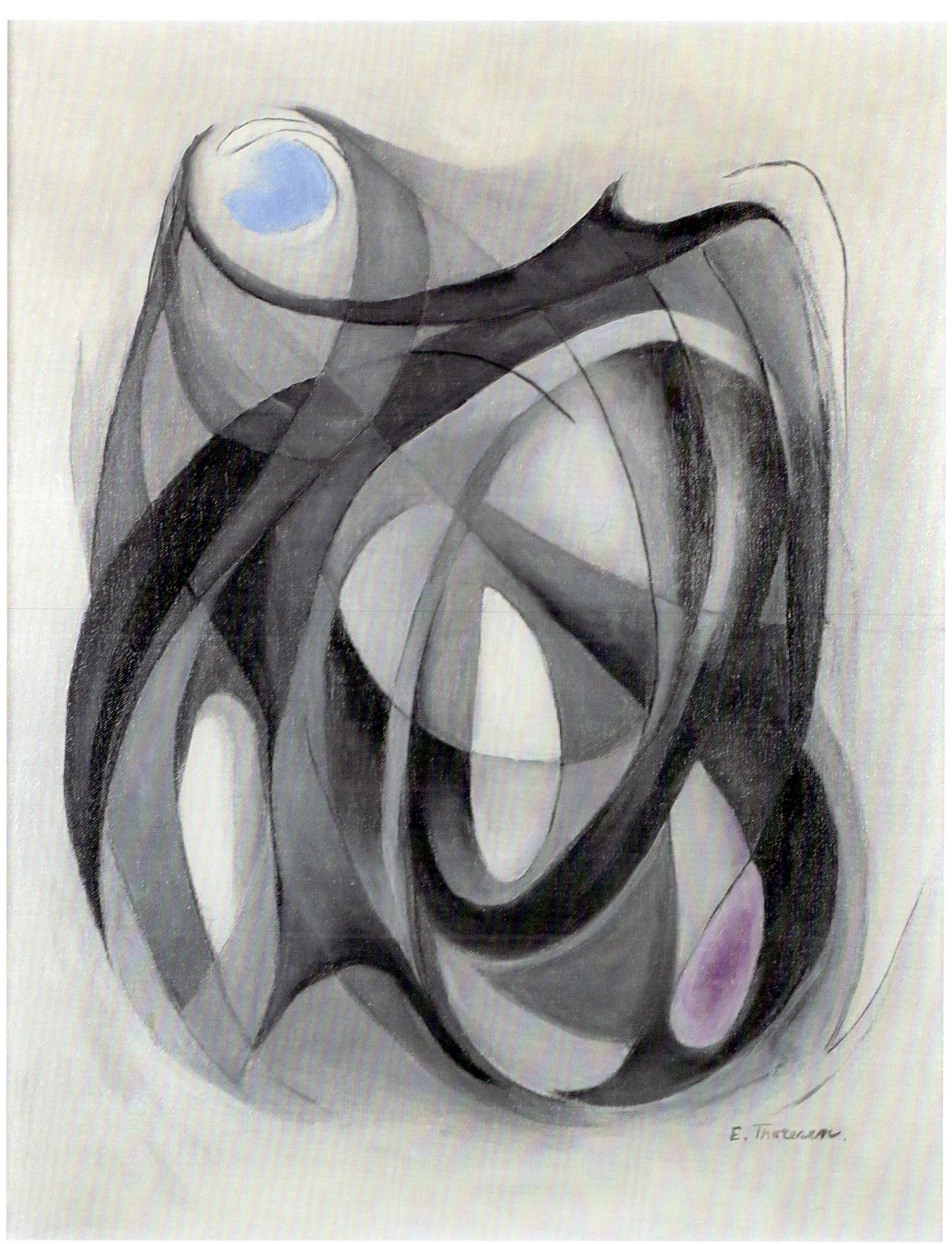

Elsa Thoresen (1906–1994), Untitled, 1980. Oil on canvas, 28 × 22 in. (71.1 × 55.9 cm).

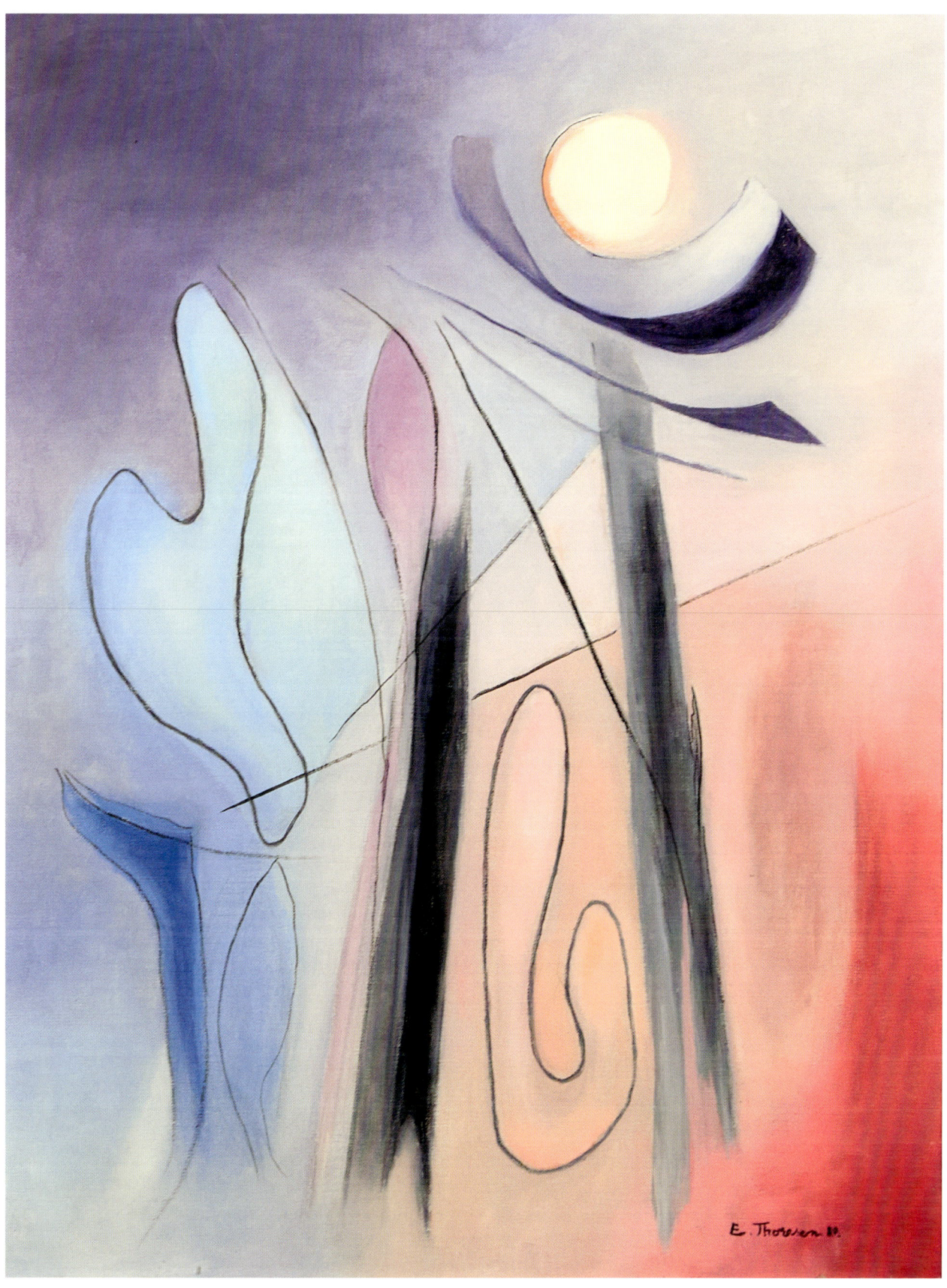

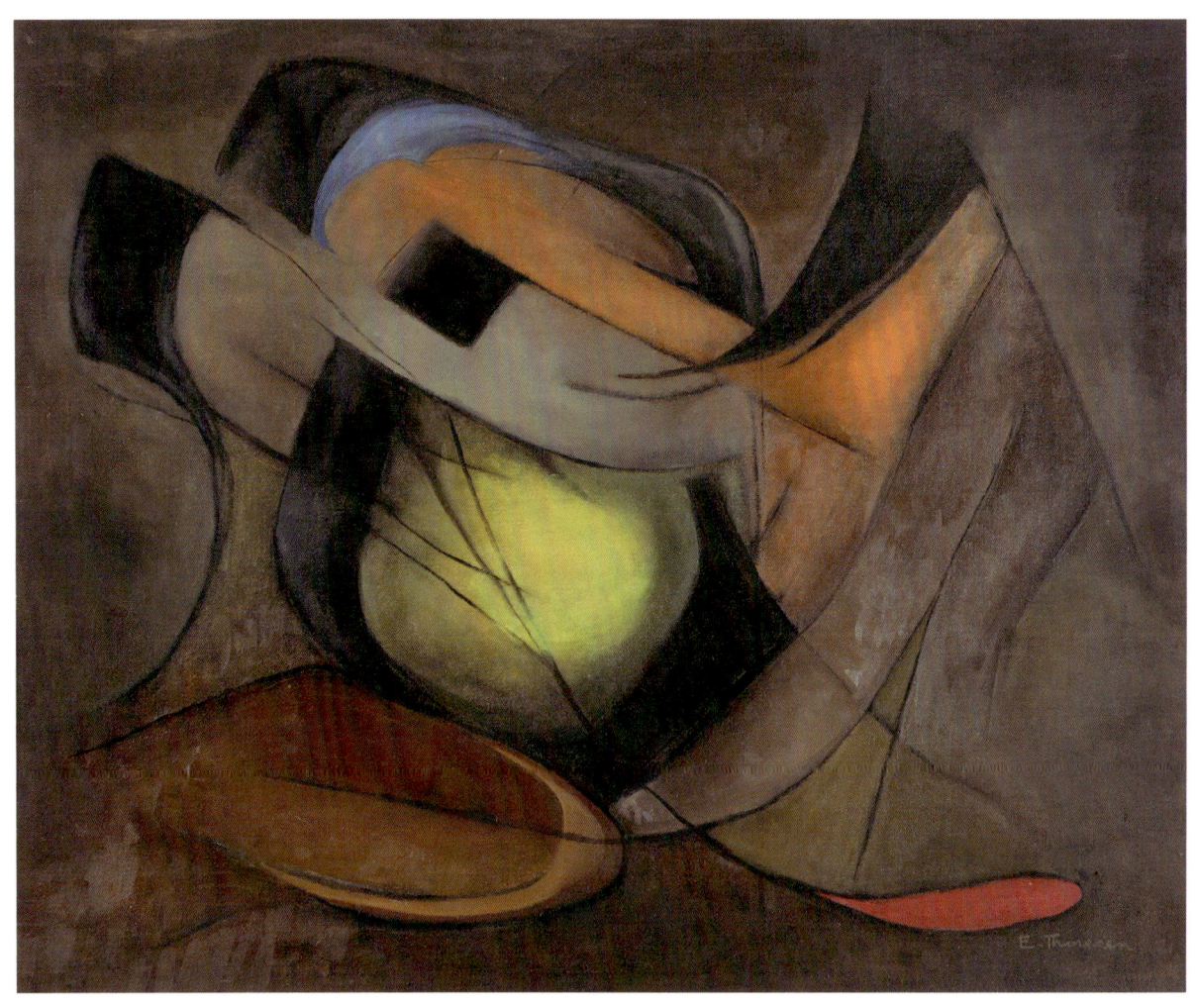

Elsa Thoresen (1906–1994), Untitled, 1981. Oil on board, 24 × 30 in. (61 × 76.2 cm).

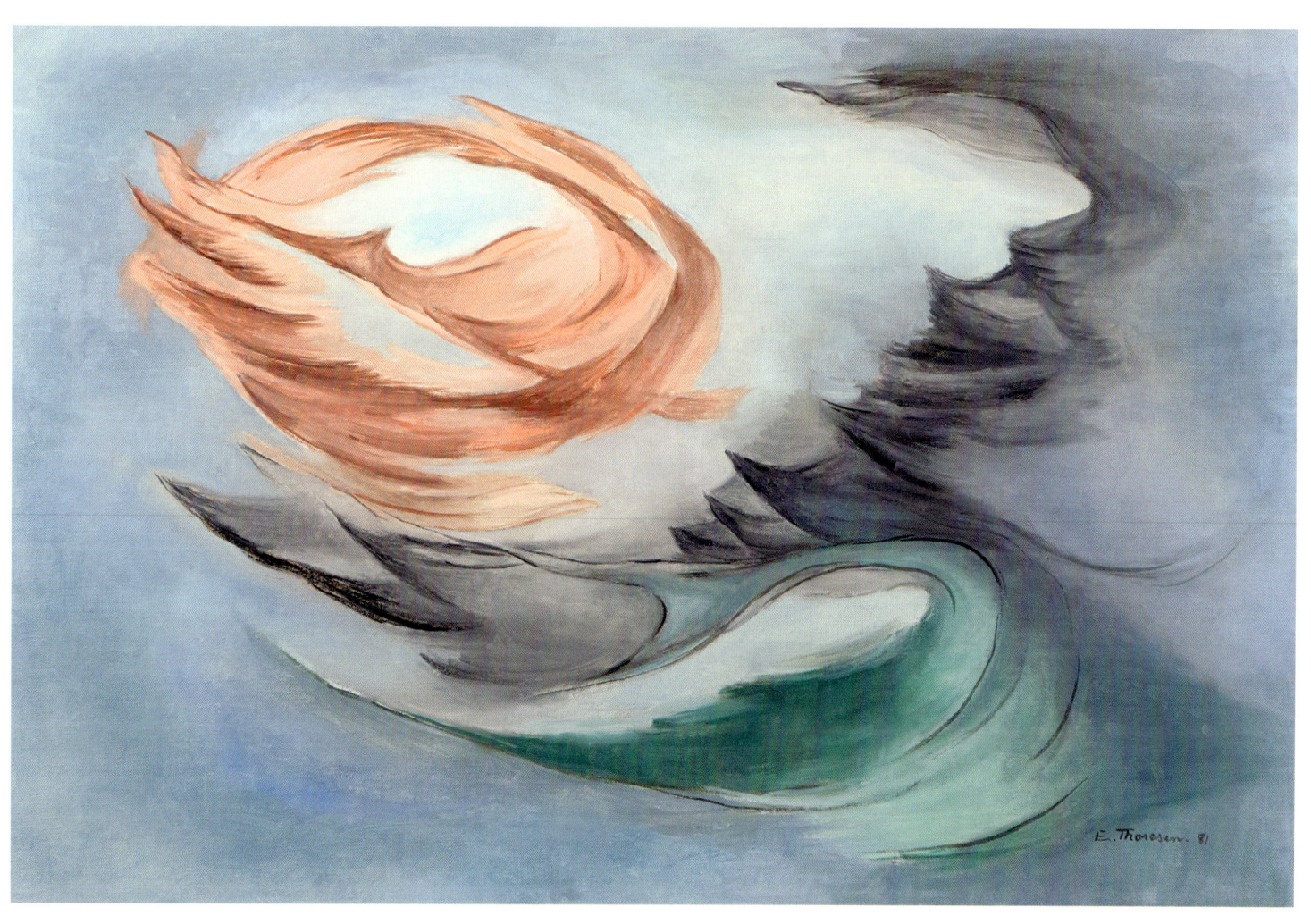

Elsa Thoresen (1906–1994), Untitled, 1981. Oil on canvas, 24 × 36 in. (61 × 91.4 cm).

Elsa Thoresen (1906–1994), Untitled, 1993. Oil on canvas, 30 × 40⅛ in. (76.2 × 101.9 cm).

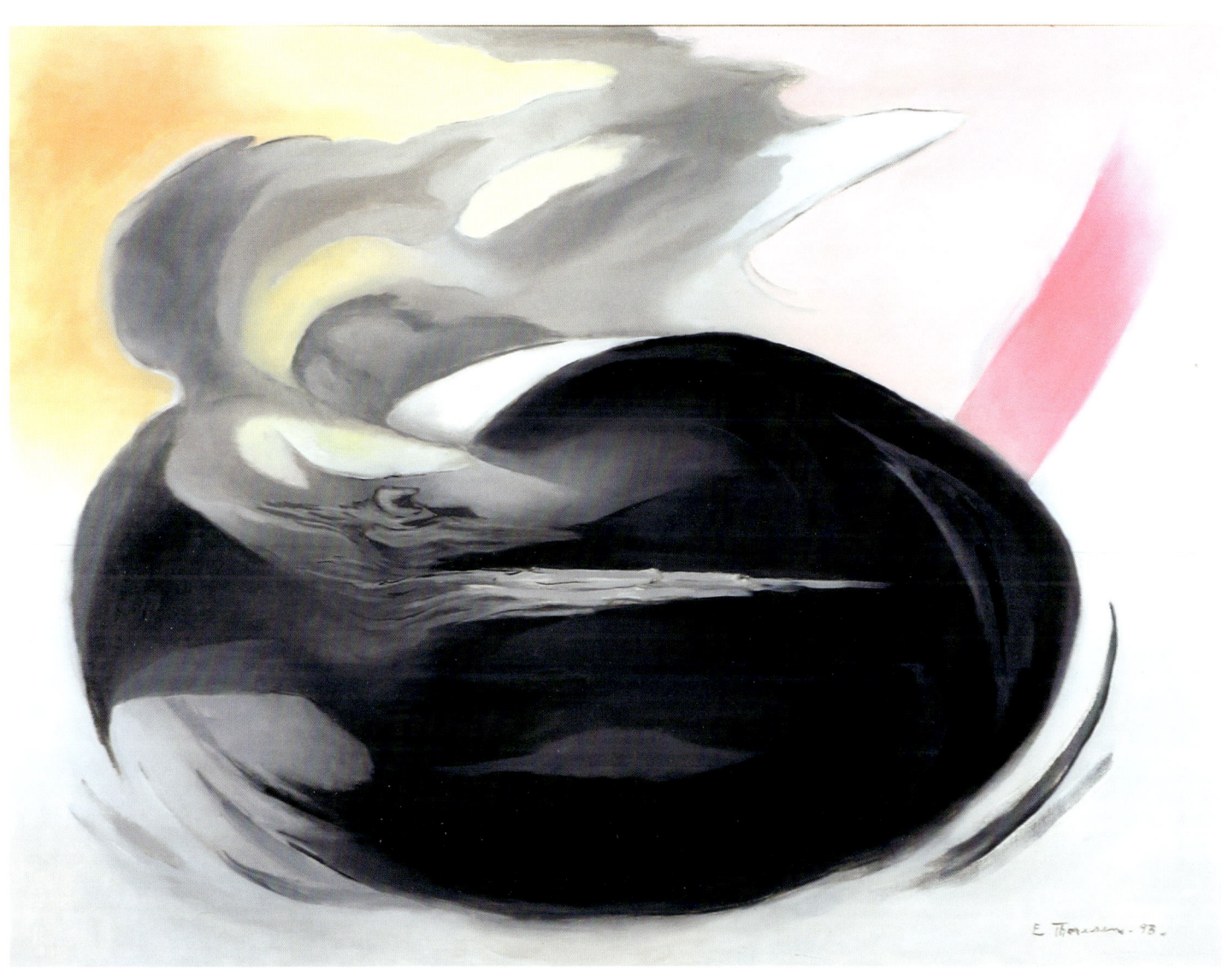

Author's Note

In May 2023, I was in Paris for the month doing research for a future project documenting the activities of several Washington state artists in Montparnasse in the early twentieth century. Through my friend Mitchell Wolfson Jr., I was introduced to Sacha Llewellyn, a Paris-based art historian / curator who had been involved with the exhibition *Surréalisme au féminin?* at the Musée de Montmartre. An important advocate for women artists, she was seeking additional information about a Seattle artist, Elsa Thoresen, who was included in the exhibition.

I had seen only a few works by Thoresen back in the early 1990s but was never able to locate much biographical information about her, especially concerning her time in Seattle. I was delighted to meet Thoresen's daughter, Alice Tompkins, through Sacha's introduction. Alice and her husband, Chuck, warmly and generously invited me and my partner Dominic Zambito into their home in Washington state to view the works of her mother and Vilhelm Bjerke-Petersen, Thoresen's first husband and Alice's father. I presented my interest to curate the first American exhibition and book on Thoresen's work. Alice agreed, since her mother is known (as is her father) primarily in Scandinavia and not in the United States. I am extremely grateful to them for their generosity and patience, allowing me to examine many never-published works of art as well as delving into their family archives.

Acknowledgments

For initiating this project, I am indebted to Sacha Llewellyn, a brilliant and prescient art historian (Rediscovering Art by Women, https://r-a-w.net).

Mitchell "Micky" Wolfson Jr. has been a friend and supporter for well over thirty years. He seems to know everyone in the art field and has generously connected many of us through his passion for art and design.

Cascadia Art Museum in Edmonds, Washington, just north of Seattle, was cofounded by Lindsey Echelbarger and others in 2015. He, the board, and staff have provided a venue for the internationally acclaimed exhibitions and books that we have collectively assembled. Their support is crucial to the revival of the reputations of countless historic Northwest artists, some of whom are now receiving international acclaim.

Many thanks to our board:
Lindsey Echelbarger, Chair; Ruthanne Weaver, Vice President; Phil Grad, Treasurer; Kasumi Yamashita, Secretary; and members Gary Faigin, Tori Force, John Impert, Gwen Johnson, Alan Lawrence, Julie Long, Marni Muir, Mark Pomerantz, Meg Rankin, Tanya K. Sharp, Janette Turner, and Silvia Waltner

And to our tireless staff:
Sally Ralston, Executive Director
Nate Hegerberg, Director of Operations (thanks for the Tompkins family interview transcriptions)
Mary Cate Babcock, Registrar
Julie Olson Anna, Director of Education
Kirsten Andrews, Donor Relations Manager
Breana Blackburn, Bookkeeper and Office Manager
Sydney Kaemmerlen, Marketing Manager

The following people have assisted me immeasurably during this project:

Nicole F. Mitchell, Director, and the staff at the University of Washington Press

Phil Kovacevich, who brilliantly designs all our publications and turns my research into works of art

Jane M. Lichty, for her expert editing and generous accommodation of our time constraints

Merch and Alice Pease

Rod Ralston, for his superb photography

Knut Ringen and Jacky Randall

Chris Walther, C. W. American Modernism Gallery, Los Angeles, CA

Thank you to the following art professionals and colleagues who were so generous and thoughtful:

Kent Belenius
Galerie Bel'Art
Stockholm, Sweden

Eirin Bergum
Registrar
Kunst Museum Brandts
Brandts, Denmark

Ewa Bobrowska, PhD
Associate Program Officer,
Convening Grants
Library Manager
Terra Foundation for American Art
121 rue de Lille
75007 Paris, France

Erika Danker
Director
Rian Design Museum
Falkenberg, Sweden

Ann-Marie Andersson Dannbring
Lund University Library, Sweden

Frank Falch
Curator
Kunstsilo
Kristiansand, Norway

Rune Finseth
Curator
Museum Sønderjylland
Kunstmuseet i Tønder

Carolin Görgen
Associate Professor of American
Studies
Sorbonne Université, Paris

Charlotte Cordua Gran
Photo and Rights Administrator
SMK—Statens Museum for Kunst
Copenhagen, Denmark

James C. Hall
The University of Iowa Library

Johan Zimsen Kristiansen
Art Historian
Denmark

Else-Brit Kroneberg
Head of Collections
Kunstsilo
Kristiansand, Norway

Thomas Breitenstein Millroth
Art Historian
Malmö, Sweden

Beate Mjaaland
Director, AKO Kunststiftelse
Oslo, Norway

Isabella Neira
Digital Project Specialist
Digital Library Services
University of Minnesota Libraries

Lena Rydén
Head of Art / Specialist Modern Art
Bukowski Auktioner AB
Arsenalsgatan 2
Stockholm, Sweden

Susanna Slöör
Artist and Curator
Stockholm, Sweden

Dr. Jana Teuscher
Curator
Stiftung Arp e.V.
Berlin, Germany

Anne Vigeland
Curator
Mjellby Art Museum
Mjellby, Sweden

And finally, to my partner Dominic Zambito, Prince du 7e arrondissement

This book is dedicated with love to Alice Tompkins in memory of her parents.

David F. Martin

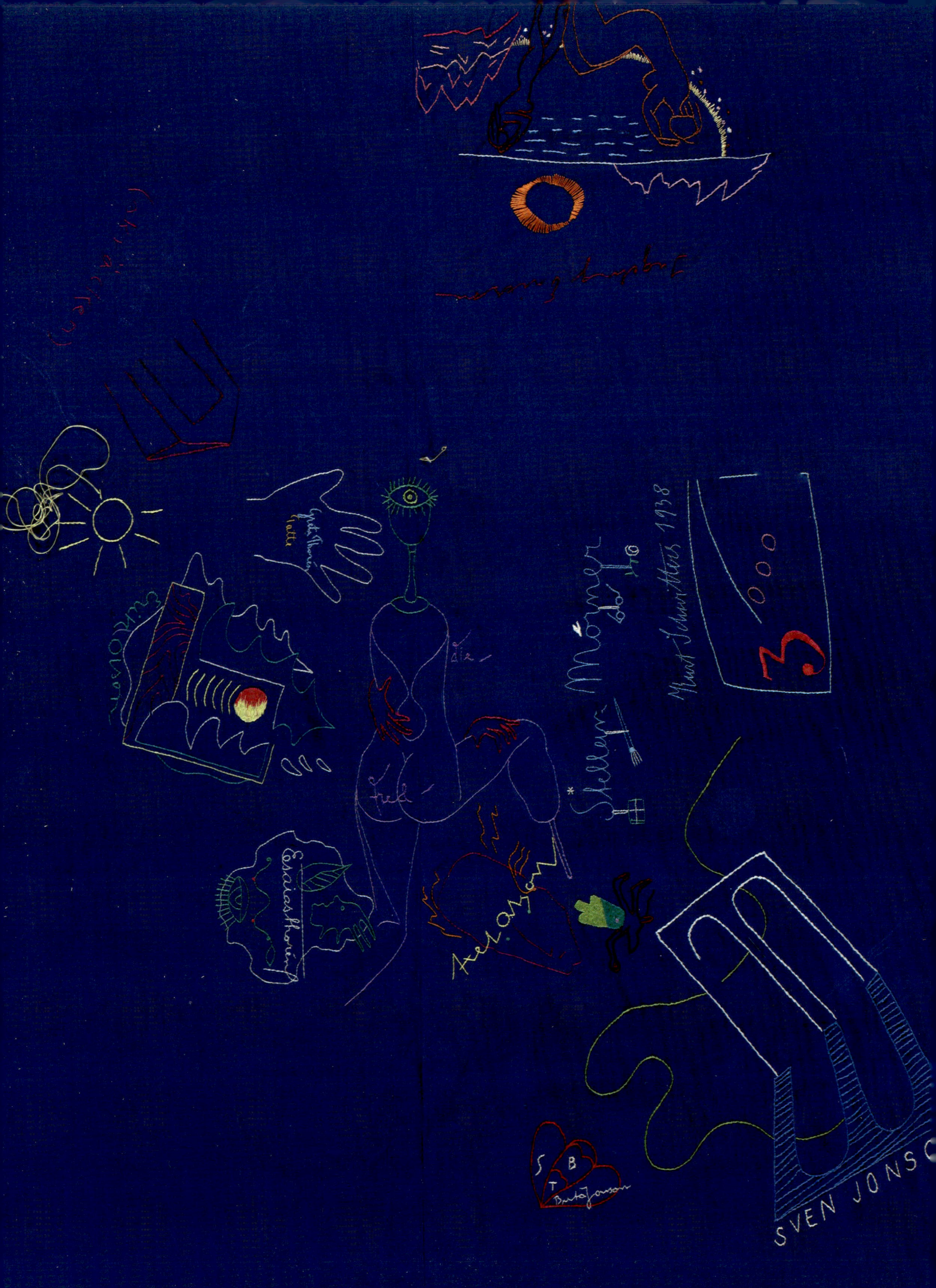

Donors to the Publication

DIAMOND

Best Western Plus Edmonds Harbor Inn

PLATINUM

Mike and Pat Green / Helen Johnston
    Foundation
Mark Pomerantz
Anne Volk
The Walker Foundation

GOLD

Paul Carlson & Shawn-Marie Hanson
Sherry Mossafer Rind
Paul Sturm & Flora Ling

SILVER

Michael Cunningham
Lindsey & Carolyn Echelbarger
Gwen & Steve Johnson
Pamela Proske

BRONZE

Andrew & Delney Hilen
Lawrence Kreisman
Lee & Sally Shobe

FRIEND

Bruce & JoAnn Amundson
Sharon Archer
Ross & Julie Case
Fred Chrysler & Bobbi Stennes
Mark Clatterbuck
Anne-Lise Deering
Alison Farmer
Randy & Jan Holbrook
Stephen Lacy
Frank & Mary Montgomery
Gary & JoAnne Nelson
Merch & Alice Pease

PATRON

Blackstone/Altwegg
Leif Erickson Lodge No. 1
Julie Long
Jeffrey & Mary Lundt
Kathleen Mortis
Julia Pierce
Tanya Sharp & Morgan MacRury
Carol A. Sund
Jeanne Thorsen & Tom Mayer

Objects of the Elements: The Art of Elsa Thoresen is published in conjunction with an exhibition of the same name, organized by Cascadia Art Museum and on view from December 3, 2025, through March 8, 2026.

Front cover: Elsa Thoresen (1906–1994), *Berget i natten* (The mountain at night) (detail), circa 1946. Oil on board, 13 × 16¼ in. (33 × 41.3 cm).

Frontispiece: Elsa Thoresen (1906–1994), *Skovens poesi* (The poetry of the forest) (detail), 1947. Oil on panel, 20⅞ × 30¾ in. (53 × 78 cm). Museum Sønderjylland.

Page 4: Elsa Thoresen (1906–1994), Untitled, 1935. Oil on canvas, 18⅛ × 15 in. (46 × 38 cm). Kunstsilo / The Tangen Collection. Photo courtesy of Bukowskis Auction, Stockholm.

Page 6: Elsa Thoresen (1906–1994), Untitled (detail), 1945. Oil on board, 10½ × 13½ in. (26.7 × 34.3 cm).

Pages 60–61: Elsa Thoresen (1906–1994), Untitled (detail), circa 1948. Oil on canvas, 21 × 25 in. (53.3 × 63.5 cm).

Page 158: Elsa Thoresen (1906–1994), Fabric with embroidered sketches and signatures of artists (detail), 1938. Cloth, 57 × 54 in. (144.8 × 137.2 cm).

Back cover: Elsa Thoresen at her easel, circa 1925.

All photographs, art, and ephemera courtesy of the estate of Elsa Thoresen, managed by Alice Tompkins, daughter of the artist, unless otherwise noted.

ISBN: 978-0-9989112-7-4

Cascadia Art Museum
190 Sunset Avenue South
Edmonds, WA 98020
cascadiaartmuseum.org

Distributed by University of Washington Press
uwapress.uw.edu

Design: Phil Kovacevich
Editing: Jane M. Lichty

Printed in Canada by Friesens